THE DREAMS OF WOMEN

OF WOMEN

Exploring and Interpreting Women's Dreams

Lucy Goodison

BERKLEY BOOKS, NEW YORK

THE DREAMS OF WOMEN

A Berkley Book / published by arrangement with
W. W. Norton & Company

PRINTING HISTORY
W. W. Norton & Company edition / April 1996
Berkley edition / November 1997

The Putnam Berkley World Wide Web site address is
http://www.berkley.com

ISBN: 0-425-16120-X

BERKLEY®
Berkley Books are published by The Berkley Publishing Group,
a member of Penguin Putnam Inc.,
200 Madison Avenue, New York, New York 10016.
BERKLEY and the "B" design
are trademarks belonging to Berkley Publishing Corporation.

PRINTED IN THE UNITED STATES OF AMERICA

10 9 8 7 6 5 4 3 2 1

*To the women
whose dreams and thoughts
have made this book*

Acknowledgments

I would like to thank the women who generously sent in their dreams for this book, including: Teresa Baldwin, Kim Beckford, Roxanne Clark, Penelope Cloutte, Sarah Colley, Ann de Boursac, Ronit Dassa, Linda Dove, Cosi Fabian, Hengameh Golestan, Kathy Goodall, Amelia and Abbie Green Dove, Alison Jackson, Kay, Lois Keith, Sonia Keizs, Jenny Kuper, Alison Leonard, Lorraine, Elinor McDonald, Heather McDougal, Barbara Marks, Marti Matthews, Patricia Monaghan, Margaret Murphy, Maxine Payne, Marie Perret, Mary Pikul, Jo Robinson, Jackie Ryan, Beth Shaw, Diana Shelley, Ruth Simmons, Tessa Souter, Jacky Taylor, Carmel Temple, Anne Wade, Eva Willer-Andersen and Mary Winegarden.

For kind permission to quote or refer to their work I would like to thank: Beata Bishop, Ann de Boursac, Jane Gilmore, Judith Hemming, Anni and Bob Moore, Inger Nolan, Stef Pixner, Jenner Roth, Morton Schatzman, Barbara Somers.

I have also been very grateful for suggestions, comments, help or encouragement from Jane Armitage, John

Barker, Diana Burski, Norma Cohen, Sue Cowan-Jenssen, Inga Czudnochowski-Pelz, Diana Dantes, Ann de Boursac, Stephanie Dowrick, Sheila Ernst, Julio Etchart, Claudine Frigère, Betty and Robin Goodison, Judith Griffies, Carlos Guarita, Patti Howe, Denis Hyde, Einar Jenssen, Marie Maguire, Gwyan McDougal, Heather McDougal, Penny Morris, Will Parfitt, Stef Pixner, Anna Robinson, Jo Robinson, Jenner Roth, Joanna Ryan, Beth Shaw and Sally Vincent.

Ann de Boursac died of cancer before this book was completed. We had shared many years of dreamwork together; her subtlety, intuition and compassion helped my understanding so much and made a particular contribution to this book.

Stef Pixner heroically helped me through last minute tangles. Kathy Gale at The Women's Press showed much patience and good will. I greatly appreciated Christine Considine's wise, sympathetic and skilful editing, and the contribution she made to shaping the book.

The love and support of Jane Foot and Stef Pixner, my daughter Corey Goodison and my partner Carlos Guarita also helped me to survive the writing of this book: thank you.

Permissions

The author would like to thank the following:

The Society of Authors as the literary representative of the Estate of Rosamond Lehmann, for quotations from *The Swan in the Evening* by Rosamond Lehmann.

Montague Ullman and Claire Limmer (editors) for quotations from *The Variety of Dream Experience: Expanding Our Ways of Working With Dreams,* as follows: excerpts from Introduction, by Montague Ullman; 'The Experiential Dream Group' by Montague Ullman; 'A Mother's Dream Group' by Jenny Dodd; 'After the Dream Is Over' by Nan Zimmerman; 'Night Rule: Dreams as Social Intelligence' by John R Wikse; 'Dreams and Society' by Montague Ullman.

Every effort has been made to trace the original copyright holders, but in some instances this has not been possible. It is hoped any such omission from this list will be excused.

Contents

THE DREAMS
OF WOMEN

Introduction
THE GIFTS OF DREAMS

A hawk means robbers, says Artemidorus in his ancient dream dictionary. Does it?

Dreams are like gifts on offer every night in wrapping which often remains unopened. Many of us are fascinated, curious, sometimes frightened by them. We want to know: can we find out what our dreams mean?

We can turn to dream dictionaries for on-the-spot translations of dream symbols; consult the advice of magazine and TV pundits; seek out the pronouncements of gurus; go to a psychotherapist; or read Freud, Jung, and other dream theorists for moulds of meaning into which our dreams can fit.

Any of these may be useful, but we also need to remember that our dreams are our own. There is a danger that by deferring to outside authorities we may be robbed of our own insights into these nightly ''gifts'' which can throw light on every aspect of our lives—relationships with friends, lovers and family; sex; work; politics; life skills; illness; decisions;

how we feel about the dead; and what we see as the purpose of life.

I have worked with my own dreams for over twenty years, run dream workshops for sixteen years, and taken part in a self-help dream group for nine years. This experience has convinced me that dreams are too rich and idiosyncratic to be decoded by set "dictionary" translations, too diverse and complex to wholly comply with any of the general theories which have been put forward. A hawk or wolf means robbers, says Artemidorus. A dream is a distorted message from the unconscious, says Freud. Dreams are shaped by eternal archetypes, says Jung. Leave dreams in the underworld, says the post-Jungian James Hillman. Everything in the dream is you, says Fritz Perls. Such theories try to account for *all* dreams, and would like to appropriate the dream experience of all cultures, all sexes, all races. Practitioners working with dreams are often drawn into "brand loyalties" and favour one theory, one master or one institution.

This is rash. The study of the human bodymind is in its very early stages. Like beginners in any field, we do not fully understand its processes and I believe that no single theory or therapeutic approach can claim to have a definitive answer.

It can be particularly difficult for women that most of these theories have been created by male "experts." Freud states that our dreams carry repressed desires, for example for a penis. Jung, that the female "archetypes" shaping women's dreams are intuitive, "negative," earthy, receptive. Such arguments suggest that all women are the same and do not portray us very positively. To be given a key to understanding ourselves can be reassuring. But we pay a price for believing that others know more about our experience than we do.

This book approaches dreams from a woman's perspective. Since men's and women's experiences are different—biologically, psychologically, and socially—I would argue that male theorists cannot do justice to women's dreams. The dreams raise issues which they perhaps cannot hope to understand, such as the experience of child-bearing and child-rearing; women's relationships with our mothers; friendships and sexual love between women; envy; and feelings about the shape, size and appearance of our bodies in a misogynist society. Some dreams are concerned with problems which men—however well-intentioned—cannot by their nature hope to solve, since women's solutions may be at odds with prevailing male norms. Women's needs may differ from those of men—in work, in relationships, in spiritual matters. They alone can embark on the process of defining what it means to be female: not the search for a pre-existent female "essence," but the opening up of possibilities previously denied. Given the differences in power and the conflicts of interest between women and men, some topics are perhaps too threatening for men to acknowledge, such as the contradictory feelings—ranging from delight to anger and terror—arising from our relationships with men. It is hard to imagine how any male practitioner, however sensitive and impartial, could really pick up the signals or resonate with these issues in women's accounts of their dreams.

My aim in this book is not to substitute my own theory for those others. Partial theories, in themselves useful and applicable to many dreams, have too often been presented as all-encompassing. My contribution is to question the notion that day and night are totally separate rather than a continuum. When sleep and wakefulness are polarised, as is "normal" in our culture, all sleep experience is lumped together, and one uniform explanation is sought for it. This blinkers us from seeing our experience clearly, and the full scope and variety of dreams goes unappreciated.

Writing this book has impressed on me that thought and imagination cover the same range of activities by night as by day, albeit there is a difference in form. Women describe some dreams as physical in origin, some as emotional, some spiritual or even divine; and our dreams' perceptions range from the ridiculous to the sublime just as in waking life. As by day, it seems that by night our imagination explores possibilities; indulges in silly fantasies; becomes preoccupied by fears and anxieties; pictures its wishes fulfilled; gets hooked into paranoias; re-runs and digests events that have happened; makes plans; solves practical questions; has insights about human relationships; tackles intellectual problems; tunes in to the experience of other people; has intuitions and occasional flashes of great wisdom; experiences deeply impressive visions; communes with the world around us; and witnesses revelations about the nature of life and death. Each dream needs to be approached differently: some interpreted, some ignored, some meditated upon, some acted out, some applied to daily life, some left to soak in whatever world created them. Each approach is useful at different times.

This remarkable diversity shines out from the dream accounts which are the backbone of this book. They were all written by women and sent in response to an open letter I circulated. The book is not a survey, but the women who have contributed are of different ages, races and sexual orientations. Their homelands range from the Middle East to the Caribbean, from Europe to the USA, as well as Australia. Some women have asked for their dreams to be anonymous, and in some cases I have changed names and details to preserve that anonymity. I hope readers are as inspired as I have been by the variety of resourceful and creative approaches these women use to reap the gifts of their dreams.

Some readers may not have the same access to their dreams as these contributors, and this book also includes many practical suggestions about how to remember dreams and work with them to discover their meaning. It provides tools, shows possibilities, and encourages you on your own explorations, individually or with friends.

I do not offer a system, but try to show the strengths and weaknesses of different approaches, and suggest a framework

within which the various theories can co-exist rather than
conflict. While existing theories have tended to compartmen-
talise, emphasising the emotional, the intellectual, the physical or the spiritual, this book suggests that all of these have
a place within the broad canvas of a whole person and a
whole life, and a dream may be concerned with all or any
of them. My aim is to ask questions, challenge assumptions,
and present material from women's lives so as to create a
space in which women's dreams can breathe. The consistent
thread is the spirit of enquiry, and the reaching beyond received theories and fundamentalisms to trust our own experience.

1

Starting to Remember and Understand Your Dreams

Despite what we are led to believe by some dream experts, we can learn to understand our dreams on our own, with a partner or friend, or in a group. Dreams do not have to be banished to the arenas of professional psychology, mental health or mysticism; they can also become part of everyday relationships, education, art, drama, storytelling, conversation, meditation, and a whole range of other activities. This chapter shows different ways of starting to recall and explore your dreams.

RECALLING YOUR DREAMS

For some women, the first hurdle to understanding their dreams is remembering them at all. In this case there are many strategies that can be tried. Some women have found that simply saying aloud before sleep that they want to remember their dreams has helped them to do so. Some ask for a dream on a particular topic. Others use relaxation or meditation techniques before sleep to encourage a receptive frame of mind. For example, you might sit quietly to empty your mind of busy thoughts, do some calming breathing, or imagine letting go of the tension from each part of your body in turn. It is a question of finding whatever works to focus your intention.

On waking, it can help to stay lying still in your sleeping body position to recall your dream. If you move and get up quickly, you may dispel whatever faint memories linger. Most people can occasionally recall odd fragments of dreams, and if you respond positively to any such fragment—however vague—this may lead to remembering more. Try saying it aloud, telling someone else, or writing it down, and see what else surfaces. You can also try drawing the dream fragment, or even acting or dancing it. The more energy and attention you give, the more your recall may improve.

If you are still remembering nothing, you can try doing an exercise from Gestalt therapy (which is described more fully later in this chapter) called "Talking to your dreams." Use two chairs or two cushions. Sit yourself on one and imagine your dreams are on the other. Try speaking to your dreams, telling them how much you want to remember them. You may feel silly at first, but if you can enter into the spirit of the role-playing, it can be illuminating. Then switch seats and speak as if you were the dreams replying. Say whatever comes to mind, without censoring or getting embarrassed. Giving the dreams a voice, let them describe themselves and tell what would help them to surface. You may be surprised at what comes out:

"We are too colourful and weird."
"We are too heavy for you to face."
"You are too busy in your waking life to make room for us."

If you can still not remember any dreams, you could try exploring your daydreams. These will bring up pictures and images which, as creations of a similar imaginative process, can be worked with just like dream images. Getting used to that process may in turn help dream recall.

KEEPING A DREAM JOURNAL

Having a "dreambook" or journal by your bed to write in as soon as you open your eyes can be a very useful way of capturing a dream. You can then refer back to it to see a history of your dream life, and also to refresh your memory if you are working on a particular dream at a later time. As one woman describes:

"Many other people put time into journal writing each day, but my priority is dream recording. Dreams seem to reach into the farthest mysteries and resources of myself, so it seems important to record them, even if I don't immediately understand them. Dreams seem a way to see more clearly the elusive parts of myself. Often in the act of recording them I already begin to recognise what the dream was about."

Not all women find it easy to keep a dream journal. For some the problems are practical, as one single mother explains:

"I still keep a dream journal, though somewhat sporadically since my daughter was born . . . You have to be able to focus on yourself in those first few moments when you wake up to keep track of your dreams, and I find this not very compatible with the conditions of motherhood! I am not so methodical and organised about my journal now; but I still find it enormously helpful and comforting to meditate on my dreams when I do manage to find time to do it."

As with any aspect of life that is hard to understand, the simple act of writing in a journal can be surprisingly helpful in crystallising thoughts and insights, as Sherry Thomas described in an issue of *Country Women*:

> What has come as a continual surprise are the moments of revelation and epiphany that happen *because of the writing itself*. A turn of phrase, a metaphor flying from my unconscious onto the page, words my hand wrote faster than my conscious self could speak: looking at these I learn from myself what I did not know I know . . . These moments of revelation . . . are extremely intense and always nourishing.

Some women find that the process of re-writing dreams and re-reading them over time can also add to understanding them:

"I leave some pages at the beginning of each notebook for indexing dreams. I kind of purposely stay two or three weeks behind in my indexing work; this gives me occasion to re-read the dreams I've had recently and often their meaning now seems clearer in light of things happening a week or so later . . . I number the pages and give each dream a name. It takes time to re-read the dream, but it's really worth it."

This woman, Marti Matthews, finds her middle-of-the-night dreams the most interesting, the ones which offer the deepest understanding into her life. They also require some effort if they are to be remembered:

"I record these dreams in the dark, so as not to disturb my sleep too much. It's very hard to get myself to record them, as I'm usually far away in deep sleep . . . I've learned by hard experience over and over that I can never remember these dreams in the morning unless I write them down in the middle of the night. It takes real desire to get myself to do it. I keep a notebook beside my bed with a pencil (once I used a pen for an important dream and found in the morning that it hadn't worked, almost nothing was recorded!). I just feel my way across the page from left to right and top-of-the-page downward.

"In the morning I re-write what I scribbled in the dark . . ."

Even a scrap of a late morning dream can be enough to set the ball rolling, and like Marti Matthews you may gradually develop your own methods for dream recording.

Historically women have been denied a voice in the public sphere, and in the private sphere they have been silenced in their role as carers and keepers of others—carrying feelings regarded as trivial, family secrets never to be spoken, and a voice that should not be raised. As a result it can be hard even to find the words to start to tell that experience. Just lifting a pen and setting some of it onto the page can be a relief as well as an important starting point for investigating dreams.

USING RITUALS AND RITUAL OBJECTS

Special objects like crystals, shells, flowers, candles or treasures with personal associations can create a shift in mood which makes us more open to having, remembering and understanding important dreams. Sometimes a simple ritual before sleep, like spending ten minutes gazing at a candle or into a glass of water, looking at a plant or flower, burning aromatic herbs, or dancing to a favourite piece of music, can help lead us into dreams.

Such self-generated rituals and objects are different from the traditional symbols of organised religion, which carry an

inherited charge and may influence or limit the imagination.
Using self-created rituals or special objects can focus energy
or give the atmosphere a lift; it can be a way of expressing
something you need, or affirming shared values; it can reflect
and enhance your experience. However, with all ritual acts
and objects—even self-chosen ones—there is a risk of becoming attached to them so that they trap our energy. When
experience changes they may need to change too; we need
to be aware when they are helping and when they are unnecessary or have become an interference. The more simple
and open-ended a ritual, the more flexible it may prove to
keep you tuned to the main purpose of being able to listen
to your dreams.

Some books about dreams recommend using the practices
of ancient or ''native'' communities as if those ceremonies
could be re-adopted now by people in the West. This approach has grown in popularity in recent years and seems to
hold both possibilities and dangers for the modern dreamer,
which are worth considering. The books sometimes imply
that people in those other cultures were or are more authentic
than us, and that their techniques will help us to reconnect
to something we have lost. Sometimes this may prove true,
but in my experience this can also become a form of ideal-
isation which cuts us off even more from our present experience—and often distorts the past at the same time.

A good example of this process is the way modern dreamers approach the practice of ''incubation,'' or sleeping in a
special place in order to have a wise or healing dream. The
ancient Greeks are often cited: at the shrine of Asclepius at
Epidaurus people would come to perform certain rituals and
then sleep overnight in an underground chamber where their
dreams would suggest treatment or provide a cure for illness
or disability. A practice that is ancient carries a certain glamour and some books suggest we might like to take up ''incubation.'' However, much of what is written about the
actual rituals at Epidaurus is speculation, a recurrent problem

when trying to re-create history. And from the records that do survive, engraved on "stelai" from the site, a rather less appealing picture of the shrine's operation is given.

The inscription on Stele I, for example, records that a woman named Ambrosia came from Athens, blind in one eye. On her arrival she laughed at some of the cures as unbelievable, but in her sleep she had a vision:

> It seemed to her that the god stood by her and said that he would cure her, but that in payment he would ask her to dedicate to the Temple a silver pig as a memorial of her ignorance. After saying this, he cut the diseased eyeball and poured in some drug. When day came she walked out sound. (Transl. Edelstein)

This is a striking story, not only for the cure but also for the implicit link to the administration and economics of the shrine. Ambrosia's dream was interpreted by male priests, and this record is what they inscribed on a stele to advertise their institution to other customers. Was she cured? We know that advertisements are notoriously unreliable. What is clear is that Ambrosia was reprimanded for her scepticism, and paid a high price (the silver pig). The whole outfit may have been as manipulative and mercenary as any spurious modern health treatment. Ancient and traditional societies faced the same issues about mystification and exploitation in spiritual matters that we face today. Incubation may have been an effective ancient tradition, but I would suggest that the only good authority now is your own experience of what works for you.

DREAM DRAWING

A creative way to start exploring your dreams is through painting or drawing them. This may be through a literal picture of people, objects or events in a dream, or it may be more an expression of the mood of the dream through shapes and colour. It is important to have a range of colours at hand, so that you can choose the one that is exactly right, and you need to draw quickly and intuitively, free from any pressure to create a "work of art."

Afterwards it can be good to talk to a friend, partner or group about what you have done, but it can be unhelpful if others try to interpret a dreamer's picture. Instead they could ask questions about it, or say what they notice or feel about different parts of it. But even feedback such as this may prove to be less useful than simply witnessing and trusting the dreamer's own creativity in exploring the dream.

This process can be seen in the following example from the Irish psychotherapy journal *Inside Out*. It concerns Linda, a young woman of 24 attending a one-off weekend group. Group leader Inger Nolan describes how Linda painted:

> a big, gray, "horrible" mist from a dream. While she was painting it, . . . she got an impulse to put in a red dot to the left in the picture. She enjoyed that and painted a few bright coloured matchstick men around this red dot and said: "They are playing. [pause] This mist is really bugging me!" I asked, "What is it about it that's bugging you?" She replied: "It's that I don't know how big it is! It was kind of everywhere [in the dream] and I didn't know where it would end." I gave Linda a choice, whether to finish or to explore further how far the mist would go. She worked for another while on the matchstick men. After a few minutes she started to add paper after paper to the original one, attaching them with Sellotape and painting the mist until it covered several square yards on the floor. The mist was big, but eventually contours all the way round developed, forming a cloud. Linda was extremely satisfied, laughed and giggled as she showed it to the group.

I view the dot and the matchstick men as Linda's successful attempt to gain courage in exploring aspects of the dark side of this dream and within herself. When I met Linda a few months later in another context she told me she had gained important insights through the work she had done that weekend.

This example shows the value of working with dreams in a responsive way, following the specific needs and impulses of the dreamer. Inger Nolan helped Linda not by analysing her dream but by empowering her to follow her experience through spontaneously. How far did the mist reach? Was it possible that uncertainty and depression could overwhelm her? Linda lighted on her own idiosyncratic way to find out, while the therapist simply provided a safe situation for her to pursue it. Painting one symbol which she remembered from a dream led Linda into looking at, and coming to terms with, broader issues in her life.

In the following example, Anne Wade describes how she worked with a variety of visual art forms to transform a nightmare into a helpful dream. Her nightmare symbol was a bird:

"I was a wounded bird who could not fly. I was lucid and I did everything I knew to transform the dream, to heal the bird and enable her to fly. I was told that, before I could be healed, before I could fly, I must go through all the pain I had denied as a child. The pain was appalling . . .

"I woke with tears streaming down my face . . . I had a bird I had carved years before out of driftwood . . . At home I drew this bird, held it and meditated on it and talked with it. I did indeed go through all that pain, never sure whether it was necessary or self-indulgent, as I worked to remember and heal the abuse I had endured."

The art work and meditation led to a different kind of dream experience:

"I had a series of bird dreams, starting with hatching out as a tiny chick. I felt beautiful and intact—this was a very important word. Gradually the bird grew, in many healing, loving dreams.

"I still often felt worthless because of what had been done to me, and did not know how to reclaim my worth securely, but the wound is healing and sometimes I fly."

Here drawing one dream symbol led into a process of releasing enormous pain and helped the dreamer towards a new sense of self-worth.

WRITING DREAM POEMS

There are other creative ways of assimilating dream messages. One is to make a dream into a poem. You do not have to think of yourself as a writer to do this. Sometimes a simple retelling of the dream may turn out like a poem, as with the following example from a dream by Ann, aged 11. Published in the journal *Fire*, it was transcribed from a tape recording made by Sally Vincent and, without any editing, was transformed into a "poem" simply by the line arrangement:

"There's a big cupboard in my room.

"I dream a woman comes into the room where
  I'm in bed.
  She's not a nice woman and
  she's a bit gnarled and
  has glasses on and a red dress

with spots and
a headdress.

"She stands at the end of the bed,
holding the bedpost and rocking herself
backwards and forwards.

"She starts to get
smaller and smaller and
starts screaming.

"It's horrible,
she opens her mouth ever so wide and
screams and screams and
gets smaller and smaller.

"Then, she jumps up to the top of the cupboard and
goes on screaming and screaming and
getting smaller and smaller."

What strikes me about this dream is how graphically it presents feelings familiar from other examples later in this book. Its themes of fear, shrinking size, and expression (the scream) all feature in the dreams of grown women; one wonders at what age they first start to haunt the dream life of a young girl. The simple act of transforming a dream into a poem can help to come to terms with such feelings: a private terror moves into the social domain where it can be read, shared, discussed, appreciated, looked at differently.

In his book *The Dream and the Underworld*, James Hillman proposes a different approach and questions the value of trying to draw any waking meaning from dreams. Do we need to bring them to the analyst, to the typewriter, to our friends, or even turn the light on them at all in the morning? He believes that the "underworld" is where the dream belongs. Again I would suggest that it is a mistake to make rules: some dreams are crying out to be brought into daylight, while others are inviting us to immerse ourselves in their nighttime world. Sometimes our response to that invitation may be a creative work which we ourselves do not fully understand; writing a poem can be a way to be drawn deeper into a dream. In the example below, Patricia Monaghan used a long poem to express this impulse to, as she puts it, ''pull the day towards night.'' Here are some excerpts:

> ''Housemagic''

> ''You descend the stairs at midnight.
> You walk through the sleeping house.
> Light surrounds you in the silent dark.

> ''Was it a nightmare woke you?

> ''You pour a glass of water.
> You sit by the window, beside that
> cobalt vase filled with blue flowers.
> Into the dark blue centre of sleep
> you slip again, into the blue
> blackness of true forms, into
> the fragmented pool of meaning . . .

> ''Now as you sleep you dream
> of a half-remembered house bedraggled
> as old lace, its stairs rot into wooden
> filigrees, its attic suffocates in private
> dust. And in its flooded basement
> the rivers, the sewers of the world
> breed terrifying marvels. Because
> the house grows wild, disorderly, all
> the gardens in the world turn treacherous
> and forests strangle on themselves.

> ''But in this house all change is possible . . .''

It is a different thing again to use a dream primarily as an aid to writing, drawing on dream symbols as a poetic resource. The following method can be used to help women find their ability to write a poem (devised by Stef Pixner for jointly run dream workshops at the Women's Therapy Centre in London): "Imagine yourself in your dream. Look around you. Focus on the background of the dream—a broken light switch perhaps, a lift shaft, patterned wallpaper or a shopping mall—rather than characters and action. Now choose 10 to 12 words relating to that background which most call your attention; let yourself be attracted to them as if you were window shopping. Write those words out. Now make a poem (or it could be a different story) starting from those words." As with all imaginative exercises, the process will probably work better if you take a few minutes to relax into your body before you begin. The following poem by Stef Pixner came out of a workshop on writing blocks using the above method. This process is not the same as exploring a dream emotionally or psychologically—she points out that when you turn a dream into a painting or poem, it takes on its own life and "you may understand it in a very different way":

> *"The day I talked to his wife"*
>
> *"I remember*
> *the rounded doorway*
> *the whitewashed wall*
> *the sleeping sea*
> *below*
>
> *"But no, it wasn't*
> *the sea*
> *it was dark strips of city garden*
> *where parachutists landed*
> *unexpectedly*
> *the day I talked to his wife*

> *"I remember*
> *the small gap*
> *between her teeth*
> *a white carpet*
> *stretched between us*
> *a blue tobacco packet*
> *a pile of running shoes*

> *"I remember*
> *the parachutists*
> *floating to the sea or the city*
> *his arms gripping me from behind*
> *his cheek on my arm*
> *his wife under the doorway*
> *the words that never came"*

USING VISUALISATION

The symbols and images in our dreams can be explored
through visualisation in a way which can give new insights
as to their meaning, or make them more accessible to change.
Imagining feeding a hungry dream animal, or cleaning a neglected dream house, can be a way of mobilising resources
to care for a part of yourself that is crying out for help and
attention. It can also be interesting to visualise an ending to
a dream that feels unfinished, as in the following example:

In my dream everyone was clustering round my sister and
consoling her as she was in some trouble. Then we were
walking outside and started digging under some earth and
grass. Some pink or red letters came into view: WILL . . .
helmina. A lost child.

This woman comments: "I think this reflects my jealousy for the extra attention given (especially by my mother) to my eldest sister, who was often ill. After this dream I remembered being told years ago that my mother had really wanted me—the fourth after three daughters—to be a boy. Hence Will . . . helmina: meant to be a boy and ended up a girl. A very 'lost' child as a result. Perhaps I made up for it with 'will' power? The letters were written or carved on a stone a bit like a gravestone—I had the sense that part of me had been 'buried' as a child and I was curious."

Feeling unresolved, this woman decided to visualise continuing the action of the dream onwards. She did some relaxing breathing, and "I imagined returning to the dream and digging under the stone. What did I find? A kitten—starved, damp, pathetic and very shaky. I was shocked. It seemed to have been there so long it was a miracle it was alive at all. So this was the part of me that had been buried . . ."

This woman might continue by drawing the kitten or acting it, or asking what it needs, to see what further insights arise. There can be a temptation to paste a "happy ending" on to a dream in a cosmetic way, to dispose quickly of any uncomfortable feelings. It is much more helpful, as here, to let the ending spring from your imagination, even if you are taken aback by the results. As long as nothing is forced, it is possible to play with and around the symbols in our dreams, like clay shapes which can be re-formed in different ways. You can imagine a different ending to the one you had, or even make up an entire dream. As London psychotherapist Jenner Roth points out, "Some people feel this method is cheating and not real dream work but it brings me to an important point about dreaming. The dream is ours, it belongs to us. We create it. We have it . . . It is there for our use."

USING TECHNIQUES FROM PSYCHOTHERAPY

Different therapies have proposed ways of understanding dreams. Each approach has a different emphasis and different insights to offer, and each has its own limitations. Here is a brief—and by no means exhaustive—introduction to three of the best-known dream methods:

Freud

Every therapeutic approach to dreams is indebted in some way to the innovative work of Sigmund Freud earlier this century. Freud believed that a dream is a message from the unconscious, but a distorted one. The task of the psychoanalyst working with a patient was to track down the real meaning that is disguised in their dreams' symbols. Freud stressed that "the remembered dream is not the genuine material" and that elements of the dream are "ungenuine things, substitutes for something else that is unknown to the dreamer." He believed that these unknown elements would very often be linked to childhood experiences and would reflect the fulfilment of wishes and impulses left over from the struggle to survive as a child. To track them down, he used a process of "free association" whereby the dreamers would let themselves freely follow the trail of thoughts, feelings and associations prompted by the different symbols of the dream. Freud's method led to the uncovering of repressed emotions such as jealousy, rage, hatred and lust.

This approach can work outside the domain of psychoanalysis. In a workshop run by Ann de Boursac and myself, the ten participants were encouraged to choose a recent or important dream and, after using a process of free association, to scan it for traces of envy, rage, murderous hatred, lust and other basic impulses central to Freud's theory. This might sound daunting, but there was only one person in the group who did not uncover something useful in this way.

Moreover, the process felt very energising: although it is uncomfortable to admit such feelings, it is also freeing to have permission to acknowledge them. We laughed hilariously while recognising that there were serious seeds of truth in Freud's theory about these "shameful" urges hidden in our dreams. In the psychoanalytic situation, those feelings are made safer by being contained within the strict boundaries of the relationship between therapist and client. Outside that situation, it is especially important that a dreamer can make her own interpretations, and that she feels safe from the judgements of others. One of the gifts of dreams is that they can show us our own denied and discreditable impulses. One of Freud's major contributions was to develop a method to track them down. Without pressure, and in a safe situation, his method can be used to bring out some liberating insights.

To find the trails that lead from our dreams into the past, free association is an invaluable part of the legacy of Freud. This is a technique which we can use ourselves constructively on our own dreams. In his *Introductory Lectures on Psychoanalysis* Freud stressed that "The work of interpreting can be performed on one's own dreams just as on other people's" and as the ideas of psychoanalysis have made their way into the world, free association has become a staple method of approaching dreams whether in a therapy situation, a dream group, or at home alone. The rich insights it can yield—even far from the consulting room—are shown by this example of a dream which an American woman had exactly ten days before the birth of her first daughter and third child:

"I must get to Cleveland in time for a 2:00 P.M. therapy session. I am at the bus station buying my ticket and spot a Cleveland bus about to leave. I rush frantically to the bus and pull out my ticket to show the driver. But I am told that it's too late; the bus is full. So I plead: 'I HAVE to be in Cleveland by 2:00 P.M.!'

"*Probably because I am so very pregnant, I am allowed to get on. This is the 1:53 bus. I note that I'll be late but at least I'll get there. The bus is small and rather plush. Most of the other occupants are women. I find a place in the back. People move a bit to make way for me. I worry that there is no way to get the message to Cleveland that I am on my way, though I will be late. Then my father gets on the bus. He moves towards the back and puts his coat and things down on the seat. Somehow he's called my house and found out that I'd gotten on this bus. He explains that even though I'll miss half of this therapy session, I'll still have to pay for it. I am silent although I realize that I have no money to pay for it. Then my father announces that my Aunt C. has set up a special fund to pay for this therapy and I am very relieved and grateful!*

"*We arrive in Cleveland and I rush to the place where the session is. This turns out to be a special session conducted by Dr. Lulu Schein, which is a performance based on my life. I enter and start to watch.*

"*A very tall, beautiful dancer is stretching her long arms up and out very gracefully and I copy her. This feels wonderful. More dancers (women) join in this section—all very graceful and happy. I am told that this is me as a young child.*

"*Dr. S. recognises and acknowledges me and I acknowledge her. She's warm-looking, 45 to 50, Jewish.*

"*Then other events happen, the many various events I've experienced. (But sadly I forget much of this section of the dream.) . . .*

"*Then FEAR. People come rushing over to me with an enormous umbrella-thing which I realize is going to trap me. I am trapped under it and I hear and see thunder, lightning, a terrible rainstorm. I am terrified: I hear my parents screaming at each other and fighting. I am about six years old, back in Oxford Street. I curl up in a tight ball and bite*

my fingers and scream: 'NO, NO, DON'T! STOP, OH NO, STOP!'
"I wake up in terror."

This woman's associations to the dream are as follows: "Cleveland is where my father grew up, and where he moved after leaving my mother when I was nine years old. From the age of nine (until college) I spent a few weeks every summer with him—so 'going to Cleveland' is about reuniting with him. Being too late is about being too late to be with him as a little girl—needing him as a father then, but now it's 'too late.'

"The bus is a 1:53 bus: in January 1953 (1/53) my father had just lost his job, because of the McCarthy witch-hunts. This was very traumatic and caused my father to suffer a nervous breakdown. For the next two years there was much fighting and anguish in the house.

"My Aunt C. (his younger sister) has always been very affectionate and loving; she represents a softer, kinder version of my father.

"The performance part of the dream was very rich and vivid and moving, though I forget (unfortunately) so many of the details! Dr. S. represents the Jewish maternal women in my life—my aunt and my grandma.

"The final fear scene represents the terrible fighting between my parents (1953–55) in our house in Oxford Street, where we moved when I was six. My father had a terrible temper and frightened me with his anger—which often erupted like terrifying, loud thunderstorms. I don't know if the big umbrella represents being safe, or being trapped beneath his anger. But it could even represent my own birth— as my mother was 'knocked out' for labour and delivery.

"I could say lots more about this dream . . . A very intense, very powerful dream about accepting myself, part of giving birth again to myself as I give birth to my daughter."

Here the dream's symbols yield a rich return, and there
seems no need for further interpretation. Indeed, the whole
dream is shaped around getting to, and experiencing, a therapy session which the dreamer has specifically created for
herself, including even a dance re-enactment of parts of her
life. The dream could hardly make a clearer statement about
its own self-contained therapeutic purpose.

If you are not confident about doing free association on
your own, here are some guidelines. If your dream is long,
choose a fragment of it. First run through the dream (or
dream fragment) in your mind, then take a sheet of paper
and write on it a phrase or heading for each different section
or element of your dream, leaving plenty of space between
each one. Now do some relaxed breathing or a little physical
exercise to let your awareness move out of just your head
into your whole body. Then sit or lie comfortably and let
your mind wander without restriction on each phrase in turn.
Don't censor your thoughts, however unexpected. It may
help to close your eyes. Allow several minutes for each section of the dream and notice every thought or image, however irrelevant it may at first appear. Afterwards, write the
associations in the blank spaces you have left on the paper.
If you have a friend or group member to work with you, she
can hold the paper and write down the associations as you
speak them, taking care not to intrude with her own thoughts
and interpretations. Free association works best when it is
really free and in the hands of the dreamer herself.

When you have all your associations written down, you
may like to see what difference they make to your understanding of the dream. You may choose to look, as Freud
did, for underlying urges, hidden wishes, repressed emotions
and a concealed "dream-message" which may have surfaced
through the associations. Or you may prefer to explore the
material through role-playing, art, meditation, or one of the
other approaches described in this book. Memories surfacing

from the past can be upsetting, so make sure you have a friend to support you if necessary.

Another tool Freud used was a series of formulae for decoding dream symbols. Working from his patients' dreams, he believed there was an ancient "basic language" according to which dream symbols could be translated. In a typical passage in *Introductory Lectures on Psychoanalysis*, he states that, "*Hills* and *rocks* are symbols of the male organ. *Gardens* are common symbols of the female genitals. *Fruit* stands, not for children, but for the breasts. *Wild animals* mean people in an excited sensual state, and further, evil instincts or passions."

The emphasis on sex is typical of Freud. This was perhaps an appropriate response to the prudery of his time; but in his writings it is disconcerting to find not only pencils and umbrellas, but also hammers, guns, knives and other aggressive tools assumed to stand for the penis, while jars, pits, hollows, cupboards and other passive receptacles are taken as female sexual symbols. Perhaps the symbols in his patients' dreams were based not on a universal law but rather on their socially stereotyped and fearful attitudes towards gender and sexual impulses.

Freud's ideas on dreams were limited by his sex, race, class, generation and personal prejudices. We see this when he assumes that the dream symbols most common in his culture are a universal language applicable everywhere. We see this when he misunderstands the experience of women, or attempts to push his own interpretations onto a reluctant dreamer (see Chapter 13). His method is not useful for all dreams—because not all dreams are concerned with the themes he was scanning for. None the less, his pioneering work has left us with some crucial dream tools.

Jung

Carl Gustav Jung, who started as a follower of Freud, developed a different attitude to dreams. He saw them not as distorted messages but as the bringers of wisdom from the unconscious, compensating for lacks in waking life and providing hope and guidance for the future. For him the unconscious was not just a dungeon of repressed unpleasantness. Though he acknowledged that difficult feelings are often repressed into it, he also saw it as a treasure-house. He had more respect than Freud for the symbols themselves, which he believed were not a disguise but were carefully selected for the qualities they embodied, and could in themselves be very healing whether in dreaming, meditation or visualisation.

If Freud's theories emphasised the digestion of difficult feelings, primitive emotions, instincts and raw physical urges, Jung focused on our "higher" qualities and more ethereal functions. He was more likely to find in dreams inspiration, vision, optimism and the potential for positive change. For example, whereas Freud saw a house in a dream as a symbol of the physical body (with doors representing body orifices), Jung in *Man and his Symbols* treats it as a more general symbol for the psyche, life activity and potential.

Many women have found this approach useful. Beata Bishop, an astrologer and psychotherapist working along Jungian and Transpersonal lines, describes in the journal *Caduceus* a dream which recurred over several years where:

She was in her home and found an extra room which she explored with surprise and delight. Over time the room changed from being small and plain to acquiring arches, garden views, beautiful window seats, an inviting spaciousness, and finally furniture. Eventually she dreamt that her home was an Italian palazzo and the extra room had become a whole extra floor, overlooking the sea.

She comments: "This recurring dream coincided with a heavy, bleak, routine-bound spell and an unhappy relationship that had nearly squashed my inner life out of existence, until at last the *palazzo* version jolted me awake. Of course, I thought, there is a lot of marvellous unused, undiscovered space within, an entire top floor is waiting to be inhabited and enjoyed (by then I suspected that the top floor had something to do with the spiritual dimension), so why do I stay in this chicken-coop existence?

"My conscious mind could no longer deny what I had long known unconsciously: the dreams had seen to that. I broke out of the choking routine and the limiting relationship then and there and rearranged my priorities. And the dream of the extra room did not return ever again."

Here the dreamer saw in her dream a pointer towards fulfillment and was able to make changes in her life accordingly. This can be an encouraging approach. To try it for yourself, re-tell or re-read a recent dream all the way through, and then scan it for a symbol of hope. This may appear as a beneficent being or a spiritual source; Jung often interpreted mandalas in this way. However, it is more likely to be a less explicit symbol, like a new room, plants growing out of a pile of dead leaves, an animal, a boat travelling through a night sea, a familiar bracelet, a song. When you have lighted on a symbol (always take the first that comes to mind however unlikely it might at first appear), explore it by talking, meditating, writing, or drawing it. Then ask yourself whether it represents a resource in you, and whether there are changes you could make in your life to express its qualities more fully.

There may also be dreams, or times in your life, when a Jungian approach is not so helpful. In an article in *New Scientist*, Morton Schatzman highlighted the differences of approach between Freud and Jung by pointing out that for Freud dreams of steps and staircases represent the sexual act because "we come to the top in a series of rhythmical movements and with increasing breathlessness." Jung on the other hand would link a patient's dream of going up stairs with "getting to the top, making a career and growing up." This contrast tells us a lot, both about Freud's preoccupation with sexual urges, and about Jung's tendency to shy away from dealing with the body directly—as if myth, history and general issues were easier to confront than the flesh. This is a weakness in his work, and a limitation when it comes to dreams about sex, the body and basic emotions.

Like Freud, Jung too attempted to construct a universal symbolic vocabulary, or map, based on the symbols he found in his patients' dreams. He developed a theory that the individual psyche floats on the sea of the "collective unconscious," a kind of pool of images common to all humanity. This collective unconscious contained, he believed, certain symbolic forms or "archetypes" such as the female "anima," the male "animus," the shadow, wise old man, witch, earth-mother and the "Self," which represent different aspects of the make-up of human beings. He used myths from other cultures to back up his view that these "archetypes" are universal and have always been there, influencing human life and shaping our dream symbols. However, his work on the anthropology of other peoples is dubious, and he offers no evidence for his opinion that the archetypes are a biological part of humans' physical make-up. The symbols in his patients' dreams may have had a more local origin, in their own social experience. Jung's "archetypes" are colourful and inspiring, but it may be limiting to take them as gospel.

Jung's ideas on dreams have had huge influence, particularly among women, and many contemporary books about dreams draw directly or indirectly on his writings. On one level his work emphasised the value of "female" qualities: he saw the unconscious and intuition as "female" and stressed that in a healthy person these needed to be integrated within the psyche. However, he did not question the stereotypes which categorise those qualities as female in the first place, along with other "primitive," physical and sexual, elements; while he linked thought and consciousness with "light" and with the male. Sadly, his followers—including many women—have tended to perpetuate his thinking rather than challenge its fixed male/female roles.

Gestalt

One of the newer humanistic therapies, Gestalt, offers another approach to dreams, suggesting that everything in a dream represents part of the dreamer's psyche. Rather than analysing and interpreting, the method involves acting out or "speaking as" the different people and things in the dream. This may sound a strange idea, but consider this example, which Sheila Ernst and I described in *In Our Own Hands: A Book of Self-Help Therapy*. A woman dreamt about standing on a railway platform. When asked to speak "as" the platform, she hesitated but finally shut her eyes and began: "I'm cold and hard and people walk all over me." This connected so strongly to her present experience of herself that she burst into tears and the dreamwork carried on from there.

Gestalt Therapy Verbatim contains transcripts of one of Gestalt therapy's founders, Fritz Perls, using this dream method. His style is rather too showy, "macho" and provocative for many women—and for many of the contemporary Gestalt therapists—but the book gives a graphic picture of this approach in action. It includes an example of him working with a woman called Nora who had dreamt about a bleak and incomplete house where the stairs had no rails. Nora—like many newcomers to Gestalt—had difficulty at first identifying with the house. The usual method is to sit on a separate cushion or chair to get into the role. Eventually she managed to speak from the position of the house, and found it an uncomfortable place to be: "I'm open and unprotected and there are winds blowing inside. [voice sinks to a whisper] And if you climb on me you'll fall. And if you'll judge me . . . I'll fall.'' She described herself as having concrete floors and solid foundations, uncomfortable but dependable. Perls asked how the house could be a little warmer? "Well, cover it, close—put windows in it; put walls, curtains, nice colours—nice warm colours." She role-played, speaking as these extra "luxuries," trying to convince the house that these extras were needed, but when she spoke back as the house, she was stubborn: "I don't think I really need you."

The Gestalt theory is that we project on to the elements in our dreams denied parts of our personality. So in this case, the house represented Nora herself. Although at first Nora felt that she was living in the house, it turned out that she actually was the house: it symbolised her and her life. Once she had recognised this, she could check out what the house needed. What is missing in a dream can be very important. In Nora's case she found that warmth and colour were missing from the house, and the suggestion was that this may have been what was actually missing from her life. Gestalt theory encourages us to act out and recognise aspects of ourselves which have been alienated (whether symbolised as a bleak house, a wild animal, a powerful motor, or warm curtains) so that, as Perls said, we can begin to re-assimilate, to re-own parts of our personality we have given away: "The more you disown, the more impoverished you get. Here is an opportunity to take back."

Body awareness is very important in Gestalt work. While retelling a dream people may suddenly screw their eyes up, or make a fist, or start wringing their hands or shivering, or become aware of a pain or ache. In this case they may be encouraged to "speak as" the eyes or the fist, or to "speak as" one hand and then the other, so that the two hands effectively have a dialogue, with the idea that these parts of the body may also be carrying disowned feelings—perhaps anger or fear—which the dreamer can re-own through the role-playing. In this way Gestalt addresses not just the head and the intellect but the whole person, keeping a focus on the physical and the present, as Marti Matthews describes:

". . . Gestalt work has the space to include whatever is relevant from the past, but it's focused on the present problem . . . The technique is so simple—'be' the different parts of your dream . . . It was your dream and regardless of what universal things can be said about dream symbols, the really important thing is that YOU chose this symbol and it has importance to you . . . Even a physical symptom, [my therapist] will say, 'BE the achey back' . . . My dreams come alive this way, and the unconscious and consciousness are bridged as the dream symbol speaks for itself TO my conscious understanding. It's so fast! And feels so accurate, powerful, and—above all—healing."

Taking the parts of different characters or elements of a dream and acting out a dialogue between them, as in the Gestalt method, reveals the possibilities of using the waking imagination to resolve dream difficulties. The method can be learned and used with a friend to help you, or even alone at home. With a dream about a house or building, for example, a dreamer can act out an empty tower block, a rickety shed about to collapse, a door that won't open or a cosy cottage with too much clutter, and then make important connections to issues in her own life. Alternatively, she may approach the dream more laterally, asking herself questions like: How did it feel in the house? When have I felt like that? How did I feel when I woke? What part of my life is empty? What aspect of my life feels about to collapse? Where in my body would the closed door be? What is the clutter in my life that I could do without? These kind of questions may help the dreamer to talk about the structure of her life and how it might need to change.

With its directness, its ability to include the body, and its emphasis on the present, Gestalt makes rapid change seem possible. However, we will see in the course of this book that there are also dreams which are not primarily an inner dialogue, which cannot fruitfully be acted out, and which need a different approach. It is a question always of finding out what works best for you or for a particular dream.

You may find that you go through a phase of experimenting with different approaches on your own to discover which suits you. During this process of getting to know your dreams and your dreaming self, you may find it very helpful to read Ann Faraday's books *Dream Power* or *The Dream Game*, or Stephanie Dowrick's *The Intimacy and Solitude Self-Therapy Book*.

CONNECTING DREAMS TO DAILY LIFE

Using techniques from psychotherapy raises the question: When is a dream a metaphor for our inner life and emotions, and when is it a comment on daily life events? Some dreams seem to be about both. Take this example:

I dreamt that we have squatted a prefab house, me and another woman. It seems very isolated and vulnerable. I go round putting on lights and drawing curtains to protect it. I am afraid.

This dreamer comments:"I had to learn to cope early in life, I learnt 'male' characteristics to survive in a male world. I get things done, I answer back, and I put men at a safe distance. But on the other side of this 'strength' there is a weakness, a passivity, which comes out at night when I often sleep in terror of a night invader breaking into the house. I have, like many women, been alone in a house during an attempted break-in. So this is partly based on experience. But

I wonder in this dream whether what I really fear is my own feelings breaking in on me?''

This is a dream which, as the dreamer herself comments, could be taken either way: as reflecting a real fear of invasion which women often experience in urban Western society when at home alone at night; or as reflecting inner processes and feelings which are threatening to ''burst in'' on her. While this dream is ambiguous, there are other dreams which seem clearly to have a practical rather than a psychological message. On occasion it is useful to remember that a house in a dream may represent—literally—a house. Here is an example from Linda Dove, from a time when she was very involved with the problems faced by her children's community-run school in Los Angeles:

''My dreams are usually vivid and complex but this one was brutally simple, a nightmare in fact.

''We had been talking and planning to add a second storey to our little Californian bungalow. The meetings with the architects were scary and exhilarating—the very idea that I should say what I want, and that I might be able to get it! A room of my own! I would go to sleep thinking about it and wake up still thinking about it, all mixed up with worries about the LA riots and the bankrupt school system.

''My nightmare began simply with a charming little house, three storeys high but quite narrow, with lots of windows, an old detached English Victorian house. It was built four-square on plain, flat ground. Then slowly, steadily it began to sink. It just quietly sank into the mud; the primeval swamp swallowed it up completely.

''I woke up in a horrible sweat but I didn't really make sense of the dream 'til I was showing the architect's model to a friend later and, trying to downplay its grandiosity, I joked that perhaps it wasn't wise to be building 'the house of my dreams in the city of my nightmares'.

"It slowly dawned on me in the next few days how true that was. Los Angeles is like primeval mud, completely unmanageable; building in it was like being the unwise Little Pig or the Biblical person who built on sand.

"Now we're planning to move to a town separate but next to LA, with a separate school system, police force, etc. And building my dream house is on hold, at least until we get out of the nightmare swamp."

Here the dreamer was helped not by any dream theory but simply by letting her dream simmer, and being prepared to listen to the comment it was making about a practical life situation. We have seen many different ways to start accessing dreams; to know which one is appropriate at any time, we need first of all to keep an open mind and pay attention.

Reading and Notes

Ann, "Dreams of Children," collected by Sally Vincent, *Fire*, 1, July 1967, published by Fire, 4 St. George's Terrace, London NW1, p. 16.

Bishop, Beata, "The Bridge of Dreams," *Caduceus*, Spring 1992, published by Caduceus, 38 Russell Terrace, Leamington Spa, Warwickshire CV31 1HE, p. 8.

Dowrick, Stephanie, *The Intimacy and Solitude Workbook*, W. W. Norton, New York, 1994.

Edelstein, Emma J. and Ludwig, *Asclepius: A Collection and Interpretation of the Testimonies*, I, The Johns Hopkins Press, Baltimore, 1945, p. 230, Ayer, Salem, NH, 1976.

Ernst, Sheila, and Lucy Goodison, *In Our Own Hands: A Book of Self-Help Therapy*, The Women's Press, London, 1993, p. 152 (first published 1981).

Faraday, Ann, *The Dream Game*, Harper and Row, New York, 1976.

Faraday, Ann, *Dream Power*, Berkley Pub., 1986.

Freud, Sigmund, *Introductory Lectures on Psychoanalysis*, The Pelican Freud Library Vol. 1, translator J. Strachey, Penguin Books, Harmondsworth, 1974, pp. 144, 143 (dreams not genuine and self-interpretation), pp. 200–203, 192 (basic language, decoding symbols). Published in the U.S. by W. W. Norton, New York, 1976.

Gestalt Therapy: for the best overall description see F. Perls, R. Hefferline and P. Goodman, *Gestalt Therapy*, Dell, New York, 1951. A very readable summary can be found in Petrûska Clarkson's *Gestalt Counselling in Action*, Sage, London, 1989.

Hillman, James, *The Dream and the Underworld*, Harper and Row, New York, 1979.

Jung, Carl G. (ed.), *Man and his Symbols*, Dell, New York, 1968.

Jung, Carl G., *Symbols of Transformation*, translator R. F. C. Hull, Routledge and Kegan Paul, London, 1956, p. 391 (archetypes) [Vol. V of Collected Works].

Nolan, Inger, "Working Creatively with Dreams," *Inside Out*, 12, Spring 1993, published by Inside Out, 23 Lower Albert Road, Glenageary, Co. Dublin, p. 15.

Perls, Fritz S., *Gestalt Therapy Verbatim*, Bantam Books, Toronto, New York, London, 1969, pp. 237–240 (talking to your dreams), pp. 102ff (Nora's dream).

Schatzman, Morton, "The Meaning of Dreaming," *New Scientist*, 25 December 1986/1 January 1987.

Thomas, Sherry, "The Journal as Source," *Country Women*, 21 September 1976, ("Woman as Artist" issue), published by Country Women, Box 51, Albion, California 95410, p. 12.

2
Working on Dreams with Others

Working on dreams with others is a tremendous resource. It can provide insight and understanding that cannot be gained from working individually. Other people may notice things that the dreamer has overlooked, bring in a different perspective or insight, give support to help the dreamer come to terms with difficulties, and—through their interaction with the dreamer—bring dream issues out into the waking world of living relationships. Working with a friend or group can be an extension of individual work, opening the possibility of using different approaches and resolving the whole dream exploration differently.

Take this dream:

I am in a shack with an aunt I do not like. Down the sides of the shack are big drainpipes with arms.

Here, with some details changed, is an account of how this woman worked on her dream in a woman's group:

"Simone started by sitting on a cushion to speak as if she were the drainpipes. They said, 'We are fat. Everything goes down us. All kinds of rubbish.' She linked this to her own

33

difficult emotions about her body, which she felt was over-weight. She talked about her problems with food. In a Compulsive Eating group she had traced her over-eating to a hidden need to make herself unattractive to men so that she would be safe from their approaches. The resulting sense of self-disgust was difficult to live with, and made her feel cut off from everyone.

"At this point one group member recalled that in the dream the drainpipes have arms. 'What do the arms want?' The dreamer replied that they want contact, but cannot have it because the drainpipes are so disgusting. Then someone asked what would happen if she went round the group and used her arms to make contact with each group member in turn. At first this seemed a very embarrassing thing for her to do, but she plucked up courage and moved round the circle, taking the hand of each woman in turn. Sometimes she spoke or just said 'Hello', in some cases she sat in silence for a few minutes or simply made eye contact. She was very affected by the experience. She said afterwards that it was rare for her to let herself feel that kind of warmth and acceptance from other people."

This technique, from Gestalt, of drawing an issue out of a dream into the group situation can help to bring problems into the here-and-now. By noticing her reactions as she went round the group, and experiencing their warmth and support, Simone could see how she needlessly perpetuated her sense of isolation in everyday life, and could question the belief that people would automatically reject her because of her weight.

DOING ROLE-PLAY WITH OTHERS

In Simone's dreamwork, direct personal contact with the group made all the difference. If it had been appropriate, the role-play could also have been set up differently from the start, with the whole group involved more actively. As psychotherapist Jenner Roth describes it, "Another wonderful way to work on dreams in a group . . . is to have group members play various roles from the dream, and the dreamer either play themselves or act as producer/director giving clear and explicit directions to each actor about their position, posture, attitude, language, etc." This can be a way of gaining a new perspective on the dream, and the dreamer can benefit from the comments of other group members who can share their own responses and resonances after the dreamer has finished working. In Simone's case, she could have had other people playing herself, the aunt, the shack and the drainpipes. They could act out a dialogue under her direction, and afterwards they could give her feedback about how they felt in the different roles. Sometimes you can carry the action of the dream onwards, which might have drawn out different insights for Simone. This kind of re-enacting was developed as a psychotherapy method—Psychodrama—earlier this century by a Viennese psychiatrist, J. L. Moreno.

Other possibilities for tapping into a group's collective wisdom include using the dream as a basis for group storytelling, with or without actions. The presence of other people also helps generate the energy needed to explore dream symbols through movement or dance.

DOING MOVEMENT AND DANCE

Jung suggested that animals and insects can represent the archetype of the "self," that is, the core aspect of who we are. Perls said that everything in a dream is us, that all the elements—including cars, stars and monsters—are symbols of resources of energy potentially available to us. In each case, the interesting issue is why one animal or object appears rather than another, and which part of the self it represents. A good way of finding out is to try moving as that dream element. Doing this as a group process gives confidence and momentum. One way is for the group to start by sitting quietly with eyes shut for a few moments to allow a creature or other symbol from a recent dream to come forward. Then, moving in a circle, each in turn can make a movement to express that symbol, while the rest of the group joins in. This gives the dreamer back-up in really entering the spirit of the symbol, finding what part of herself it represents, and how she feels about it. In one workshop which I led recently, the group ''moved'' in turn like a crab, a fog, an earthworm, a mountain, a tree, a triangle, a horse, a mermaid, a candle and a fireball.

Sometimes when the group has met more than once, and people are familiar with some of each other's symbols, a drum can be used to call the changes in this exercise. Anyone in the group can bang the drum and call out a symbol from her own or another's dream, and then the whole group switches to moving like that symbol. In due course another woman will feel prompted to bang the drum again and call out a different symbol, and so on. Having everyone join in on a difficult dream symbol can make it feel less horrible and easier to accept, while sharing a pleasant one gives a chance to enjoy it. One can also learn a lot from trying out other people's symbols. At the end of a session each person might choose a symbol to take away as an emblem—perhaps representing a quality they would like to have more of in their life. Meditating with that symbol after the session can help to carry what has been learnt into daily life.

Another approach is for the group members to move together like a large organism in recreating one person's dream scene or symbol. In one workshop, for example, a woman had dreamt an uncomfortable symbol of a black train travelling relentlessly. She directed the whole group to form the engine with our bodies. Interestingly, she asked us to face

inwards so that the outside of the train was all our backs
turned towards her. She realised that some of the "charge"
of the symbol for her was about feeling excluded from
things. But she also realised that although the train was passive on the outside, there was a lot going on inside (all our
limbs, faces and attention). Some people see black as a "negative" colour, but in my training I have been taught to see
it as very positive, absorbent and protective, especially useful
at times of transition. From this exploration through movement, the train emerged for this woman as a symbol of
changes happening for her: it was inward-looking, apparently
sealed-off, but none the less powerful, motivated and pur-
poseful. As a result, she felt more able to trust the processes
of change in herself.

DEALING WITH ANGER

Some dreams reflect a disruptive or painful anger, which
needs to be released before we can contact a full sense of
our personal power and creativity. Sitting on such anger can
be paralysing. Working with such dreams is rarely easy, but
the presence of other people can help to make the dreamer
feel safe to explore it in a way that she could not do alone.
The following example, based on a dream which a woman
explored in a group in London, shows some of the difficulties
and possibilities.

*"A person had been captured by a terrorist. She was lying
on a bed in an attic all tied up with heavy stuff. The door
was locked and the telephone was broken."*

The dreamer, "Diana," started by acting out the two main
characters. She found that the person tied up felt like herself—a single mother overburdened with responsibilities.

The terrorist seemed to represent her anger. In the dream work she ran into some common problems. One was that although both characters were angry, she found it hard to express that anger from either position. Instead it came out indirectly, as complaint, self-justification, or contempt, with phrases like: "It's not fair, I don't deserve this," "You asked for this," "It serves you right," "You're pathetic," and "You're not worth getting angry with."

Another problem was that in the re-enactment the kidnapped person wanted to simply "dump" her burden: she found it very hard to let herself feel the full anguish of her situation and was tempted to short-circuit the process of the dreamwork by quickly getting rid of it: "I realise I don't need this load. It's gone. I'm free to leave the attic." Such a high-speed shortcut to happy endings is rarely helpful, because it is hard to move forward without first experiencing the difficult feelings of being where one is. Through the use of breathing and body awareness—which often help in such situations—Diana eventually found that she could express some anger, as the terrorist, moving from "You're pathetic" to "I hate you!" Since opening up one emotion can help to release another, this led to the "victim" feeling free to express some of the pain of her life as a single parent geared towards the needs of others with very little for herself. Both the characters were communicating more, but at this stage they were still locked in conflict between "bully" and "victim," and the dialogue went round and round.

When this happens it can be helpful to look for something in the dream that is being overlooked. In this case, as one of the group pointed out, there was a broken telephone. When Diana moved on to speaking as the telephone, she found herself saying: "You could use me to phone for help, but I'm broken. I'm not working. You can't get through me." In this role Diana could identify with the part of herself which was paralysing her with resentment, which stopped her from communicating to ask friends for the support she needed. This inability to ask for help is what had left her feeling as isolated as a kidnap victim. While other parts of her are working overtime, this part is "not working": it is expressing anger in a passive way by blocking her contact with the world. As London psychotherapist Ann de Boursac has commented on this issue of owning your anger in dialogue work: "People will generally find it much easier and more comfortable to identify with the victim than the persecutor role. It is always useful to play out both sides. Sometimes we get stuck and are so caught up in the drama between the characters that we ignore an object—like an open window or a broken telephone—which seems to be just part of the setting but actually holds a vital clue."

In this case acting the telephone helped the dreamer to take responsibility for the way she was resisting doing what she needed to do, and the way she was actively cutting herself off from other people. Being the telephone drew Diana's attention to the possibility for action, for taking practical steps to improve her situation. Unexpressed anger can block the ability to make such practical changes. As women we are not generally encouraged to own our anger, but doing so can be a positive experience, one which a group can facilitate and accommodate.

OVERCOMING SHAME ABOUT OUR DREAMS

Sometimes dreams offer disgusting images, horrible events, unpleasant creatures. This may prompt the feeling that "deep down I am a horrible person," and we may carry these images around with us as a secret shame. Dreams should not be taken literally, and feeling judged or blamed for creating an unpleasant dream can be distressing and unhelpful. Here other people can make a big difference, either by making us feel worse or by helping us to come to terms with what seems so unpleasant. Look at the difference between the two following examples.

Gestalt Therapy Verbatim includes an account of Fritz Perls' work with a woman named Liz who recounted a recurrent dream of tarantulas and spiders crawling on her. In the dreamwork, she was very reluctant to act the spider or own it as part of herself ("I'm not aggressive . . . I'm not black and shiny . . ."). But she eventually did take the spider role and developed what Gestalt calls a "topdog—underdog" dialogue. Typically this is a dialogue between two inner voices: a bullying, righteous, judging voice in the head— in this case the spider, who criticised Liz for not doing things well enough—and a manipulating underdog voice who whines and sulks ("I try my best"; "I forgot"). Liz eventually recognised the topdog spider voice as that of her grandmother pressurising her to behave "correctly." Over years she had internalised that voice as part of herself, so now it was always with her—denigrating everything she did and killing her pleasure in life. In this way, as Perls put it in one of his more damning summaries, the grandmother "killed your soul, and the whole potential of your soul is missing. It's all mind . . . You are a 'good girl'. And behind the good girl there is always the spiteful brat . . . So this is where you are stuck, between compliance and spite." The next line of the transcript I find painful to read: "L: Thank you, Fritz," and Liz stepped down. One wonders where she might have found to go with this diagnosis. Gestalt emphasises the value of *feeling* your impasses and letting yourself fully experience your stuckness as the only way to move on. But when we lose our autonomy, when an authority figure tells us things about ourself, when we are made to feel a hopeless case, then sometimes we feel robbed of the resources even to face the stuckness, let alone move on. A woman who already has low self-esteem may not be helped by being told that her soul is missing.

Compare Liz's dreamwork with the following example,

where a woman was helped by her friend to draw something constructive out of a cruel dream scenario:

"I dreamt that there was a brown, nasty, rubbery flying monster with a pug face which was banging round my head, bothering it, annoying it. Someone told me about how they set up a fight in an arena between this monster and a beautiful coloured butterfly. The butterfly got beaten to pieces, it was very cruel. Though I wasn't there, I could imagine it, it was horrible."

The woman who had this dream commented: "This dream troubled me so much that I asked a close friend to sit with me to help me explore it. I was particularly affected by the cruelty in it. I started by acting the butterfly. I felt powerless, hurt, a bit like I used to as a child when my family—especially my father—pressurised me. As for the monster, I didn't want to act it, I was repelled by it. When I did, at first it said things like 'Don't get in my way' and 'I'll crush you to get what I want', and expressed hatred for the weedy little butterfly. My friend asked me as the monster what I was after with such ruthlessness; the monster replied that it couldn't let her father down, had to be super-competent or it would be nothing. I could recognise it as a part of myself, a bit like the voice of my father inside me. I hate myself when I am like that. My friend encouraged me to really get into the role physically, which I did with a lot of energy. The dreamwork came to a helpful resolution, partly by my friend helping me to identify the good things about the monster (it is very energetic and capable, it *does* take care of things and get things done), also partly by her encouraging me to release some of the fear lying behind that relentless activity. The monster and the butterfly were not such extreme contrasts in the end, and ever since then I recognise that 'monster' part of me—with a special nickname—whenever I start acting like that."

While some creatures glow more numinously in our inner world, and may attract us more as symbols of the "self," other less pleasant ones may be equally important in unlocking something inside us. In the dream above, two symbols—one beautiful and one quite unpleasant—represented different parts of the dreamer; both had something to offer and, although initially in conflict, they started through the dreamwork to move towards integration. It was her friend's compassion and generosity in accepting the dream monster which helped this woman towards accepting herself.

CAN PEOPLE WORK TOGETHER ON DREAMS WITHOUT PROFESSIONAL TRAINING?

Unsung and unpublicised, in many countries groups of lay people meet to share and explore their dreams. The women who belong to such groups speak highly of the benefits:

"I've been in the same self-help dream group for about eight years. We meet about once a month, taking it in turns in the homes of the four of us . . . We always start with a meal . . . then we meditate for twenty minutes . . . and then we divide the remaining time by the number of those present and each person can bring a dream . . ."

"The dream group has been a marvellous source of warmth and support in my life—even though we only meet about four or five times a year now, and live quite far apart. But a rather special relationship develops between women who have met through their dreams—we know each other in a way that is different from other friendships. We have, if you like, got to know each other through the language of symbol, and have had to be very gentle with each other, because dreams come from such deep places. Also, it so happens that the lives of the women who are in this particular group have all been unusually adventurous and dramatic.''

All you need to set up a dream group is goodwill, the ability to pay attention to others, and a few simple ground rules. The priority of any group is to establish a safe environment (warm, comfortable and undisturbed) and firm boundaries (about starting time, ending time, how you work with the dreams, and confidentiality outside the group). A clear decision needs to be negotiated about where you are going to meet, how often and for how long (evening? lunchtime? early morning? afternoon with one group member looking after children? weekly? fortnightly? monthly? for two hours? three hours?); also how you will divide the time between group members (some groups prefer to spend the whole session on one dream). It is good to have a regular time and a commitment to attending a certain number of sessions, because consistency is an important factor in helping people trust each other to share their dreams.

Montague Ullman, who has done pioneering work organising dream groups in many settings in the USA and Scandinavia, is convinced that ordinary people can work fruitfully with their dreams. He suggests that the necessary skills, and the ability to appreciate dreams, become accessible in any situation where understanding and compassion are valued, and the benefits are huge:

> ... by going beyond the privacy of the self ... we can have a most satisfying experience, one that meets a universal need to unload personal secrets in a safe environment and to meet others at deeper levels than in ordinary social intercourse.
>
> This need is largely unmet in what we somewhat euphemistically regard as a civilised society. When a supportive and stimulating structure is offered, it is amazing

how responsive people are to dreamwork . . . (*The Variety of Dream Experience*)

Members of lay dream groups may find they are helped by reading books, by attending occasional professional dream workshops to learn new approaches, or even by asking a professional therapist to come in and help the group for a few sessions if they get stuck. However, in my opinion the single most important skill needed is the ability to listen to others with respect and compassion. This gives the dreamer the support she needs to make her own discoveries about her dreams. Listening in this way is harder than most people imagine, so it may help to give some guidelines.

HOW CAN A GROUP LEARN TO HELP EACH OTHER WITHOUT INTERFERING?

It is very tempting to interpret another's dream for them. But it is easy to get it wrong, and far more useful for the dreamer to be helped to make her own sense of it. When you have heard someone's dream, useful comments are the kind which start:

> "I noticed . . ."
> "I felt . . ."
> "I wondered whether . . ."
> "I am curious about . . ."
> "Your symbol of x inspired me to . . ."
> "Your symbol of y made me think about such-and-such issue in my own life" (owning your own problems rather than laying them on the dreamer).

Ullman stresses the importance of group members respecting each other's experience, and emphasises two factors:

safety and discovery. The first makes the second possible. Interventions by group members concerning another's dream should not be invasive.

At every stage of the dreamwork, control rests with the dreamer. Commenting that it is the sign of a beginner to probe too deeply, Ullman recommends that the group follow rather than lead the dreamer, and that they avoid grinding axes, posing searching questions, or pursuing waking prejudices about what might be important to the dreamer. This lays the ground for discovery, because the dreamer needs help from the group to "make discoveries about himself [*sic*] that are difficult to make alone."

To achieve this, Ullman worked out a specific formula for groups to use in tackling dreams, which may be useful when starting out. First, the dreamer volunteers a dream and the group asks any questions they need to clarify it. Secondly, the group play a game in which they imagine that the dream is their own. Speaking to each other, they offer their own projections about the dream, which the dreamer may in due course accept or reject. They share feelings or moods which the dream arouses in them, and imaginatively explore the dream imagery and any possible links with life situations.

In the next stage the dream is returned to the dreamer who can respond to what the others have said as much or as little as she wishes. She can share how far she has come in understanding the dream. If more work is necessary, she can proceed in a dialogue with the group, where they ask open-ended questions to help her make links to the real-life context—such as: "What were you thinking as you fell asleep last night?," "Did anything happen recently which affected you emotionally?" or "Do you want to say anything about . . . in the dream?"

Notice that in Ullman's method there is no interpretation of the dream by others. What the dreamer gets from the group are feeling responses to her dream, which she can use as she will. Ullman believes that it is not interpretation but

the "process of engagement with one's feelings in a supportive and cooperative milieu that makes for change."

The final stage of the dreamwork is the next session, when
the dreamer is invited to share any thoughts that have come
up since the last session.

Ullman's approach is one of many for exploring dreams
in a group situation. You might decide to do activities (such
as dream drawing, or movement) together as a group, or just
allot time fairly to group members to use as they will. A
group might at different times use any of the approaches
described in this book, from free association to problem-
solving, from art work to role-play. In *In Our Own Hands:
A Book of Self-Help Therapy*, Sheila Ernst and I discussed
many of the issues which arise when starting a self-help
group, and offered exercises to try out different ways of
working together with respect for each other's needs.

CAN A DREAM GROUP HELP ME
TO MAKE POSITIVE CHANGES IN MY LIFE?

Winifred Rushforth, who was running analytically-based
dream groups in Scotland while in her nineties, suggested
that being in a dream group could go on indefinitely and that
group members can perhaps expect "increase of wisdom,
understanding, ability to forgive, freedom from anxiety, release of tension, occurring progressively as we are mindful
of our dreaming." However, she acknowledged that there
may be painful revelations along the way.

The "dream dictionary" approach sometimes seems to
suggest that by unlocking your dreams you can make easy
strides towards positive changes in your life. But in reality
it can be more of a slow and winding process, which cannot
be rushed. If the quest to understand ourselves through our
dreams leads to the possibility or need to change, then ex-

periencing the difficulties our dreams present can in itself be helpful and healing. Gestalt therapy's ''paradoxical theory of change'' suggests that the best way to change is to begin by truly accepting where you are at in your life. If you are depressed, let yourself feel really depressed; if you are stuck, tell yourself ten times a day how stuck you are; if your life is like an incomplete house, as in the case of Nora in Chapter 1, let yourself fully feel the discomfort of that. Only then may you be able to start to change. Denying the situation, trying or pretending to be different, leaves you with no basis or ground from which to start; as Gary Yontef put it, ''Trying to be who one is not is not self-supporting.''

Through doing regular dreamwork, positive changes may—and probably will—happen, but for a group to push someone into changing provokes resistance and gives the message that they are not acceptable as they are. Changing to please someone else simply does not work because you do not have resources of your own to maintain the change. To help someone change, a group needs patience, an accepting attitude, and trust that people will eventually move towards what they need. To make any wished-for changes in yourself, it is not a question of feeling ''wrong'' and working hard to become ''right,'' but rather of letting yourself be open to strengths in yourself which your dreams point out. I am going to close this chapter with an example of a woman who let her heart go into this process—and made huge gains as a result. It concerns a dream character who became a constant companion and source of strength for Beth Shaw:

''I now own the house I was brought up in, but people have moved into it without my permission. My mother and sisters are in one part, the cast from the community musical show I've just been in are in the playroom. But I'm most disturbed by a voluptuous Brazilian woman who's sprawled on the landing half-naked making long-distance calls to Brazil. I'm tearing my hair with anxiety over how I'm going to pay the

bill. Even though I yell at her, she invites me out to a beautiful Italian cobbled square with her boyfriend, a skinny young man, and we all dance together in star formation. I feel this is just wonderful, and I'm still very surprised that she takes me to the dance when I've yelled at her. Then at the end of the dance I feel my mouth fill with glass cutting my skin. She says, 'You can't worry about the bill anymore when you're hurting yourself so much with the glass in your mouth.'

"When I woke up, I felt horror at the image of feeling the glass in my mouth, so I called it a 'nightmare,' then I thought of the beautiful scene in the square. It led me to think that experiences weren't always *either* good or bad but a mixture of what we like or don't like. I think the influence of the Brazilian woman stayed with me to the end of the day when I went out with some of the cast (of the community show) to dinner. Afterwards, even though it was past midnight, I invited those who wished to back to my flat where the stage manager mended my old guitar and we sang till 3:30 A.M.— which was lovely! I don't think *I* normally would have thought of inviting them, though of course the Brazilian woman would stay up as long as she liked!

"When I took this dream to my next dream group, I was astonished when they said, 'But Beth, we see *you* as the Brazilian woman!' Then they suggested that I might try some 'acting as if' I was the Brazilian woman.

"It began to dawn on me that perhaps I had a choice of either acting the skinny, anxiety-ridden, fearful Beth, or be more the Brazilian, relaxed at spending money, just being sensual rather than needing reassurance, enjoying eating, eating to her fill, lovely luscious food . . . I have a glimpse that the Brazilian woman doesn't feel so competitive with other women because she is sure of her sexuality—she knows there's plenty of love, sex, food, money in the world for her!!

"I am amazed at the power the Brazilian woman has, just by having her feet on the ground and being solidly in her body. Because she is secure about her place in the world, she moves through it with grace and ease. She can forgive those who yell at her like the skinny Beth with glass in her mouth, and she doesn't hold resentments. She isn't a snow-white goody-goody—somehow good/bad is irrelevant in connection with her. She is. She doesn't need to manipulate anyone because she feels secure in herself and knows that if she wants something, she will ask for it directly. She generates excitement, so she doesn't need to wait for exciting things to happen to her.''

Six years after having the dream and writing the above, Beth Shaw returned to what she had written:

''Re-reading it now, I realise I had forgotten the beginning about the other people who had moved into my house without permission. I have often thought of the rest of the dream and have remembered it pretty exactly. For about nine months after I had that dream I 'lived' with the idea of becoming more like the Brazilian woman fairly intensively and this brought some changes to my life. For instance, I had long wanted to go on certain walking adventure holidays but had felt afraid to do so, because I thought I wouldn't manage to put up my tent. But now I thought the Brazilian woman would ask someone to help her the first time and that way she'd learn. This is what happened and I had a wonderful holiday, on the last morning of which I was sitting by the campfire after an icy cold dip in the River Dove in Derbyshire, thinking sadly, 'Well, I suppose this is all over until next summer.' Then I thought, it's only June now, and if the Brazilian woman enjoyed herself as much as I have, she would book up another walking holiday *this* September! And so I did and had an even more marvellous time roving over Exmoor . . .

''I would say that the Brazilian woman has never quite left my consciousness in the intervening six years. And just

the day I began typing all this up, a friend came round to
give me a massage and we were talking about how my arms
were strapped up soon after I was born (to stop me sucking
my thumb after an operation on my hare lip), and thus they
have always felt extremely wobbly to me. The masseuse suggested I might make two drawings: one of my wobbly arms
and one of a stronger image. I puzzled about the stronger
image and then I thought what rounded strong *full* arms the
Brazilian woman has (her skimpy top shows off her arms
well) compared with the skinny Beth in the dream, rather
shrunken inside herself. So I've decided to borrow the Brazilian woman's full arms for the next few months, I'll just
spend a few minutes at the beginning and end of each day
visualising my arms as 'full of themselves' as hers.

"I've not yet become the Brazilian woman of my dreams
but my life is certainly a lot richer since she appeared in my
dreams. I eat much better and am not so skinny (I'm more
rounded). I still worry about bills but I enjoy spending
money more, which means I have to work a bit harder to
earn money but that's okay as I enjoy my work. I don't think
she would have had so conscious an effect on my life if I
hadn't been in a dream group and if I hadn't taken that dream
to the dream group to receive the revelation that they saw
me as the Brazilian woman even if I didn't . . . yet."

Reading and Notes

Ernst, Sheila, and Lucy Goodison, *In Our Own Hands: A
Book of Self-Help Therapy*, The Women's Press, London,
1993, pp. 9–56 (ways in to working together as a self-help
group), pp. 194–212 (brief summary of Psychodrama theory and practice, giving further references) (first published
1981).

Jung, Carl G., *The Archetypes and the Collective Unconscious*, translator R. F. C. Hull, Routledge and Kegan Paul, London, 1959, p. 187 [Vol IX, Part 1 of *Collected Works*].

Perls, Fritz S., *Gestalt Therapy Verbatim*, Bantam Books, Toronto, New York, London, 1969, p. 87ff.

Psychodrama: See under Ernst, Sheila and Lucy Goodison.

Rushforth, Winifred, "The Analytic Dream Group," *Self and Society*, Vol IX, 3, May/June 1981, ("Dreams" issue), published by Self and Society, 39 Blenkarne Road, London SW11 6HZ, p. 133.

Ullman, Montague, "Introduction," Montague, Ullman and Claire Limmer (eds.), *The Variety of Dream Experience*, Continuum, New York, 1989, p. x.

Ullman, Montague, "The Experiential Dream Group," Montague Ullman and Claire Limmer (eds.), *The Variety of Dream Experience*, Continuum, New York, 1989, pp. 1–26 (I quote p. 5).

Yontef, Gary M., "Recent Trends in Gestalt Therapy in the United States and What We Need to Learn from Them," *British Gestalt Journal*, Vol I, 1, 1991, p. 14.

3

Remembering the Body

There is a wealth and diversity of dream life which can be explored, as we have seen, in creative and ingenious ways. Some women choose to apply or adapt existing methods, others to invent their own. The search for meaning can take many paths, and it often starts with the insights offered by dreams about the body.

In the nineteenth century a French aristocrat Marquis Hervey de Saint Denys published his book *Dreams and How to Direct Them* with a colour frontispiece which showed a young woman appearing naked at a sophisticated dinner party. The picture is part of our legacy of male dreams about making the female body vulnerable, exposed, available. Women's dreams present the other side of the same story: how we feel about our bodies which can be so vulnerable, in fantasy and in reality. Dreams remind us of parts of our body we neglect; they tackle taboos, assimilate changes, and debate unresolved sexual or moral dilemmas. Their memory is long: they can also recall long-forgotten abuses and help to heal historic hurts.

The traditional theories of psychoanalysis place emphasis on women's alleged feelings about their lack of a penis. It is interesting that many women's dreams seem to suggest a very different concern: the process of reclaiming their own *female* bodies, especially their lower half, legs, anus, genitals, and womb.

RECLAIMING THE BODY

Marie Cardinal, born in Algiers, arrived at a Paris consulting room after escaping from a sanitorium, in distress and with the symptom of menstrual bleeding which had continued constantly for three years. In her classic book *The Words to Say It*, she tells the autobiographical story of how psychoanalysis gradually helped her to escape from the constrictions of her Catholic background and re-own her body. Near the end of the process she had a dream which largely relived an actual incident. She had been staying in Provence with good friends, and had gone to visit a dovecote with one of those friends, an artist who creatively used in his work ''found objects'' (''garbage''). Stepping in from the glorious countryside on to the earth floor of the dovecote tower, she had a realisation which connected the beauty of the place with an unlikely element, excrement: ''It was the bird droppings which must have fertilized the soil in here.'' In the beauty and silence of the roofless dovecote, she had a sense of being ''part of the Whole . . . complete.''

In the dream she recreated this visit and found herself:

standing alone in the dovecote with water washing down round the inside of its walls, carrying glittering oblong objects which she realised were finely worked silver cases, each one containing a turd: she was standing in the middle of a magnificent toilet bowl.

She woke full of joy and satisfaction. Puzzling the meaning of this dream afterwards, and trying to understand how harmony and excrement could go together so well, she reached the understanding that "there was an entire area of the body which I had never accepted and which somehow, never belonged to me. The zone between my legs could only be expressed in shameful words, and had never been the object of my conscious thought."

The acceptance of this "shameful" part of her body was what opened the possibility of feeling satisfaction and a spiritual sense of completeness.

As she ruminated on the dream, a picture came to her mind of the circus clowns who pretend to think themselves clever while seemingly unaware of a little red bulb lighting up at their rear ends:

"They are grotesque, because they appear to ignore what is happening at the base of their spines . . . Poking fun at myself was delicious. I'd lived until the age of thirty-six with an opening in my body with the horrible name 'anus.' I had no ass! What a farce! . . . I had a front and that was all, I was flat like the queen in a pack of cards . . . with a big bosom, broad hips, a crown on her head, a rose in her hand, hieratic and no behind!"

Marie Cardinal's dream drew together the spiritual and the scatological to reaffirm the value of her lower half in grand style. Linking physical functions—even "unpleasant" ones— with emotions and the psyche, dreams show the body not as a machine but as a living organism charged with thought and feeling. Apart from reclaiming lost parts of our bodies, the dream world also seems able to confront taboos and guide us towards taking pride in body processes.

TACKLING TABOOS: FROM SHAME TO PRIDE

Here is an example where the experience of menstruation— generally considered a shameful one in our society—is as-

sociated with a dream affirming creativity, self-expression
and connectedness. As the dreamer, Australian-born Roxanne Clark, explains:

"This dream had a special significance for me as I dreamt it
in the early hours of the morning I began menstruating and
it involved a friend, F., who also began menstruating that
same morning.

*"F. and I are standing talking in her front room, which
is green, light and soft. I am upset about something and have
been crying. We see two men approaching through the front
window and F. says they are from the wheel-clamping de-
partment coming to return her car. She goes to answer their
knock at the door and I stay in the room, embarrassed at
being seen while upset. I press up against the wall, almost
behind the door, not wanting to be seen, and am shocked
when one of the men walks into the room. He is surprised
to see me, but then takes no more notice of me as he walks
up to a large exquisite urn standing against the opposite
wall. I had not seen the urn before.*

*The man is young, black and quite ordinary to look at,
but he picks up the urn and begins handling it with deftness
and confidence, lifting and turning it around. I forget my
shyness and am overwhelmed by a feeling of protectiveness
for the urn. I walk over to the man. The urn is exquisite; it
stands as tall as my shoulder, has funnel-like ends and a
round, pregnant-shaped belly. It is made of the finest white
clay and has a fine, textured matte patina. Encircling the
middle is a shadow relief of traditional Aboriginal life in soft
charcoal, blues and greens. The scene is a man standing with
a spear and women and children sitting in a circle. I am
awed by its beauty and sacredness, and afraid the man will
break the urn as he twists and turns and pushes it to fit into
a hinged slatted wooden support, which looks like the old
clothes horse I use for drying my laundry. However, he seems
very relaxed and confident in what he's doing, and though I*

can't see his face—he looks sideways at me—he looks up
with his right eye which is beautifully cat-Egyptian in
shape—elongated and almond-like—and which strikes me
with power, light and intensity in one single glance. He con-
tinues working and fits both funnel ends into the frame se-
curely. The belly, huge, remains unsupported on its side.
Satisfied with his work the man takes the urn out of its frame
and returns it to its original place and leaves the room. I
rush from the room to look for F. and tell her of the scene
on the urn. I find her washing dishes in the kitchen sink . . .

"When I awoke from the dream my hand was resting on
my belly. I knew I had begun menstruating and felt very
peaceful . . . I discussed the dream with F. and we both felt
the urn was a potent symbol of spirituality, creativity and
fertility.

"F.'s front room where myself, the man and the urn in-
teracted is a place in which I feel safe and inspired creatively.
The urn definitely represents the embodiment of my life's
potential—my creativity, spirituality, self-expression, connectedness. It feels quite ancient and appears fragile but is
very strong, as the man's handling of the urn proved. I am
unsure of this man, but feel he has two levels of significance.
Firstly he came from the outside world, and an authoritarian,
controlled system—'wheel-clamping division'—which I was
afraid of being exposed to; but he was also gentle, confident,
relaxed and was a dexterous craftsman. The initial significance is of the external world 'clamping,' holding me in
place, but then I feel this man went on to show me I could
creatively fit all the potential of what I see in the urn into
formal structures—the domestic wooden frame—and just as
easily return safely to a safe and solitary place. I believe he
was also showing me I could use my own masculinity in a
confident non-threatening way, as he had transformed once
he entered the room. His beautiful, intense eye was enigmatic
and shone with an ancient, spiritual light. It was 'other-
worldly' and I think a very strong spiritual link. I feel a

connection between the ancientness of the eye and the scene of traditional Aboriginal life on the urn's belly. That there is a link between myself and seemingly disparate lives, times and places . . .

"I felt very empowered after this dream, with a stronger sense of my life's direction and purpose, and acceptance of this."

After this dream, Roxanne Clark and her friend established a monthly ritual to mark the menstrual process. The dream moves through feelings which will be familiar to many women in our society, such as shame (hiding behind the door at the start of the dream) and vulnerability (the fragile urn) to reach a point of celebration of menstruation as symbolising her own creativity, which can be integrated with external structures.

It is interesting that in traditional interpretations of the vessel as a female/womb symbol, it is usually the receptive, containing aspect of the vessel which is emphasised. Here however it is the creative, outward-going aspects of the urn which come forward for the dreamer. The main function of the womb is to give birth: an outward-moving, pushing, exertive action. In my research into the woman-oriented society of prehistoric Crete I found that the vessel was often shown with something growing out of it. Perhaps the emphasis on a passive and receptive rather than active and creative vessel is another example of the way Western culture has defined women's roles and symbols according to its own prejudices. I would suggest that only women can explore what the symbolism and meaning of the womb is for us, and very often it is dreams which will bring those meanings forward.

FACING SEXUAL DILEMMAS

Another gift of dreams is that they can help us to face honestly some difficult issues in sexual relationships. Sometimes they encourage us to do this by replaying in detail real-life problems, as in the following example:

"Last night I dreamt Brian and I are trying to make love in the van in the driving seat but it doesn't work out. Maybe it's the position, we try again on a patch of grass at the end of a field but he just can't get it on, he isn't into it. I feel inadequate, it's my fault, I'm just not good enough, there's nothing I can do (the way I have felt when he's been 'off' me) and I feel despairing about the relationship. I can't go on, it can't go anywhere. Despair."

Many women may recognise the tendency this woman has to blame herself when things do not work out sexually with a man. By replaying for her the pain this sexual scenario is causing, the dream is perhaps pointing out a problem which needs attention.

Sometimes the issues raised are of a more general nature— for example about morality, or power—as if the dream were using a hypothetical sexual encounter to raise a discussion topic. Here's an example:

"I am sleeping next to K., the 18-year-old stepson of one of my best friends. This is not on, so I move away from him although I found it exciting. He says, 'Sex is just like eating, there don't have to be many hassles about it' or words to that effect. I say "Well, eating is one thing, but if you're eating human flesh there is quite a lot to talk and think about."

The dreamer comments: "I had this dream at a time when I was experimenting sexually, and I think part of me was trying to warn me that although I thought I was being free, I was playing with fire and perhaps making too light of the emotional after-effects and human factors involved."

Here many interpreters might focus on the complex relationship between sex and food, kissing and eating, on which the dream plays. It has been suggested that since feeding is one of the earliest and most rewarding sensual acts of the baby, this sets a mould which is perpetuated for women later in life, the penis more or less standing in as the nipple.

However, the dream also clearly raises the issue of morality. In traditional Freudian interpretations, dreaming of making love with someone might be taken as reflecting a secret wish to do so in real life. The original Freudian view was to see dreams as wish-fulfilment, expressing primal, childlike, often disruptive or destructive impulses and instincts. Such a wish may well have been present in the dreamer above. But what is interesting is that the dream also contains a very adult debate about the human cost of indulging such lusts indiscriminately. This more thoughtful dimension of dreams, which is often overlooked, is discussed more fully in Chapter 7.

LIVING WITH BODY CHANGES

Throughout our lives our bodies change. We become taller or shorter, fatter or thinner, our eyesight changes, we lose parts through surgery or accident, our faces look different. For women, these changes can be particularly problematic, because society places such an emphasis on youthful female beauty. Older women are often represented as ugly and worthless. Dreams can help us adapt to such changes. They remind us what is changing, they help us adjust, and sometimes they can return to us parts of our body that are no longer functioning in waking life. This is what seems to happen in the following example where Diana Shelley explores associations linking the womb to creativity and to grieving.

Despite a hysterectomy, in her dream her womb is still there to play its part in a process of mourning her dead father:

"I forget the beginning, but there I suddenly was, feeling that old wet feeling between the legs. I didn't see it as blood, but of course it was. But I didn't have a womb, so it wasn't menstruation, it was haemorrhage—from what, through what, how? And then the dream was about stopping what I was doing to find a hospital, or a doctor at least. We did and we didn't, it's unclear. But I was having to get home, I was with people, but I had to walk, dragging along, when suddenly I felt a shock of a large, soft object come between my legs from behind and rise between them. The dog who was with us—a big mongrelly, long-haired golden retriever—was offering himself as a mount. I steadied myself astride him and held the fur at his neck and we moved towards home.

"Before I completely stopped dreaming, in the moment before waking, I knew and remembered my fear before I lost my womb that I would not be able to grieve properly. And now I feel myself unable to grieve properly, so is it true?

"This is the dream as I wrote it down at the time, two months after my father died just over a year ago. For much of this time I have felt unable to grieve for him 'properly,' openly, in the light of day. Working on this and other dreams, alone or with my therapist, I have come to realise that my grieving has been done mainly in dreams.

"Most of them repeat his dying, over and over again, which I see as a process of coming to accept his death, though I still don't truly believe he has gone. The dreams have helped to loosen the tightness and let the sorrow flow in a way which usually feels impossible in my waking life: paid work, political and trade union work, living with my partner, the commonplace things that do go on, more than anything the way my grief has been obscured by my mother's needs.

"This dream means something more complex than the repetitive dying-again dreams or the dream, on my birthday, when he came back alive, looking as he did when I was a child, to hold me. Set aside from the actual process of grieving, I think the dream is about how to grieve.

"The dream is also linked by the dog to others I have recorded over a period of more than 20 years. I quite often dream of animals, most frequently cats, sometimes horses, less often dogs or wild animals. They are present in the dream either as needing my help (to escape or complete a journey) or as helpers. This animal arrived in just this helper role, mysterious, unknown and with the quality of an equal, not a pet. I must have bled on his golden coat, but it made no difference to the quality of the help he gave.

"Six years ago I had a hysterectomy. I was fortunate in being able to choose when this happened as it was not an emergency. I had time to do the therapeutic work I needed first, and with my therapist I worked on what I feared about losing my womb. I had come to understand some years before I would never have a child, so it wasn't that which was so hard. What I identified with my womb was my capacity to write, to create, to express my deepest feelings and to grieve. In the women's movement, I feel we share some responsibility for creating these fears: in reclaiming our power, one of the things we have done is identify our wombs as a principal source of this power. But what of the women—so many of us—who for one reason or another (some bad, but some necessary) have our wombs taken away? Do we now lose our power? Like the images which conflate eyesight with discernment, this image can be discriminatory.

"Many years ago, when I was a member of a theatre group, an Irish woman taught me to keen, to grieve for the dead (and we used this in a piece on Northern Ireland, keening on the word Belfast). When I keened, kneeling on the ground and rocking backwards and forwards (as you can see grieving women do around the world), I would feel the grief

starting in my womb, at my centre, and rise through my body
till it came out as a cry, a word, the name of the dead.

"So what I feared, facing my hysterectomy, was losing
the centre of myself from which the grief (or the other forms
of the inner made outer, like writing) could break. Since my
womb was taken away I have not—as far as I can remember—dreamed of it bleeding. Then the need to grieve properly came and so in my dream, even without my womb, I
had to bleed."

Diana Shelley's account raises some important issues. She
points out that while we reclaim our female sexual body, we
do not have to fetishise it, for example by attributing magi-
cally "fixed" powers to the womb. We can watch our experience and make symbols to reflect it; as our experience
changes, so can the symbols. We do not have to accept the
tendency to fix symbols and rigidify them into systems and
institutions in the way that religions and therapeutic theories
have loaded a heavy meaning onto symbols like the cross
and the penis. Diana Shelley continues to write creatively in
waking life without her womb; in the dream she grieves and
has a womb which bleeds. This is another issue: the way in
which she is drawn into the dream world to do something
(grieve) which is hard to do in daily life. And in that world
she finds a magical helper available to her: the huge golden
retriever who appears from nowhere to carry her home. Like
the young man who handles the urn in Roxanne Clark's
dream, the dog is a "saving grace," a symbol of succour
and hope who inspires confidence in the act of living.

A common view of dreams is that they are an escape from
the realities of daily life. But for Diana Shelley and the
woman in the following example they appear rather differently: as a means of coming to terms with important life
changes. Rather than providing a means to avoid the body
we have to live with, they seem to teach us to live with the
body we have. While non-disabled people might imagine that

someone who cannot walk would dream of running or flying, Lois Keith wrote a dream poem which she sees as part of a process of accommodation to changes in her body after an accident:

"When I was 35, on holiday in Australia with my family, I was run over by a speeding car and badly injured. Most of the wounds healed but I had damaged my spinal cord and had no sensation and no movement below the break, about a third of the way down my back.

"I remember lying flat in the hospital bed, barely conscious with my head fixed in place by sandbags, trying to comprehend this completely altered state of being. I had been brought up in the 'mind over matter' school of thought—my mother had taught me that it was willpower that got people through difficult times. With all the strength of mind I could muster and with total concentration, I instructed just one of my toes to move. When they stayed exactly where they were, I knew with complete certainty that no message from my brain was going to change this and I was never going to walk again.

"It wasn't easy to get used to this but I had a very supportive partner and two young daughters and I knew that I would have to find a way. Two days after the accident, the neurosurgeon said to my husband, 'You will have a good life but it will be a different life.' This is what we hung on to then and indeed, it has proved to be true. I also understood instinctively, although it took me a while to articulate it, that despite messages from the media, there was no use thinking about 'cures.'

"But of course, dreams have another way of talking to you. About six months after my accident, I was at home surrounded by women friends with pens in hand. We had met the year before at a writing group run by Michèle Roberts at the City Lit Institute in London and some of them carried on supporting me by meeting together at my house.

The writing I did then is all about loss. I rarely wrote unless
I was with them and when I did it all came pouring out onto
the paper as if I had been saving it all up in my head. This
poem is one of those pieces. It wrote itself in 15 minutes,
just as it appears here.

"Dreams"

> *"I dreamt I was alone*
> *At the foot of the stairs in Daleham Gardens.*
> *Eight wide stone steps led to my mother's flat.*
> *But I didn't know how to get up them.*
> *Dead nerves crushingly refused to make my legs*
>   *move*
> *I couldn't do it, I didn't know how.*
> *I would just have to sit, sit alone and wait.*

> *"But somehow it wasn't impossible.*
> *If I took it carefully I could do it*
> *Why had I thought I couldn't?*
> *Take it slowly, slow and careful*
> *If I held on to the bar with one hand,*
> *If I held a stick in the other*
> *I could do it. It was easy.*

> *"One step forward.*
> *First one leg then the other.*
> *Easy easy easy*
> *Easy as winking*
> *Easy as dreaming*
> *Why had I thought I couldn't?*

> *"I dreamt I was at a party*
> *Lots of people drinking, talking and laughing.*
> *I needed a pee.*
> *I planned a strategy like a campaign*
> *And then I was there in the lavatory,*

Moving with help onto the seat
Narrow and white.

"*My muscles moved.*
A freak, a delightful freak.
Swish went the pee,
In a noisy rush like a fountain.
I smiled as I heard it splash into the pan
My muscles had moved.

"*Later that day I did the same again*
The rush of the fountain.
Easy easy easy
Easy as peeing
Easy as dreaming
Why had I thought I couldn't?

"*Waking, waking with a slow sense of truth*
My smile soon fading.
Just a hint of the truth
Shadowy frameworks around my real life.
A frozen smile
My dreams deceive."

"It's a sad dream and some of us cried when I read it out. But reading it now, I don't connect with the feelings and ideas in it. I see it as part of a process of accommodation to a different way of life and a different way of looking at my body. I remember a doctor for whom I have a high regard, telling me that this process, conventionally described as 'coming to terms,' usually took two years and although at the time I rejected the neatness of this forecast, I think now that it was true. I stopped thinking about how this could possibly have happened to me and started to accept myself.

"I'm not a very good rememberer of dreams but I know that I haven't dreamt about physical loss for many years and there are no 'miracle cures' in there either. In my dreams, I am neither hurtling over the hills nor am I in a wheelchair. There is usually some vague physical restraint but it isn't clear and it isn't the issue. Somehow, I leave my physical body out these days. The landscape or the room setting is often very real and detailed but—like many women, I suspect—the real subject of my dreams is relationships and attachments. I am in there and so are my feelings but other people are always clearer.''

SURVIVING VIOLENCE

Western culture glamourises and sells, but does not love, the body. As Sara Gogol put it in the American journal *Country Women*, ''We live within a society that sees the body as disgusting. Where the larger body we all live within, this planet, is not cared for lovingly but ruthlessly plundered; where women are defined as inferior to men; where a tiny minority of people have power over the rest . . .'' The control of the few over the many in society is mirrored in the image we use of the head controlling the body—as if the body were an ignorant and unruly population which needed to be suppressed. This body-denying, body-hating attitude is reflected in our social history of persecution and cruelty. It also resonates in individual acts of domestic violence which can have a long-lasting effect on the victims, usually women. Dreams can recall, and help us come to terms with, such experiences.

The following example brought to the dreamer's attention unresolved and painful feelings from an event which had happened many years previously:

''We are in the snow. We come across a block of ice, it is coffin shaped. There is a body inside, facedown. We turn it over, it is a boy about 9–12 years old. I think he is dead.

But he's not. I then feel stuck in the ice like him—intense restriction. I'm—we're—frantically trying to free the ice from his face so he can breathe. Quickly, help. I feel as he would—or am I him? We free the ice from his face, he can breathe. Now I feel my legs crushed, not able to move—get me out! End of dream. (I don't know who 'we' are—just a few other people.)"

The dreamer comments as follows: "This dream, I believe, is as a direct result of an event which took place when I was in my teens. My father came home drunk. I was lying on the couch, my mother was sitting nearby on a chair. My father, at some stage, got on top of me—full body contact—and would not get off. He was crushing me—my head was being pushed into a corner, I was desperate for him to get off. I thought I was going to suffocate. I started to panic and then scream. It was not until this point that my mother intervened.

"I am in my thirties and recently came out as a lesbian. The actual event happened about 20 years ago. The dream I have written about here happened very recently and is the first of its kind, but I know what it is associated with. I recalled it the next evening when a friend was leaning on me and I couldn't move my legs. It came back to me immediately. I have done some 'role-play work' around the actual event. I managed to vent some of my anger—at my mother mostly—and recognise the sexual implications of the events. I need to do more as it is still with me and often crops up."

An incident such as this may take a long time to work through and recover from. Other women's dreams reflect similar themes—that their bodies have been taken away from them, maimed, or killed—even without the direct experience of violence or abuse. Here is an example:

"It's a time when I'm really angry at a friend because of her rigid judgemental authoritarian attitude—like my father! Before sleeping I was full of murderous rage.

"I am in the front garden of my old kindergarten building. I am trying to dispose of my dead body. I have to butcher it, carve the flesh off the bones, and cut off the head in order to get it into a box to hide it. It smells disgusting of butchery like a charnel house. The box is the one we use to take the cat to the vet. I pack the pieces of body in and take it to hide it down by the gate. Must get it out of the way. I wake up out of disgust/fear and realise that it was my father that had killed me."

Feelings of self-disgust and hatred towards our own bodies—in which, as here, we sometimes end up being the aggressor—are perhaps not surprising given our society's attitudes towards women. While the previous dreamer described actual physical violence, this dreamer mentions only her father's "judgemental authoritarian attitude," and the butchered body in her dream shows that even this can effect a symbolic "killing" in which women can feel deeply hurt and damaged. Other examples seem to highlight the dreamer's pain at being a sexual female:

"Last night I dreamt I was a prostitute in New York and had a series of clients, all women. One was quite beautiful, in a frilly nightie. She lay very still and said 'What can you do to turn me on?' I moved closer and fondled her, she said, 'Don't touch my cunt it hurts.' I was shocked to see it was like an open wound, a broad slit with pus and blood."

Here the dreamer commented: "I think this is saying something about how easily I can be hurt sexually, however much I try to protect myself from hurt in other parts of my life."

This could be read in a variety of ways. For example Freud might have seen this image of bloody genitals as an image of castration, but the dreamer understands it as reflecting her experience of being hurt sexually and her symbolic sense of

her genitals as a wounded part of herself. While psychoanalytic theories reflect male preoccupations, such as the fear
of castration, my reading of the women's dreams sent to me
suggests rather different concerns, such as their own vulnerability, and issues about and between women, which our daytime culture marginalises.

Traditional male theories have been preoccupied with the
heterosexual experience, and seem to have regarded sex between women as something unmentionable or unspeakable.
Women's dreams acknowledge no such limitations. The freer
atmosphere of the dream world makes it possible for all kinds
of body and sexual experiences to be explored and experi-
mented with, as in this woman's dream:

*"I am making love with my mother. She is old, as she is now
in real life. I come to an incredible orgasm which wakes me,
and I find that my lover is asleep with his hand resting on
my crotch."*

Such dreams may touch a nerve of discomfort and embar-
rassment and may be too physical for some. However, there
are also body dreams which are not really about the body at
all: where the body is no more than a symbol for something
else.

DECODING BODY SYMBOLS

The newer, humanistic, therapies stress that dreams are often
not to be taken literally. A dream about making love with
someone might express wish-fulfilment, as Freud would have
it, but may just as likely be reflecting metaphorically a wish
to re-unite with a part of yourself symbolised by that person.
A dream of murdering someone does not mean that you are
a murderer or even that you secretly wish to kill someone:

the dream may be pointing out that you are killing, or letting go of, or ending, something in your life or a part of yourself. This raises questions about ''body'' dreams which are perhaps not very much concerned with the body at all.

Freud devoted much energy to showing that seemingly innocent dream imagery like bushes, hills, church spires and so on, could serve as a disguise for sexual parts of the human body. He also suggested that a dream symbol of one part of the body could be a disguise for another: for example, pulling out a tooth represents castration as a punishment for masturbation, presumably because with a stretch of the imagination a tooth is penis-shaped (female masturbation does not seem to be included as a possibility).

One of the revolutionary aspects of Freud's work was his courage in pointing out the importance of sexual symbolism in dreams—especially in the more prudish atmosphere of his times. However, since then things have changed. We are perhaps freer to dream about sex directly without needing such disguises—as the examples in this chapter show. Meanwhile dream dictionaries have trivialised Freud's ideas by concentrating on simplistic ''x means y'' equations, and some schools of psychoanalysis have pursued Freud's ideas to absurdity. The result is a lot of confusing misinformation about what body symbols mean.

Take the example of hair. American psychiatrist Morton Schatzman quotes with amusement (in *New Scientist*) a discussion recorded between five psychoanalysts about a patient's dream of having a bald patch on the back of his head. The interpretations they suggest range from an anal preoccupation, a fear of homosexual impulses, and inability to cope with rage, to a fragmentation of the self and an identity crisis: one suggests, ''I think the patient was saying 'I cannot cope with my loss of control, my rage; so I'll have to submit into a feminine homosexual position in order not to precipitate a fight that will destroy me.' '' Turning to the popularised version of this approach, the dream dictionary, we find interpretations that are less far-fetched but no more helpful. In Tom Chetwynd's *Dictionary for Dreamers* (one of the best of a dubious bunch) we find the suggestion that loss of hair indicates loss of virility. This is a plausible and modest suggestion, but not much use to women who also dream of hair loss. Jung's work has also influenced the dictionaries, so that "ancient myths" are sometimes brought in to provide interpretations. In one dictionary claiming to "unlock the language of your soul," I read that "Maidens originally sacrificed their Virginity, dedicating it to the Divine Powers in a Greek Temple. Later they sacrificed their hair instead . . ." From my own research work on ancient Greece, I am not sure which maidens or what Greek temple that might have been, and suspect this is another of those half-truths which get repeated so often at second hand that they are assumed true. It is also hard to see how this ancient Greek symbolism might help us in the present.

Is there any one fixed system for interpreting dream symbols? And if there were, is it necessarily helpful for people to have their dreams interpreted in this way? I think not. This point came home to me when I took part in a phone-in dream panel on BBC Radio Four's *Woman's Hour*. One woman telephoned to ask the meaning of a recurrent dream in which her teeth were falling out. Now I have found that one of the most useful guidelines in investigating body symbols is to look simply at what that part of the body does. Thus the teeth are used among other things for eating, biting, talking and smiling. Another guideline is to ask what issues you have experienced people working on in relation to their teeth; for example, I have seen people using their teeth when exploring their anger, grinding them or feeling an impulse to bite something. Based on those two lines of approach, one could say that this woman might have problems with anger or expressing herself generally; or she might be anxious about her appearance, perhaps with the fantasy that a pleasing "front" conceals something rotten. Or one of many different dream theories may hold the key: the mouth might indeed, as the Freudians would have it, be standing in for another body orifice. Or her unconscious might simply be reminding her that she needs to go to the dentist. One could not possibly know which is the correct interpretation without talking to her. Moreover, any interpretation that she was given by another person would be unhelpful and perhaps very upsetting unless she had a chance to make the connection for herself, and think about how that issue (e.g. expressing anger) comes up in her daily life. Sometimes people need to find something out for themselves before they can make use of it or decide to make a change. Sometimes they need time to work on an issue and absorb it, so that a one-line interpretation gives them nothing. For all these reasons, an off-the-cuff interpretation given by someone on the radio—or by a dream dictionary—may be useless or worse.

The key question is how the dreamer chooses dream symbols. Both Freud and Jung—in different ways—suggested that there is a fixed universal language of symbols, waiting for us to use to express or disguise our night experiences. Jane Roberts in the ''Seth'' books (a series of contemplative texts dictated in trance) presents a more flexible view. She too suggests that there is a process of translation going on, but not in any cut and dried sense. Her view is that dreams are energetic experiences which are not in themselves visual or dramatic. As we wake, we translate those elusive experiences into a form our conscious mind can grasp. To do this, we clothe them in the symbolic material that is most readily available to carry the dream feelings and thoughts into wakefulness. I understand this as an amoral process in which the waking mind unscrupulously grasps at any symbolic material that is at hand, with no respect of persons, to convey the thoughts, qualities or sensations of the dream experience. Because of a common culture, people in the same society may often use similar symbols. Because of different life histories, we may also use very different symbols sometimes. There are few rules. The dream symbol of a gun may stand for a penis, as Freud suggested. But a very different symbol might also be used to stand for a penis. And equally the opposite may be true: the dream symbol of a penis may represent something completely different. There are dreams using sexual or body imagery which turn out to be not only or not primarily about the body or sex. They are using that symbolism to comment on other issues.

In one workshop a woman's dream about a disappointing meal, with different elements which failed to blend into a satisfying whole, turned out to be reflecting frustration about a life whose various experiences had not added up to fulfilment. The dreamwork led into her imagining a meal that she *would* like, and talking about the different ingredients—suggesting different aspects of her life, work and relationships—which she would like to blend together. So here the dream was only ostensibly about food, and turned out to be more concerned with a general life situation. One could, of course, argue that the symbolism was not accidental: eating is one of the earliest experiences which confront us with the issue of what we do or don't want, and attitudes may be formed then which spread beyond food and resonate in our approach to people, work and so on later in life. We talk about "an appetite for life" or being "greedy for life."

Similarly there are examples where a dream about peeing was about being "relieved" of a personal burden, and where having a baby in a dream was about "giving birth" to an emotion which needed to be expressed. Sex in dreams may reflect more general feelings about how we relate or commune, intercourse in a dream may mean social intercourse, nakedness in a dream may be saying something about how we feel exposed in a more general sense, and so on. As an example here is a dream which I had myself, just before the publication of a book which had taken many years' work.

"I was going round and trying on clothes which were somehow left in piles and I put on a suit which was pink. End of dream."

In my dream group I was asked to imagine putting on the pink suit. Immediately I felt very uncomfortable: "Now I feel really naked. The pink suit is my birthday suit!" I realised that the dream was about finishing my book and being exposed by its publication. Until then I had never had to make a public statement as an individual about my beliefs and ideas (I had been "going round and trying on" various identities). But now it would all be out there in the book and, after so much work, I felt terrified about the book's reception.

In this dream again body symbolism was used to say something about a very different process, that of having a book published. Of course, one can argue that all feelings of shame and exposure derive ultimately from physical feelings of exposure and body shame; but my most pressing concern at the time was my book, and feelings of body shame were primarily a symbol or blueprint for my feelings about its publication.

If we are to glean the gifts of our dreams' insights about our bodies and our lives, we need to pay attention without assumptions. I am going to close this chapter with an example of just such an open-ended approach, one which listens without preconceptions, even to the point of using a person's active imagination to create a daytime "dream" associated with a particular part of the body: a knee.

LETTING THE BODY DREAM ITS OWN DREAMS

This account is from a woman, whom I shall call Kath, who was attending a dream workshop run by Barbara Somers at the Centre for Transpersonal Psychology in London. In this very interesting exploration, Kath started not with a dream but with a body symptom: a left knee which intermittently seized up, making her almost faint with pain. Asked when

the symptom first came up—often an important indicator—
she told the group that it first happened when she was eleven
years old. She was on a riding holiday. Her father, a priest,
always had sexy books hidden in the drawer of his desk, and
she had borrowed *Peyton Place* and then bought the sequel,
which led to him confronting her and telling her off. Presented with this symptom at the knee, Barbara Somers suggested that the knee produce its own dream.

Kath had an image of a scene with a vague white floating
figure on the right and on the left a black metal vice. As she
let the image fill out, Kath described the white figure as grey
and ghostly, with no clear boundaries. Behind the vice there
was an enormous dark energy. The vice was always chasing
the floating figure, haunting it, but could never quite catch
it. As Kath sat still and let the image develop under its own
momentum, she became aware that there was a dark forest
and rocks to the right, and that there was a path between the
black and the white figures, down which a horse could come.
As the path emerged, she saw that the figures had lost their
relationship to each other and were no longer fighting.

After Kath had begun exploring her image in this way,
Barbara Somers suggested that Kath speak "as" the knee in
the way familiar from Gestalt dreamwork. Imagining herself
the knee, Kath felt caught between the two figures, not wanting to be pinned down and trapped. "Let me go," says the
knee. "Let me go on my way, let me do my job. Be a knee.
Be a bridge so that energy can flow from top to bottom. Let
me be who I am. Leave me out of it. I'm not your battle-
ground." At this point Kath realised that the two figures
represented her parents—her father rigid and immoveable
like the vice, her mother a grey cringing martyr figure adapt-
ing to the father. "Let me be myself," the knee goes on.
"Have sex with each other, not with me." The feelings expressed by the knee were related to Kath being sexually
abused by her father when she was quite young. The words
of the knee, and it seems the painful symptoms of the knee

in Kath as an adult, reflected unexpressed feelings and tensions from her childhood.

Now that these connections had been made, Barbara Somers asked Kath if she had any thoughts about what she had experienced. Kath talked about her difficulty in her adult life in defining herself: it had become a habit with her to consider first what others wanted her to do. Barbara Somers then took her back to the complete dream: what would the knee like to do now? Tuning in again to the scene, Kath said that a powerful horse, black and glistening, was coming down the path. At Barbara Somers' suggestion, she visualised getting on the horse. She talked about the sensation of power in her pelvis as she felt the contact with the horse. "I feel more defined. The path is clear. It is something to do with finding my own sexuality."

The last stage of the piece of work was to gather the threads together. Kath was encouraged to check out how her body was feeling. She commented that her jaw felt looser, as if trapped energy were being released, "It's something to do with finding my own voice. My body feels more alive than at the start." She said that freeing herself from the web of abuse in her childhood would enable her to separate her father from God: "I could find a different definition of God. I could be less allergic to God." It would also help her to be more open to a relationship with a man. She said that she realised she needed to worry less about the meaning of experiences, rather let them soak in, experience the sensations, and stay in her body in the present tense. She did decide to take some riding lessons to let the symbol of the horse find a place in her life.

This kind of creative visualisation sounds difficult if you are not used to it, and some people may not take to it. However if you take time to relax, breathe fully, and let yourself focus your attention on the issue at hand—in this case an awareness of the left knee—it is possible to come up with a telling and relevant symbol. Kath was the only person who could have traced what her symbols meant for her, and a dream dictionary opened at "k" for "knee" would not have helped her.

Reading and Notes

Cardinal, Marie, *The Words to Say It*, translator Pat Goodheart, Van Vactor & Goodheart, Cambridge, MA, 1984.

Chetwynd, Tom, *Dictionary for Dreamers*, Thorsons SF, San Francisco, 1993.

Gogol, Sara, "The Air That Enables Me to Sing," *Country Women*, 24 April 1977, ("Personal Power" issue), published by Country Women, Box 51, Albion, California 95410, p. 4.

Roberts, Jane, *The Nature of Personal Reality*, a Seth Book, Prentice-Hall, New Jersey, 1974, pp. 439, 452ff.

Saint-Denys, Marquis Hervey de, *Les Rêves et les Moyens de les Diriger*, 1867, Bibliothèque Nationale, Paris.

Schatzman, Morton, "Everything You Ever Thought About Psychoanalysts Is True . . . ", *New Scientist*, 25 December 1986/1 January 1987, p. 38 (quoting from Jules Masserman, *Dream Dynamics*, Grune & Stratton, 1971).

4

Finding Lost Parts of Ourselves

How well do we know ourselves? Do bits of untypical behaviour surprise by popping out of nowhere? Do we have hidden resources that we are not aware of? The characters and objects who inhabit our dreams may have a lot to teach about parts of ourselves that have been lost, whether they are symbolised by babies, cars, film stars, or members of the opposite sex.

FINDING A LOST "MALE" SIDE

"I am driving down Coast Highway One from San Francisco to my parents' house. It's getting late in the day. I stop to telephone my mother to tell her I'm not going to make it. There's a phone booth by the highway, all by itself in the narrow strip of land between the highway and the shore. The area all around is fairly desolate; dune grass covers the slopes and it's very windy in a steady, swishing way. The light is that funny grey half-light that happens sometimes late

*on a hazy afternoon, when the sun is just a disc. I tell my
mother I might stay the night here.*

"*As I hang up I see a figure coming down the road towards me—a distant man. All of a sudden I feel extremely
vulnerable and alone, so I decide to hide until he passes.
There are no trees or bushes around, only the grassy hills
sloping down to the ocean, so I set off up a faint track,
walking east and inland. I stride quickly uphill, trying not to
look back and walking nonchalantly, the way you do in bad
parts of a city to stay invisible. The wind is hissing steadily
in the grass. All this way I can feel him following, I feel his
dangerous presence, but I tell myself that I'm probably
wrong, just giving myself the jumps, he's probably passing
by along the highway. As I top the rise I look back, and I
see that he's started up the track after me; with that horrible
drop in the gut I realize the truth of my intuition. Hurrying,
I start down the other side. Suddenly everything is quiet. I
am in a dead space out of the wind. The grass, instead of
bending and fluttering, is standing still, and all is silent.*

"*Suddenly I am seized from behind. Strong arms wrap
around me from the back, and my breasts are cupped in his
hands. I am forced downwards as he sits, until I find myself
seated between his knees. I still haven't seen his face. I can
feel his chest against my back. I can feel his breathing, and
a kind of power emanating from him.*

"*Then he says 'Stand up' which I do. He tells me to turn
around. I do that too. I feel a curious lack of fear: instead
I feel a great danger and a kind of curiosity. 'Take off your
clothes', he says, so I slowly take them off and hand them
to him, without ever taking my eyes from his; then I stand
quietly, looking into his eyes and waiting.*

"*This is where the remarkable thing happens. I know this
man is completely psychotic; he is dangerous, not rational,
capable of anything. His violence and insanity go very deep.
He is also completely trustworthy and safe, with an enor-*

*mous capacity for love—and all of this is simultaneous.
There are no contradictions in it, he is a completely integrated whole . . .*

*"So I'm standing there looking into his eyes and I'm
watching him decide. It's as though there's a thin line
stretched between our eyes which he is walking, and he could
fall one way or the other. Whichever way he falls will de-
termine my safety. He is sizing me up, weighing my heart. I
know I have to stand my ground without pretence. All I can
do is stand and wait. After a time I see him decide. I see it
in his eyes. I'm safe. And I know that I am now safer than
I ever was before . . .*

*"He's mine. We have claimed each other. We spend the
rest of the dream travelling together, and I am happy. At the
end of the dream I am preparing for marriage, and I am so
excited and anticipatory! I'm going to marry my psycho! But
at the last moment I discover that my groom is not my psycho
but another man, one who seems disconcertingly boring by
comparison. My psycho has arranged the marriage, knowing
that it's the right thing for me. I feel a little betrayed, but
after my initial disappointment I become resigned, because
I know he's probably right, though I wish he wasn't."*

This dreamer, Heather McDougal, comments as follows: "I
had that dream in 1988. This 'psycho' appeared, in one form
or another, in numerous dreams after that. I always knew
when I woke up that he'd visited me again. In each dream
we seemed to know each other better, though he was always
dangerous and always different.

"About what he meant it is hard to say, because your
interpretation of dreams changes so much over the course of
time. I haven't had any dreams with the psycho in since I
got together with my present partner. I think that figure had
a lot to do with a certain bitter edge I had in my life. I was
going out with a man who made me feel invisible and—I
can see this now looking back—there was a lot of irritable

teeth-on-edge energy in me then. Things sometimes had a vicious cast in them that I didn't admit to. I would get drunk and do extreme things. The psycho is to do with having that clawing biting energy being okay. In my dream I was waiting to see if he was safe or not—and he *was* safe and he was good and he really had that kind of clawing biting energy.

"I am now accepting it as a good thing rather than something to be suppressed. Before that I always thought I should be like the girls in *Little Women*—never cry, never be sharp or unkind. In fact, I have a lot of that acidic energy in me. It's like making friends with the darker side and having that a safe and wonderful place to be instead of something to be avoided. I think I've always been in love with that aspect of life, but I've always been a little afraid of it, I didn't think I could deal with it or let it out . . . I think for the most part it's a society-influenced thing. Society tries to dictate what's female and what's male, but I think all people are a spectrum. Of all the dreams I've ever had that one made the deepest impression on me. It's the one I carry through my waking life more than any other. There's a part of me feels I'm dangerous. Whenever I find myself getting invisible or getting to that 'good girl' place, I remember that psycho and keep myself from sliding into being invisible."

Five years later, she had a dream about:

an unpredictable and dangerous man with whom she and a group of women were at war. After fear, fighting and confusion, the dream ended with her throwing him to the ground in an Aikido grip and beginning "a process that seems to be a combination of making out with him and taking him apart into little bits (basically disincorporating him), and distributing him into the dirt, until he is gone."

She comments that "He's a kind of a sequel to the psycho, another face of him. But there are differences. In the first dream the psycho comes up behind me and seizes me; in this dream with the man I come to him, I come to conquer him, I am much more active . . .''

Here Heather McDougal clearly identified the male ''psycho'' in the dream as a vital and enriching part of her own personality: one she became less at the mercy of, and more able to incorporate, as it became more familiar.

Jungians might explain him as an ''animus'' figure, an ''archetypal'' male part of the dreamer's self. This term is used to describe the internalised ''male'' aspect of every woman, which Jung suggested is based not only on her own experiences of her own father as her first model of the masculine, but also on her innate capacity to produce an image of man. The ''animus'' is described as having traditionally ''masculine'' characteristics (''thinking'' as opposed to ''feeling''), while the ''anima'' (the female aspect in men) has traditionally ''female'' characteristics. Jung believed that the image of the ''animus'' will mediate in any relationship a woman has with a man.

An alternative is to see the ''psycho'' as part of a dreamer's self which is symbolised by a man because such behaviour is supposedly appropriate to men in our society. The question is: is the symbol primordial or social in origin? Here the dreamer herself managed to gain a lot of understanding from her dream without the concept of the ''archetypes.'' She both owned the qualities of the ''psycho'' as being quite particular and individual to herself, and—with her references to boyfriends who made her invisible and to the standard *Little Women* version of feminine behaviour— gave reasons for seeing the suppression of those sharp-edged qualities as a social phenomenon. By exploring her dream in this way, she was able to progress in her waking life towards a more positive and powerful self-image.

Although many women have found the ''animus'' a useful framework, in some cases it sits very uncomfortably with women's dream symbols:

"In the first part of the dream Simon (an ex-boyfriend) and I nearly make it to get into bed together, but then some hearty friends of his arrive for a drink. Then Simon and I are crossing a very heavily trafficked road in the dark. We get halfway across and can't quite make it across the other half. The traffic is four lanes deep and travelling fast with glaring headlights. It brushes past us, motorbikes swerve. Then we fall over and I am afraid the cars won't even be able to see us now and we will get smashed to pieces. Cold terror. I try to roll Simon over to the white line at the middle of the road to be safer, then I will put my hand up so that they see us. Everything is slow and difficult, he seems help-less, I am trying to reassure him."

The dreamer comments: "This dream is historically true in that in it we don't make it in bed or across the road, and in real life we never got it together sexually either. But I don't think it's just about that relationship. I feel it's also about two aspects of life or two parts of myself: the gentle and tender (Simon was very gentle) versus the crass and aggres-sive. The tenderness is under threat."

It is interesting that in this dream the male character repre-sents tenderness and vulnerability, i.e. "feeling," and the dreamer herself ends up trying to rescue him from the traffic. Not the "hero" rescuing the "princess," but the other way round. This does not fit in at all with Jung's archetypes of male and female. He sees man and woman as a fixed duality, the man representing "Logos," the woman "Eros," and each needing the other to complement themselves. He sug-gests that:

> The woman is increasingly aware that love alone can give her her full stature, just as the man begins to dis-cern that spirit alone can endow his life with its highest meaning. Fundamentally, therefore, both seek a psychic

relation one to the other, because love needs the spirit, and the spirit love, for their fulfilment. (*Psychological Reflections*)

This view sees heterosexual women and men bound together by mutual lack and the inability to become whole, for it is not seen as possible for either sex successfully to take on the qualities belonging to the other: "just as the anima of the man consists of inferior relatedness, full of resentment, so the animus of woman consists of inferior judgements, or, better said, opinions."

In this view of the world there is no encouragement for men or women to expand beyond gender typecasting, and little space for the gentle, feeling Simon or for this woman's understanding of her own dream. It seems important to acknowledge when lived experience does not fit in with theories, just as real people do not always fit into male/female stereotypes.

BLACK PEOPLE IN WHITE PEOPLE'S DREAMS

While certain stereotypes of behaviour are rigidly assigned according to gender, other stereotypes are often attributed to certain races; and these stereotypes may be reflected in dreams. The issue of certain behaviour being assigned to, or denied to, certain groups is very critical in relation to black people. Jung suggested that a black person appearing in a white person's dream represents the archetype of the "shadow," that is the most denied, unconscious, sometimes unpleasant part of ourselves. In *Journey of a Dream Animal*, for example, Kathleen Jenks gave a Jungian interpretation of the following dream in which:

*she, her family and friends, and an entire Vietnamese village
are fighting off an attack by the Viet Cong. They are inside
a stockade at night. The villagers start digging a tunnel out
under the stockade so as to surprise the enemy from behind:
"Will they have the courage to stay under there in the darkness?" someone asked. "After all, they are a simple,
primitive people." At this point a song wells up from deep
inside all of them, together with "a powerful release of human energies. Our voices fuse in song, reaching towards the
gods—both mine and the villagers' archaic, chthonic deities."*

Kathleen Jenks was describing a time of personal crisis, and
she believed that "The dream indicates very clearly that I
had come under attack by deadly forces . . . But the unconscious mind was fortifying me by sending in the shy, dark
villagers." She clearly saw the Vietnamese villagers as representing a lost or hidden part of herself, an unconscious
strength which was needed to come into play to fortify her
as she verged on breakdown in reaction to an unhappy love
affair. The memory of the dream song was sustaining for
her, and she was encouraged by the sense that her dream
made her aware of such forces available to help her.

This was evidently an important and useful process for
her. It is a different matter, however, to construct universal
theories out of such a process. How do we understand her
choice of such symbolism for the unconscious forces warring
inside her? And the use of words like "shy," "primitive,"
"simple," "archaic," "chthonic" and "unconscious" associated with the Vietnamese villagers? One way is to take
them as suggesting that non-white people have some intrinsic
kinship with the "dark," primitive and unconscious side of
life—which is what Jung sometimes seems to be saying. This
idea has no basis apart from mysticism and white chauvinism, and has racist implications. Sometimes when a symbolic

association seems "instinctively" right, this may be due to prejudice rather than intuition.

Another way of taking such dream symbolism is as evidence of the way that white people use black people as a symbol onto which they project unaccepted and unknown parts of themselves. That white people have such symbolism in their dreams would seem to be empirically true, not only from Jung's fieldwork but also from the dreams recorded by women in recent decades. Of course, such dreams give information about the projections of whites rather than about how black people actually are. In this they have much in common with men's dreams about women. In both cases, women and black people are merely drawn in to the dreams of a dominant group to play the role of the unknown, the "other," and to crystallise whatever feelings the dreamer has about that "other." Such dreams reflect the fantasies of white people. None of the black women's dreams sent in for, and included in, this book happen to comment on how—in turn—white people may be represented in black people's dreams.

Without these understandings, such dream symbols as those in Kathleen Jenks' dream can be taken as an endorsement of the very prejudices which gave them birth. Montague Ullman suggests that dream representations of social stereotypes—such as a black man appearing as a rapist or a female as a cow acting out a domesticated function—play a two-way role both reflecting and then apparently validating certain attitudes in society: "Exploited by the dream in attempting to resolve a conflict the stereotype is further enhanced. A mutually reinforcing influence is at work."

If such dream symbolism arises from deeply ingrained racial prejudice, if it is indeed socially created in the waking world, we would expect it to be present but perhaps questioned or modified in situations where racist attitudes have been questioned in real life. Even women who have a strong awareness of and opposition to racial stereotypes and dis-

crimination may find such symbolism in their dreams; but
there may also be some challenging of that symbolism within
the dream itself.

Here is the dream of a white woman where such a process
seems to be taking place:

*"The children come in. They are doing an African project
at school.* THEN: *Africa. We are on the side of the Africans,
getting into an area to spy, over a wire fence and with forged
passes. In the area: horses, etc., it is exciting. Later, coming
into a settlement, the women are doing formation dancing,
but in modern dress like the black women I know. I go
through the jungle to where I am sleeping, a kind of timber
bunk bed with a door. Have picked up a rucksack with foreign fags in, etc. A black guy comes and picks out from my
clothes something he would like for his wife, I say okay but
he ends up taking things I want.*

*"I am a bit scared of the jungle, but then—looking at the
nearby motorway—it is just as scary and dangerous. Then
the white soldiers come (in white topee hats, etc.), I try to
escape but they catch me, I will be sent to jail for being in
African territory. Then the white leaders arrive and more
women. One white woman says to her husband 'You never
take me seriously, this time I'm serious' but she's looking
over her shoulder at a songwriter."*

The woman who had this dream frankly admits its racist
symbolism: "I am an anti-racist activist and I was shocked
by the racist attitudes suggested by this dream. The setting
in Africa is a dead give-away suggesting excitement, etc.,
whereas in my own experience I have only ever known black
people as my neighbours living in the city. At the same time,
it's almost as if my unconscious is aware of the anachronism.

"I think the dream is about power. At the time I was not
confronting issues of power in my relationship with my husband. I felt vulnerable and threatened by him but couldn't

express it. One way I masked it was through doing a 'Lady Bountiful' routine, pretending to be very kind and helpful to other people instead of taking care of myself. Really I couldn't afford to give that much away, as the dream showed (the scene with the clothes). There was a needy, deprived part of myself, ready to scavenge for anything, which I was too 'proud' to admit to. The dream also showed another game I was playing: by having an affair with a musician in real life (the songwriter in the dream?) I was sabotaging any serious attempts to confront my husband (looking over his shoulder instead of really trying to get him to listen). The dream was nothing to do with Africa or black people: they were simply cast as symbols of the invaded, powerless, rebellious side of myself, waging a guerrilla war against a white male. My unconscious is using a racist cliché.

"At the same time part of it is asking itself, for example when I see the women dancing: 'What are you doing? These people are in modern dress!' And when I think about the dangers of the motorway, it's as if part of me is saying 'Why use the jungle as a symbol of what is scary? The city is just as wild and dangerous.' So there is a voice inside which is questioning the cliché even while I am using it."

The clichés of a dominant culture do have a damaging effect on the oppressed. Male images of women and white images of black people do damage. Writing about their black women's workshops in London, black counsellors Janet Hibbert and Dorann van Heeswyk describe the importance of tackling the insidious effects of disinformation by raising the question "What are black women really like?":

It is moving to see a black woman share her grief and rage as she tells of experiences of selling herself short . . . of her fear of really not being good enough, that maybe it is true that she's second class; of the energy that goes into being twice as good all the time to be half-way good at all . . . Through the mantle of self-loathing, each woman can make her way to her supple, early pride. This pride is radically different from the defensive pride that many of us display for survival. (*In Our Experience: Workshops at the Women's Therapy Centre*)

From the point of view of white dreamers, it is one thing to acknowledge that the unconscious can function with clichés which are inaccurate and damaging, and which need to be challenged in dreams as in waking life. It is another matter to do as Jung did and suggest that those clichés have a metaphysical stature and carry an absolute truth. Montague Ullman comments that:

such imagery tells us something about the unsolved problems both of the dreamer and of society. By clarifying the role that social stereotypes play in our dreams and by seeing the way that socially derived biases and prejudices influence our lives, we shift some aspects of our social unconscious into the realm of social consciousness.

The gift of dreams is to show us how things are: To do that they use symbols which reflect our emotions and social attitudes, rather than being in themselves "true." Perhaps those clichés will not disappear from our unconscious minds until they are eliminated from our society. But perhaps also working at the dream clichés will help to transform waking attitudes.

FIGURES TO LOOK AFTER OR UP TO: DREAMS ABOUT BABIES AND FILM STARS

We have seen that almost any element in a dream may represent a lost or denied aspect of our personality. Ever since

Artemidorus, Western culture has produced dream dictionaries giving prescriptions about what means what, such as
that the butterfly represents the soul; the snake, sexuality;
rats, disease; dogs, doggedness; and so on. One of the questions raised by this book is whether these, and the Jungian
"archetypes," are any more than a record of associations
common in our culture. What tends to be missing is a recognition of the differences in dreamers' experience, and in
their relationship to the symbol.

Take these dreams about babies and children:

*"I had a little baby whom I forgot to feed. It got smaller
and smaller."*
*"I was carrying my daughter back from the West Country
on my back, alone on an open road at night."*
*"I had a child but I lost him. I suddenly remembered him
with a shock and tried to think where I had left him."*

Looking in a couple of dream dictionaries I find the dream
symbol of a child or baby translated as "the beginnings of
new life within," "the unity of opposites," "the penis which
'produces' the child," and "the child within you. Those inner aspects of yourself such as playfulness, joy, openness."
One of them refers to Jung's theory that the archetype of the
"Self," an individual's potential of wholeness, may be represented in dreams by a child.

In these approaches the symbol is taken as a "thing." But
in fact all the examples above give prominence to a *relationship*—the relationship of caring. For a woman such a
dream may reflect concerns from her role as carer in waking
life, expressing the anxiety of carrying the main responsibility of child-rearing and nurturing, which she often does in
isolation in an uncaring society (like the long walk from the
West Country?).

Or the dream may express concerns abut the other side of
the relationship: being cared for. Some women report having

more dreams about children at times of illness, pain or stress, when protection and nourishment are issues at the forefront. Often such dreams seem to be about not our core "Self" or innate qualities but our "inner baby" who reflects our life experience of receiving—or not receiving—care. The child within may not represent joy but vulnerability, waywardness or neediness; for each of us these patterns take a different form, depending on our experience of love and childhood. The "inner baby" is often the part whose needs get pushed to second place in our role as carers for others, and those needs will vary from person to person. Giving them a clear voice can be very helpful. Try re-entering the dream and— perhaps speaking as the child or baby—check out what it needs. Then ask how that relates to what is missing in your life in the present.

Figures the dreamer admires, like film stars, may also represent an unfulfilled need, often an aspiration—but this again may vary considerably, and may not coincide with media stereotypes of beauty and glamour. I read in one dream dictionary that a glamorous figure like a film star often corresponds with the individual's "dream man of woman". The following example, however, suggests a more complex process:

"I meet Jane Fonda and she tells me that for all her socialist beliefs she would like to do 'star roles'. Something happens. Then I say 'What was that about star roles?' but she goes quiet."

This woman comments: "I think this dream is about my ambivalence about recognition. Despite my own political views, and knowing that all that stuff is rubbish, part of me would apparently like to be a 'star'."

The topic of recognition can be a difficult one for women in the West, as it is often tied up with personal élitism and hierarchies of "merit," and gaining it usually involves "buying in" to dominant male values. While film stars may be used in our dreams to give voice to our more extravagant aspirations or our more outrageous desires, there is no predicting what those may be. Here Jane Fonda carried the can for some attitudes which the dreamer was reluctant to own up to. Even when a "star" features in a dream as an idol, it is impressive to see how flexibly dreamers can take a well-known symbol and use it for their own ends.

A case in point is a recent study on the way women dream about the pop star Madonna. Kay Turner, while researching a thesis on folkloric interpretations of the Virgin Mary, discovered that large numbers of women were dreaming about this latter-day Madonna. Her book *I Dream of Madonna* described how, contrary to preconceptions, the singer appeared mainly not as a "dream woman" nor as a sex symbol but as a chum. "Even at times when her work got very involved with erotic stuff," says Kay Turner, "women didn't react with dreams of sexual transgression . . . Some women did give me dreams with sexual content, but the most consistent thread was the sense that Madonna was a pal." Not following male preoccupations about Madonna, women's dreams were using the symbolic material available to them in a creative way to acquire a powerful dream ally; not using the received image, they were forging their own version corresponding to their needs.

Again, we see that while inherited symbol meanings—fixed in theories and dictionaries—may be relevant, dreaming is a dynamic collective process whose symbols cannot be frozen into any system.

FINDING LOST POWER AND CREATIVITY

Despite what we read about the arrival of "equality of the sexes," it remains very hard for women to spread our wings in the world at large: to take the space, make the noise, reach the achievement and find the fulfilment of which we are capable. While we put a brave face on it, or try to find indirect ways to get what we need, our dreams remind us of the power and creativity waiting to be expressed. In the following example, a striking dream helps a woman understand how she has used shoplifting as an indirect way of registering protest, "grabbing" what no one would give her and reaching for a means to express herself.

This woman's pattern was to shoplift occasionally in a disconnected way, so that she was not really aware of what she was doing until afterwards. She often stole pens, and wondered whether there was a phallic symbolism or any link with sexuality, which she often experienced in a similarly cut-off way. She wrote:

"I feel intensely distressed at the thought of having to deal with the shoplifting. Not ordinary shame/guilt at crime. I have wondered whether it is connected with my sexual splitting-off, because what I almost always stole were pens, and I queried a phallic connection. But then while I was out walking the dog one day I heard a voice in me say, 'You were trying to give yourself presents to make yourself feel loved.' I sobbed and sobbed—I called the dog and went home and cried for hours."

The shoplifting had started during schooldays, and this woman linked it with being pressured to study subjects she didn't want, as well as to an early childhood of intense deprivation, about which she had never been able to speak. She experienced the need to be both "held" and "heard":

"Why is this part of me that shoplifts no trouble when I am in therapy? What does therapy do to satisfy that part of me, that otherwise is met by shoplifting?

"I wrote about shoplifting and slid into ranting on about

school, parents and government. Shoplifting as an angry protest. I hadn't noticed the anger in it before. 'Giving yourself presents' is about feeling held. Screaming in my belly: if I don't grab I won't get it.

"It doesn't answer the question about how shoplifting makes me feel heard. Pens—writing—being heard . . . I am desperate to have my version heard. To find clarity myself, to say it, to write it, absolutely precisely. I must untangle exactly what did happen, and know that I am heard, that what I say is accepted, and then perhaps I will be able to let it go.

"I didn't get anywhere with phallic symbolism and sex. What I did get instead was a dream:

"I was a bottle of beautiful multi-coloured ink. I met occasionally with another one, and we mingled some of the upper layers of ink, and enriched each other. The different colours stayed separate—they didn't blend into a mucky mud as they would in reality.

"I realised that I'd been seeing creativity as a male domain. I was afraid to write because it belonged to men. My dream was telling me that in stealing pens I was trying to steal male creativity, and that I didn't need to because I had all this beautiful womanly creativity. It was saying how diverse and beautiful women's creativity is; and that ink is as necessary for writing as a pen."

This woman's dream showed her a resource of creativity inside waiting to express itself, a reservoir of multi-coloured ink which would be able to make a mark on the world in her own way.

Do we need pens or ink? In the next example male power and expression are symbolised by a huge flying Rolls-Royce. Helped by Gestalt therapist Judith Hemming, the dreamer Eva Willer-Andersen explores ambivalent feelings, such as many of us feel, about taking her full size and embracing power when it commonly presents in such showy, selfish and polluting forms. In owning the symbol, and stretching herself, she confronts the physical conditioning which teaches us, since childhood, to be "good girls": to hold back and to hold in from expressing ourselves unacceptably. The dreamer is a painter, but the issues she raises about self-expression will resonate for women in many different lines of work. This almost full-length transcript of dreamwork—with pauses and mumbles largely uncut—gives a rare insight into how a session can work.

The session starts with Eva describing how being stuck with her painting work feels like being small and being stuck behind doors. She wants to explore her dream image of a flying car:

"It was an ENORMOUS car, ... you know ... these enormous sort of Rolls-Royces with cocktail cabinets and swimming pools, and the whole thing, inside them? It didn't have that but it was as wide as a house and it was really long ... and it was flying." [laughs]

The dreamwork starts with Judith Hemming noticing the way Eva is telling the dream; awareness of body language in the present is a theme throughout the session:

J: What are your laughter and your looks to me saying?

E: Because there was a man inside it, and ... I was really *angry* that people allowed things like that to litter the sky. And it wasn't until I'd thought about it for a while that I realised ... what this huge flying car was!

J: What was it?

E: [laughing] It was me! It was that whole feeling of growing in size, ... and it was my reaction to it which was sort of "What the *hell* was that thing doing up there? Get it down! That's *disgusting*!" ... I

couldn't *bear* the man inside it. I thought he was
everything sort of showy and . . . ostentatious and . . .
I also was very worried that it was polluting a lot . . .
yet this guy was really enjoying it. [laughs] It was a
strange dream.

The dreamwork so far shows Eva's mixture of elation and
disapproval at this symbol which is suggesting a more expansive expression of herself. When Judith asks her to act
the driver, she is reluctant to identify with him:

E: [laughs] I'm trying to *be* him but it's . . . [groans] It's
[laughs] funny because . . . I'm just aware of the fact
that I *hate* him. I'm in conflict here. [laughs]

J: But you look excited too.

E: Yeah, I feel terrifically energised. [laughs] [Bangs
fingers on side of chair] It's like he's sitting in this
big Rolls . . .

J: "I'm sitting . . ."

E: *I'm* sitting . . . [pause] [laughs] . . .

J: So what's it like sitting there in your cockpit?

E: It's like I'm just sitting in the back of this car. It's a
very, *very* big car and . . .

J: Speak as if you are the car too . . .

E: Well I'm very big.

J: Take it *all* in . . .

E: Right. Well, I'm, yeah, I'm up in the sky and I'm
really, I'm up in a beautiful bright clear sky. And
there's nothing else around here. And there's just
endless space. There's space everywhere. And I can
just . . . GO . . . in any direction at any speed. I can

just go really really *fast*. And there's *nothing* to stop me.

J: How do you feel when you say that?

E: [pause] I feel a mixture [laughs] of "I can't do it" . . . I can't really *be* it. I'm trying to. It fluctuates. If I can really put myself in the position of . . . just being able to [excitedly] *completely* HURL myself, you know, there's *nothing* to stop you. You can just go ROAR [she growls and roars] like that . . . Like completely supersonic speed . . . You're *there* before you're even there, you know.

J: "*I'm* there."

E: *I'm* there. [laughs] I'm *there*, before I'm even there! I can go that quick, you know. It's just like ROAR— [she roars and growls again] like that, you know! ROAR. [laughs] [In a quiet voice] That's what it's like.

Throughout this chapter we have seen how easy it is for women to be made to feel small. Here Eva finally managed to own as hers the size, energy, mobility, speed and freedom which are carried in the symbol of the car and its male driver. It is perhaps unsurprising that a dream symbol for power should be male in a society where men are powerful. But Gestalt theory stresses that the energy in any symbol is the dreamer's own, and can be reclaimed. Judith and Eva have started the dreamwork by following where the energy lies in the dream, in this case the car. But this is not the whole story: to stop here would be to give a false impression that we can simply shed inhibitions and conditioning, and voluntarily decide to "be different" by aligning ourselves with a powerful dream symbol. That is not easy until we have also explored what has been stopping us, our resistance, which may be connected with messages we were given as children about how to control and restrict our behaviour. It is also useful to trace where in our body we have internalised those messages, often held in muscle tension and physical constriction. This is what Judith and Eva explore next.

J: And the part that's stopping you? What's that doing? Be the bit that's saying no to all this energy.

E: Right. The bit that's stopping me is very much in my body. And it's here. Right here. [She puts her hands on her upper chest.] It's right across my chest.

J: So be that, be your chest in answer.

E: And it . . . feels like . . .

J: "*I* feel like . . ."

E: *I* feel like I'm made of, ummm . . . [pause]

J: You stop breathing.

E: Yeah, I'm . . . Well, it's like an armour. It's like a . . . an armour-plate, which has been cast to a certain size to fit a small size and if you try and go past it you come up against the pressure of it . . . because it's not flexible material, it's a very set hard metal kind of iron.

J: So as this constraining iron armouring, speak to the man that's in the Rolls-Royce that's up in the sky.

E: Yeah.

J: Be the voice of constraint.

E: Yeah. Okay. Yeah. [in a voice of strength and indignation] What are you doing up there? You are really *foul* and obnoxious. You're polluting the sky. *Get* down! What is that ridiculous car? What do you think you're doing showing off in a *stupid* car like that? You're just *one* person. You do not *need* a car the size of a castle. That is just sheer *waste*! . . . You

are obnoxious. What on *earth* are you doing? You
don't need to travel at that speed. You can get down
here and walk like everybody else. We don't need
people like you . . .

J: [pause] What's it like to say that? How do you feel?

E: That's good. That's how I feel. Against him, yeah, I
think he's *ridiculous*.

J: Very clear.

E: Yes.

J: Very articulate.

E: Yeah. It's a very definite attitude.

J: Mmm. Do you recognise it?

E: [laughs] Yeah, yeah. [pause] I think it's my stepfather, yeah.

J: He spoke to you like that?

E: [pause] Well he was always going on about waste.
Yeah. "Waste not want not." [sarcastic voice]
"How lucky can you get?" [inaudible] Waste. . . .
that picture just represents *utmost* waste, extreme
waste.

Eva has located the constriction in her chest, and has realised
that the internalised voice of her stepfather being angry and
judgemental helped build up this constraining "armour" in
her body. The angry voice of disapproval in us—the "topdog" voice in these internal conflicts—is sometimes so powerful that it drowns out any other voices. Eva finds it difficult
to follow Judith's next suggestion, that she answers back to
the "topdog," speaking as the man having a good time in
the air. Instead she fiddles—and Gestalt is interested in noticing everything that people do with their bodies during
dreamwork, as it often reflects their internal drama. In this

case, while Eva is squashing her energy down, she starts rolling a hair into a tight little ball.

J: So, as the man in this wasteful flying Rolls-Royce, answer. Answer your stepfather. Or answer your armour. Just take some time to feel your way into the other place.

E: [long pause]

J: What are you doing?

E: [laughs] Having difficulty getting into that other place . . .

J: What are you doing with your hands?

E: I'm rolling a hair into a little ball. Which is something I often do. [laughs] A little tight ball which I can then throw away. [laughs, and throws it into bin] Ahm . . . this man . . . first of all I can't bear people who drive in Rolls-Royces. [J: Mmmm] And also I can't bear people who fly in Concordes, and this is worse than a Concorde, you know . . . And also he's dressed very much like a sort of umm [laughs] he's dressed in this kind of brown sheepskin coat, umm . . . Actually, yeah, like my stepfather *did* used to wear. It was a certain type of businessman-look . . . slightly sporty . . . It represents everything I dislike.

J: And to identify with him for even a moment just feels more than you can bear.

E: I *can't* identify with him. I don't think so.

The parental male figure—Eva's stepfather—is not only the voice disapproving and restricting her expression, but is also monopolising the model of power and freedom presented by the dream in the form of the flying Rolls. The voice of disapproval is so overwhelming that it has at this point silenced everything else. Judith does not try to push against the tide, but goes with what is happening and suggests that she return to the attack:

J: So, attack him a little bit more.

E: Right. Umm. Okay . . . Where are you *going*? You're not *going* anywhere, you're just *fart*-arsing around [contemptuously] up there in the sky! [pause] . . .

After a few more minutes of this, Judith again asks Eva if she can recognise herself in the dream:

E: [pause] I don't recognise. I'm finding it very hard to recognise. I'm very confused about what's me, what's my stepfather, what's what . . . where else did it come from?

J: Your expression on your face looks as if you don't want anything to do with any of it. "Ugghh." [she mirrors]

E: Yeah. It's people like that that are destroying the world. That's what I also feel, you know.

It can be uncomfortable to recognise that unpleasant figures in dreams are also part of us, and that otherwise we would not need to be arguing with them in our sleep. However, Gestalt suggests that where there are unpleasant elements, or elements which we perceive as unpleasant, this is because their energy has been denied. By identifying with that energy and following it through in the role-play, reconciliation becomes possible. This is what happens next, when Eva imagines developing the action of the dream and lets her anger come through powerfully. Like many women, she has some difficulty at first in taking that anger seriously. Judith prompts an awareness of what she is doing at each stage by commenting and "mirroring" her actions:

J: Mmm . . . If you had power in the dream, if you could go in as that furious armour which you described in your body, what would you do to the man? And the plane? What do you want to happen? Go back into the dream and really encounter him.

E: What, to go up there or something?

J: Yup.

E: Okay, well, I'll just close my eyes. [pause, grunts] [laughs]

J: You laugh . . .

E: [laughs] Okay well, I'm just going to . . . [pause] [excited voice, laughs] Shall I just tell you what . . . Just make it up? What happens is like I would go to some kind of controlling force and I'd make them bring the plane down, and then I would go up to this guy and open the door to the car and . . . I'd say "*What* are you doing. Look will you *stop*, will you *stop* [shouts, laughingly] will you STOP POLLUTING MY SKY!"

J: You're laughing.

E: [stops laughing, still shouting] GET OUT OF MY SKY! Get away from my beautiful sky, with your stupid car. I don't . . . I have enough cars down here on earth. I don't want cars up in the sky. I do not want to see *you* in front of my window. [pause] Will you, will you just get a bit *smaller*! Why do you need such a big car? How much space does a person like you need? . . . Why do you have to travel so fast? Why do you have to wear those stupid clothes, stupid *Sunday Times* clothes? [pause] Why don't you just buckle down! [to J, in quiet voice] That was the word that came that made me laugh earlier. [to man, in loud voice again] Why don't you just buckle down? [contemptuously] Why don't you try walking! You might discover something. About natural speed. [pause] You will NOT be allowed to drive that aeroplane again. It will be grounded . . . Ah, another thing. You think you're more important than everybody else, swanning around up there, don't you? Well it's about time you came down to reality.

J: *Is* he down, as you speak to him?

E: Well, yes, he's sort of standing, looking down a bit, listening to all this, like a little boy. Yeah, he's down.

J: He's down and he's a little boy now?

E: He's very much a little boy, yes.

J: And what are *you* like?

E: I'm like a grown-up mummy.

J: I've never heard you speak to your daughter like that. [pause] Mmm. What's it like to be this powerful mummy to the little boy? [pause] You've really changed roles now haven't you? You seem bigger than him.

E: Mmm. Yeah, I feel . . . he's having to listen to what I'm saying and he's having to . . . I *do* feel bigger than him. I feel very angry at him.

J: Right . . . Can you speak as him now? Now that he's a bit smaller?

E: Ummm. [pause] [in a wistful young voice] Well, I was just having fun. I was just enjoying being up there. I wasn't really thinking about anything much . . . just enjoying what it would be like to be up there and travelling at that speed.

J: You sound a little sad.

E: Mmm, yeah.

J: What is your sadness?

E: Well, because I didn't realise that I was causing any pain to anybody . . . I was actually. just thinking about the fun of it . . . and now I feel . . . I didn't realise anybody'd see it like that.

J: You look pained.

E: Mmm . . . It's like I just saw a small part of it which was the fun part of it and . . . it seems now there was a whole other side of it which is the price of the fun . . . I don't really feel I can do it so easily. I feel like . . . that's really destroyed that game.

J: You've taken on what this angry Eva said to you?

E: Yeah.

J: Have you replied to *her*, or is this going on separately? Is there anything you want to say to her?

E: Well, I would want you to know that I'm not a monster, I'm not flying up there to destroy your sky at all, and that I . . . it's a wonderful feeling to fly up there, and that I would invite you to come up there with me, and to see what it's like to fly around, so that you could see that I wasn't doing it umm . . . to show off or to . . . I was just doing it 'cos it's wonderful.

It is interesting that once Eva's anger has been released, the hatred she felt for the man in the sky has evaporated. He has become a boy who wanted to have fun but did not want to hurt anybody. Reconciliation between the different voices now becomes possible, and this is what we see slowly happening as the dreamwork moves towards its close:

J: Be Eva and reply.

E: [pause] Well . . . I don't know about that . . . umm . . . I don't know if I *want* to go up there . . .

J: How are you feeling?

E: A bit stuck about what to do . . . because I can't really just back down completely . . . You know, do I . . . [pause]

J: Breathe . . . Do you?

E: [pause] Do I want to be seen swanning around in a supersonic Rolls-Royce? [laughs] In the sky?

J: Tell him your predicament.

E: Look, if I go up there I'm going to be making a fool of myself. I'll be doing all the things I hate you for doing . . . How can I possibly justify that to anybody, to myself?

J: Who in particular would you not be able to justify it to? [pause] Is there someone who came to mind?

E: Well, I think my stepfather. How could I justify it to him?

J: Well, have a word with him now. [pause] Try. [pause] Is he there?

E: Great trouble really. I can't quite bring myself to communicate with him.

J: He seems very present in the dream. Both in the armouring and in the pilot.

E: Right. Okay. Umm. Okay. I'm not going to call you Daddy this time. I just don't want to call you Daddy. I'm going to call you by your first name. I'm going to call you Graham. Okay Graham. Here's the problem. The problem is you . . . wouldn't like to see me flying about in a Rolls-Royce, at supersonic speed.

Umm [laughs] . . . especially if it was with your money that I bought the Rolls-Royce!

J: You looked devilish for a minute! [E: laughs]

It is at this point in the dreamwork that Eva finally volunteers that she feels able to try speaking as her stepfather:

J: What's he like? Spend a moment just being him. Are you dead or alive?

E: Well, this is it. [As stepfather] I am both dead *and* alive. And I have two answers. One is a dead person's and one is a live person's. As a dead person I could say "It really doesn't matter . . . I think that, you know, I'm somewhere else and I'd be quite happy for you to enjoy yourself, even if it's with my money because quite frankly, my dear, I don't need it anymore." And umm . . . as a live person who worked very hard to get that money . . . I would say, "No . . . if that's what you wanna do you've got to find your own way of doing it—you know, not on *my* back."

J: Mmm. What's it like to hear those two messages?

E: [long pause] What it is, is that it's quite clear that when he was alive he wasn't really going to help me get happiness. I don't mean just by money but, you know, I would have to find the happiness myself, whatever way that was—it wasn't to rely on him for any of it. And as a dead person he really doesn't care anyway. [laughs]

J: I want to see what it's like for you to hear those messages—from *me*, so that you can give yourself a chance to receive them in a slightly less convoluted way. Okay? [E: Mmm] As Graham . . . if you can

create me as Graham, just let me know—am I dead
or am I alive?

E: [pause] Well, you're dead, as Graham.

J: Okay. So I'm going to give you Graham's dead message.

E: Yeah.

J: As dead Graham I want you to know that you're free
to use my money to have any happiness that you
want. In fact I *want* you to have happiness. It doesn't
matter to me *how* you use my money. Because I'm
dead. [E: Mmmm] [long pause] What are you feeling?

E: I feel somehow that that's too simple—it's very
clear, but there's something about it that's not really
the answer. In the end, maybe it's not just money—
maybe it's more than money.

J: What's the "it"?

E: Well, [pause] maybe money doesn't buy happiness.

J: Go back to the man, and talk to him about this question. Because I'm . . . aware of time, and wanting you
to see what kind of closure you can get on the dream.
[E: Mmmm] So speak to the man who's invited you
up in the sky. [E: Mmmm] See if there's anything
else you want to say to him.

E: The one thing that I . . . I do *like* the idea of, I do
like the idea of being able to travel up in the sky at
supersonic speeds. I *do* think with you it's a wonderful idea . . . but it's funny I keep coming back to
the pollution . . . So I was wondering if there was a
way you could do something about that. Maybe you
could umm, maybe it would be possible to do

this . . . in some way that didn't . . . dirty up the air,
umm . . .

J: You sound very gentle and really wanting to talk to
this man now.

E: Mmm, yeah.

J: How does he reply? Be him.

E: Mmm. [long pause]

J: Take a deep breath.

E: Umm. [breathes] [As man] Well, I think we could
do it in a different way. I hadn't thought of that. I'm
not quite sure how we could do it . . . Maybe we
could think of something together. Maybe there *is*
some way we could fly about up there? [sneezes] In
a way that wouldn't be quite so offensive to you, but
which would still be as much fun. Umm. I think
maybe we'll have to change a few things. What do
you think? [to E]

[As E:] Well for a start I don't think we need the
Rolls-Royce to fly. Nobody ever did in the past. [gig-
gles] Maybe . . . let's just look at this . . . maybe we
could just have something that was part of *us* . . .
umm. [touches below throat]

J: You put your hand to that very same place.

E: Yeah. [removes hand]

J: Put it back.

E: Maybe we could have something that was part of us
that could make us fly up there . . . so that it was
actually us who could fly, in some way . . . maybe
we could get enough speed just by diving around on
the currents of air that the thermals and stuff up
there . . . that would give us enough thrills to actually
go as fast as we wanted. [pause]

J: What are you aware of in that part of your chest as you have your hand there? [pause]

E: Umm. It's a feeling of space. A feeling of endless space.

J: I'm remembering your tiny space with the closed doors [at the start of the session] and comparing it.

E: And, I still get the constriction. It's still there, but . . . I had an image of swooping around up in the air with some kind of wings and it was like endless unobstructed space. I feel like it was also inside here. [points to chest]

J: Mmm. You look very moved.

E: Mmm. It was like it was continuous. It was like there was no . . .

J: "In you" and "out there"?

E: Yeah, there was no, umm, *wall* . . .

J: In terms of your painting, which is where we began, if you bring that sense of openness to your painting? We've only got a moment, but just see whether spending a moment with it is any use to you.

E: [pause] Yeah. You see, I had this idea which has been germinating for a few months which would be that paintings would extend beyond their boundaries, which would be like triptychs and diptychs, it would continue in some way, and I have been wanting to, I have done some like that, and that's something I want to develop further.

J: Okay . . . Just give me some feedback on your experience of what you've done today. We've ranged far and wide, from voices to dreams to paintings to stepfathers . . .

E: [pause] I think it just comes up . . . my mind . . . it's

just *collaboration*—that's the way I feel, what I got
out of it, something to do with collaboration . . . that
there *is* a friendly solution. [she giggles]

J: How d'you feel?

E: I feel good.

J: Okay. Is it okay to stop now?

E: Yes.

Eva Willer-Andersen's comments on the session suggest
good effects on her body; progress towards feeling "bigger"; and being able to "fly" in her own more organic way,
linked to better expression from her throat and chest. The
session suggested that it was possible for her to negotiate
with dominating figures from the past in order to take up her
own space in the world. It also became clear that she could
get bigger through a process of collaboration and without
poisoning others. She comments:

"I most benefited from expressing the anger and hatred I felt
and the shift in power and relative sizes this brought about
(of the two dream characters, the man and me); also the
ensuing collaboration about how we could fly together. Also
an insight in the body of release from tight chest constriction
which I experienced a lot at the time, not that it disappeared
overnight. The next flying dream I had about four months
later wasn't in a Rolls but in a huge hollow kite in the shape
of a big black bird like a dark tube filling with wind."

Once again we can see the healing power of expressing anger
in a safe situation, which the dreamer feels made these benefits possible. The dreamwork also shows that we do not
have to see ourselves as victims in our own dramas. We all
contain contradictions. When we ally ourselves with what is
positive in our dream symbols of power, they are trans-

formed and a *Sunday Times* driver in a polluting limousine in the clouds becomes a roar, free flight, a painting that stretches its boundaries, a huge kite in the shape of a black bird.

Reading and Notes

Artemidorus, *The Interpretation of Dreams: Oneirocritica*, translated and commentary by Robert J. White, Noyes Classical Studies, Noyes Press, Park Ridge, New Jersey, 1975. Artemidorus of Daldis was a professional dream interpreter of the second century AD.

Hibbert, Jane and Dorann van Heeswyk, "Black Women's Workshop," Sue Krzowski and Pat Land (eds.), *In Our Experience: Workshops at the Women's Therapy Centre*, The Women's Press, 1988, p. 98.

Jenks, Kathleen, *Journey of a Dream Animal*, The Julian Press, New York, 1975, pp. 90–91.

Jung, Carl G., *Psychological Reflections*, Jolande Jacobi (ed.), Pantheon Books, 1953, pp. 98–9.

Turner, Kay, interviewed by Cynthia Rose in the *Guardian*, 8 September 1993. See also Kay Turner, *I Dream of Madonna*, Thames and Hudson, London, 1993.

Ullman, Montague, "Dreams and Society," Montague Ullman and Claire Limmer (eds.), *The Variety of Dream Experience*, Continuum, New York, 1989.

5

Understanding Relationships

A women in her late thirties was feeling some ambivalence about embarking on a new relationship with a man. She had a dream which included the symbol of *her father seated on a swing surrounded by four female relatives dressed as cancan dancers*. In *The Variety of Dream Experience*, Montague Ullman describes the work this woman did on her dream. It brought to light two important images from her childhood which seemed to be influencing her attitude to starting the new relationship: "One was that of the male, derived from the image of her father as privileged to flirt and become involved with other women. The other, that of the female victimized by the profligate male, was her mother . . . The privileged male and the victimized female are still available social stereotypes."

One of the gifts of dreams is that they can help us to understand what is going on in our relationships with the people close to us. Some writers have set the dream world as a kingdom apart—mysterious and primitive, peopled with creatures innate to it, swept by timeless human emotions and primordial elemental forces. To see dreams only in this way is to miss what they have to tell us about our life now in this place and time: where our relationships, like those of the woman above, are affected by the past (her father and mother) and society (current stereotypes of male and female). Montague Ullman emphasises the social aspects of dreaming, not only in group sharing but also in showing how many of the difficulties we wrestle with at night are derived from our culture. While other writers have traced dream events to universal mythic patterns or individual neurosis, Ullman—using a concept of the "social unconscious" developed by the theorist Eric Fromm—sees dreams as bringing to the fore "all what we do not let ourselves see of the emotional fallout from the social arrangements and institutions about us." Ullman points out how convenient it is for society that unpleasant by-products of social arrangements are experienced as personal and private—so that individuals are left to process and dispose of "garbage" which is social in origin. In Sweden he found that social pressure on mothers to return to work was reflected in dreams by feelings of individual guilt on the part of individual mothers who were leaving their very young children at day-nurseries. As Ullman puts it, "This privatization of what may be regarded as social waste products serves society." One could point out that making a "universal myth" out of a painful social arrangement serves society in the same way. In the case of the woman's dream above, if her father's behaviour is seen as part of an archetypal pattern rather than as a common pattern in society, she as an individual is again left to process her difficult feelings as a private problem.

This chapter looks at what we can learn from dreams about our relationships and their link with society: how they are shaped by past and present experiences; what happens when dreams bring forward problems and feelings which are normally kept private; how we can go beyond prevailing stereotypes to get more of what we need.

GOING FOR WHAT YOU NEED
IN RELATIONSHIPS WITH MEN

Often in a relationship with a man we may feel called on to
deny ourselves, whether by following traditional roles or by
acting according to new social norms of what is "indepen-
dent," "restrained," "unemotional," "undemanding," or
generally "cool." However, our dreams can cut through the
masks we construct to defend ourselves, and help us to gain
a better sense of what we actually need. In the following
example the dreamer cogitated on her dream at a computer
to explore the viewpoints of the different characters. The
result illuminated the dynamic of her current relationship and
enabled her to go beyond the superficial scenario to assess
her own needs and boundaries within it.

"At the time of my dream I was at the initial stages of a
new sexual relationship. I didn't consciously know where I
wanted our relationship to go, it seems to have developed
very casually. We had mutual friends and when we'd all go
out together, B. and I would seem to end up at the end of
the evening in a sexual encounter. It was as if it was coin-
cidence that kept bringing us together in bed. I did not know
what he thought about this, about us, and I too did not ven-
ture my feelings and thoughts. So for all I knew, he may
have seen our encounters (that's how I thought of it, not as
making love) as a physical gratification, like having a meal
or going out for a drink, and for all he knew I too may have
been indulging a physical sense rather than an emotional one.

"In my dream I and B. were at a party. I could see B.
talking to a woman. She was being very 'girly' and cloyingly
clingy, touching him in a very blatant manner. B. turned
away from her and she clung on to him and said she'd wait
for him there till he returned. He came towards me and I
walked towards him, he had a look of disgust on his face
and I pitied the girl because I knew that he could not abide

the way the girl was clinging on to him and the way she was willing to stay in limbo while waiting for him. "Doesn't she know," I thought, "that the way to keep him with her is not by showing him how much he means to her and how much she wants him with her." He needs his own space and her need is demanding too much of that space, he finds it off-putting . . . Whereas I give him his own space and I let him do what he wants, go where he wants and be with whom he wants. Which is why he comes back to me.

"When I woke up the next morning the dream lingered like a bad feeling. I decided to look into my dream. I realised that all characters in the dream were parts of me, parts of my unconscious. I too was the girl. She/I was willing to wait for him . . . She did not see this as a shameful thing, she did not feel embarrassed to show her feelings. Whereas I didn't want to show him how much he meant to me, but I was waiting for him just as much as she was. Everything else was 'in between' being with him . . . I realised that I was the girl, wanting him to acknowledge that I'm his and he's mine, but I was too scared . . . he would reject me and show disgust for my weakness. I obviously see my need for him as a weakness.

"Thinking of a past relationship when my need was not fulfilled by my partner, remembering how my need made me weak and pushed my partner further away from me till I clung harder, until his respect for me turned into disgust, until I learned that needing someone makes you weak and takes away your strengths, until you would do anything to keep that person in your life and your self-respect goes.

"People always tell me what a strong woman I am with admiration and as a compliment, but my fear is that one day they'll find out that I'm not strong, that inside I'm weak, because I need. I now know that I'm the girl in my dream, needing. I am him in the dream disgusted by that part of me that wants to cling and never let go. I am me pitying myself (the girl) for being weak and allowing myself to be vulnerable. But I am also the person who realises that it is me, not him, that needs space to do what I want and go where I want and be what I want.

"My past relationship has taught me that when I rely on someone I become completely dependent on them to fulfil all of my needs instead of looking inside of me for that fulfilment, and now that I've learned how to be completely self-sufficient I am scared to need someone else in case it makes me weak again.

"But as I'm thinking in the dream about how he needs his own space, I realise that it's not about him, but about me, that even though I need him it doesn't mean that I will suddenly become completely reliant on him, because it's me that really needs my space to be myself.

"And now I have to create a balance between my needs from him and my needs for me."

WHEN THE PAST INTERFERES IN PRESENT RELATIONSHIPS

In dreams, characters from different periods of our lives often get amalgamated or confused. What does this tell us about how past experiences may be affecting our current relationships?

"I meet Mick, an ex-lover, late at night at a tube station and feel enraptured . . . At the bottom of a shaving bowl he has a Brazilian drug, grey fluff, he shows me how to suck it in. I realise he isn't going home, just breaks ties. I am loving him, fluff on lip."

The woman who had this dream commented: "I had this dream four months after we broke up . . . I think the important thing it is saying is that the relationship with Mick is addictive, and also why . . . The fluff is sucked in like cocaine. The mark it leaves on my lip also reminds me of the white moustache you sometimes get after drinking milk and the sucking is like breastfeeding which I watch my own baby doing. I think part of me had fixated on Mick as a 'Mummy' figure and I was hooked and dependent like an infant. His pattern of long absences felt like the abandonments I experienced as a child. When we eventually separated once and for all, it was a terrible wrench. I don't understand the shaving bowl, except that Mick had not yet grown a beard when I knew him. The smoothness of his skin made him a good substitute mother.''

Here the dreamer suggests a dream message that feelings she had towards a lover were actually about her childhood relationship with her mother. The dream clearly seems to be speaking about both present and past at the same time. Her comments suggest that the unresolved feelings from her abandonments as a child left her vulnerable to—perhaps even addicted to—becoming desperately attached to a relationship where she experiences similar abandonments. The gift of the dream is to show the pattern, and to show the link between then and now. Here a male lover triggered a pattern of feeling associated with a mother; in the example below, a relationship with a husband is linked to that with a father. In this case, the dreamer had two dreams within the same month, which she saw as a pair:

"I was having a bath in our bathroom here, feeling very relaxed. Suddenly my husband K. and my young daughter came in and rushed up the stairs. K. opened the door, turned on the light and an electric shock went through my bathwater, my body started to become limp, but I just managed to roll out of the water and woke up in panic."

The dreamer commented: "I had just had a few days of peace and quietness—my husband and daughter had been on a bus trip to see his mother and I expected them back the day I had the dream. Their coming back, especially K.'s coming back, I dreamt as an intrusion which almost killed me!!! I tried to forget this dream and my interpretation, but told K. about it in order to get rid of it.

"But my feelings towards him are very fragile. He has started his new job, works long hours quite often now, and goes out to eat with his colleagues in the evening. He brightened up a lot and I became more depressed. Not only because of these changes, but also because things were going badly at work and were making me feel terribly rejected. Tonight I dreamt that

"I was in Frankfurt, my home town, dancing with my father, who was young and very good-looking. He pressed me towards his body, for a second I wanted to respond to his sexual desire, but refused at the same moment. Woke up, very bewildered. K. brought me a cup of tea to my bedside, which is quite unusual.

"I have been thinking about this dream all day long. Never during all my therapy sessions did I ever have a dream like this. I never had a glimpse of sexual desire towards my father. I came to know feelings of guilt and hate and even love towards him during therapy, but never had any sexual feelings.

"I think the category for my dreams is 'never-ending conflict.' Though I know about my always-changing feelings, my ambivalence towards K., the second dream told me a lot of the origin. The trouble is that I have chosen in him a man who nourishes these ambivalent feelings. He is the one who very often hates me if I remind him of his mother, and it could be just a word or gesture which triggers these feelings off.

"I don't know whether this second dream will help me reduce the wall I have built between myself and K. Most nights I sleep on my own, but almost every night our daughter comes into my bed at some time during the night. That's a very good reason for not wanting to sleep together, but it complicates our relationship a lot."

These dreams touch on issues about children's demands and lack of space which will be familiar to many mothers; the dreamer also suggests that her ambivalent feelings towards her partner originated with her father. The dream has offered a clear insight about her actual relationships, past and present, which she can use.

GOING BEYOND HETEROSEXUAL STEREOTYPES

Dreams can also offer insight into relationships less "conventional" than heterosexual ones. Most therapeutic theories work with "norms" of male and female and have explicit or implicit views about what is a "normal" heterosexual relationship. Most also have homophobic aspects, and the tendency of conventional psychoanalysis to see homosexual relationships as an illness or a perversion has aroused justified anger in the lesbian and gay community. It has led many in that community to question the value of any form of psychotherapy. It was about 20 years ago that gay men and women disrupted psychiatric conventions in San Francisco and Chicago demanding the abolition of psychiatry as an oppressive tool: "the cops . . . call us queer; you—so politely—call us sick. But it's the same thing . . . We are convinced that a picket and a dance will do more for the vast majority of homosexuals than two years on the couch." (*Gay Flames*)

It would be good to be able to believe that the therapeutic prejudice which provoked those remarks has been banished, but after nearly two decades of backlash against the liberation movements of the seventies, assisted by public paranoia about AIDS, it is not clear how much has changed. In the psychoanalytic tradition homophobia is fed by the continuing attempts to establish universal theories of "normal" development; and in newer therapies by their tendency to use the male/female couple as the basic unit and template for dualistic theories of positive/negative, active/passive, thought/feeling. At least in some countries the growth of a self-help movement in therapy, and of institutions dedicated to antisexist therapy, has contributed to the building of a practice and a theory which challenges those prejudices. In *Wild Desires and Mistaken Identities* Noreen O'Connor and Joanna Ryan offer a positive analytic approach to homosexuality, and in *Moving Heaven and Earth: Sexuality, Spirituality and Social Change* I attempted to deconstruct some of the heterosexist assumptions of the "new age" and human potential movements.

In areas where traditional theories betray prejudices and value judgements, for example when exploring dreams that deal with lesbian relationships, it may be more helpful to use a more open-ended dream method like Gestalt. Gestalt theory does not challenge heterosexism, but equally it lays down no overt dogma about gender, and because the approach is experiential, and leaves the authority with the dreamer, it can be used in an antisexist way. While some therapies approaching a dream about issues in a lesbian relationship might start with the premise that to be a lesbian is a problem in itself, the next example shows how Gestalt offers a way to look at such issues as they present themselves, without questioning the relationship. It also allows space to acknowledge the effect of the pressures placed on that relationship by society's prejudices.

As we have seen, Gestalt theory suggests that while the "I" in a dream represents the dreamer's conscious self, all the other objects and characters reflect unconscious aspects of herself. These may be qualities which she does not recognise herself as possessing and which she projects outwards, attributing them to other people and things. By acting out the different elements, the dreamer can re-own some of those unrecognised qualities. She does not need to be able to "act," but simply to imagine herself into a character or mood and then try out how that element would feel or speak. This example is based on a dream which a woman had during a crisis of confidence; it shows how it is possible to use the Gestalt method to explore a current relationship and reclaim power which has been projected onto a partner.

"I dreamt that I was on a rocky seashore with my lover Maeve. She was running ahead, leaping nimbly from rock to rock while I, Midge, was left behind, stumbling, trying to catch up and very frightened of falling into the sea."

Midge had this dream at a time when she had just moved, and when her self-esteem was at a low ebb. Things were going well for Maeve, while Midge felt a failure and was afraid that she might lose Maeve. Using the Gestalt method, she would start exploring this dream by breathing deeply, relaxing her body and telling the dream in the present tense to make it more vivid. Then she might speak as the "I" in the dream: "I'm Midge. I'm feeling pathetic. I can't keep up. I'm scared that Maeve will leave me behind, scared that I will fall and drown. I keep losing my footing. I seem to be helpless and floppy."

"I feel helpless" might be an important phrase for Midge to repeat at this point, to help contact her feelings in her current frame of mind. She could then try speaking as the rocks, perhaps changing position to sit on a different chair or cushion for each role, and shutting her eyes for a few seconds to help her imagine the part: "I am the rocks. I am sharp and spiky and hard. If Midge falls on me she'll get hurt. I am hard and dangerous. Maeve had better watch out for me too."

We have seen that body awareness is important in this

method, and Midge might notice that she is holding her body very differently now from her earlier, floppy role. As she acts out the rocks, she may recognise them as expressing a sharper side of herself which is the opposite of the "pathetic" role she is stuck in. The idea that dream elements represent unconscious parts of the personality was derived by Gestalt from the work of Jung, who pointed out in *Man and his Symbols* that the role of these elements is to balance us and help restore psychological equilibrium. They do this by exaggerating our present course—revealing its dangers— and by showing what is missing. Thus by playing the role of the rocks Midge might be able to balance and compensate for the one-sided role she is playing at the moment.

She might then move on to acting the sea, again perhaps shutting her eyes and breathing deeply for some moments to help her contact the feelings: "I am the sea. I am wild and free and powerful. I could swallow Midge up." At this point she might be reminded to address the "Midge" cushion directly, and keep eye contact with it, to make the dialogue more vivid: "I don't mean to harm you, Midge, but if you keep on panicking and slipping around you will fall in and drown." Then she might address the rocks: "I wash round you. I can embrace you and include you. I can just watch it all happening."

After playing the sea, Midge might find she has contacted a broader perspective on her situation, an inner strength from which she had been cut off. This may enable her to tackle her difficult situation more effectively.

When it comes to playing Maeve, Midge might well protest that surely this dream figure represents the real Maeve rather than a part of her own personality. Of course dreams can often reflect real people and situations, in this case a real-life issue in Midge's relationship with Maeve. However, the aspects of the situation which Midge has singled out, the symbols she has chosen, and the story, are her own. She is the playwright of the whole drama and will have put something of herself into each part of it. So she might act out Maeve: "Things are great. I'm really enjoying this run along the shore. Everything is working out fine. I'm not sure what is the matter with you, Midge. I wish you were up here with me."

Again, Midge might notice how her body posture and sensations change when she is playing this confident role, and she may find that she contacts a confident part of herself which she has not had access to recently, while she has been projecting that quality onto Maeve. Another possibility is that she might develop a dialogue between Maeve and Midge, which might throw some light on the dynamics between them at this time.

Of course Gestalt is not the only valid method to explore dreams about lesbian relationships: it can illuminate certain issues, but most dreams can be approached in a number of different ways and how you tackle them will affect what you find.

UNDERSTANDING OUR RELATIONSHIPS WITH OUR CHILDREN

Here is a fragment from a longer dream which Mary Winegarden had about her son Jonah a month before her second child was born:

"It is a holiday, probably Christmas. We've been with friends (John and Jo?) for a dinner/celebration and now Jonah and I are going home to change. We are riding on an elevator; no, it's the subway. Jonah leaves the subway car we're in and will ride in another car. He seems okay; I seem to feel that it's okay; he's big enough to meet up with me.

"But after he's gone I am worried and scared. I remember the huge space between the subway car and the platform; I

am afraid he will hurt himself or get lost and I AM SORRY I
LET HIM GO AWAY FROM ME. I WISH HE WERE WITH ME!

*"Then he reappears in his little red jacket and I am very
relieved. His face is full of tears as he says he couldn't find
me. I'm so glad he's safely back and lovingly reassure him.
I say that we are going to John and Jo's for dinner. He asks
me, 'Are we going to have . . .' He stumbles, trying to say
'pancakes', and says "pan-cookies." I smile and say yes,
realising he is thinking of the Christmas cookies we make
together.*

"Writing this I am in tears; I am sad to be letting go of
Jonah. Tomorrow he will be three years old and very shortly
he will be a big brother. I know he is going through lots of
different feelings about all this, anticipating the real loss of
his own babyhood. And I am feeling the loss of his babyhood
as well . . .

"The dream clearly reflects my coming to terms with the
loss of that special, intense, solitary relationship with Jonah,
my firstborn, and of course my guilt about that."

The effect of the arrival of a sibling is often seen from a
child's point of view, but the change and loss affect the
mother too. As children grow up there are many such difficult situations to face, and sometimes our intimate relationships with them can buffet or threaten to engulf us. Our
culture offers few opportunities to discuss them. Sometimes
a dream can shed light and perspective, and sharing the
dream may help weather the difficulties. In *The Variety of
Dream Experience*, Jenny Dodd describes the meetings over
four years of a mothers' dream group, weekly every Friday
morning. Up to ten women, with a number of small children
in tow, met at each other's houses and each week one woman
looked after the children. Despite tiredness and childcare demands, attendance was consistently high and the women reported real benefits from participating in the group: "We
were not seeking advice or solutions, but just the opportunity

to air our worries or joys and accept the conflicts and apparent contradictions in our lives.'' One mother dreamt about:

her children running into the house covered in mud, after which a woman appears displaying two beautiful handmade dresses.

In the group this dreamer described how her children had done exactly that on the previous day prior to a family outing; she discussed her anger and her ambivalence about punishing them, and talked about her frustration that she no longer had time for dressmaking.

Another mother had a haunting dream about:

a pyramid of beautiful red apples on a tabletop, bathed in light. A child's hand reaches out to take the top apple, and the dreamer says to herself "She's going to bite it, and it's rotten."

The dreamer told the group that all her life she had been fascinated by light. She recently read an article linking lack of light with depression; her eldest daughter (the top apple?) suffered depression most often in winter, and had "turned rotten," leaving home and losing touch with the family. She told the group that, for her, apples were magical and "core" things and that "approaching middle age, she now felt she was discarding the frills, discarding doing what she'd always been told to do, was coming to the core of herself. The dream was speaking of something creative emerging, to do with light. She concluded poignantly by saying that she'd had to get rid of the most beautiful part of her family, her oldest daughter, in order to preserve the whole."

This kind of group can be especially important for mothers whose daily lives are largely colonised by the needs of others and who receive little attention for themselves. Jenny Dodd felt that the group satisfied both personal and social needs and helped to lessen the mothers' sense of isolation.

NASTY OR NICE: WHERE DO DIFFICULT FEELINGS COME FROM?

Even in our closest relationships, we have ambivalent feelings. Sometimes it is hard to understand why people (including ourselves) behave as we do. One of the gifts of dreams is that they can sometimes offer insights about underlying feelings which may be motivating certain behaviour. Here I will take as an example the much-denied but insidious emotion of envy. This is the account of a woman who was hurt and surprised when one of her friends slept with her lover:

"The Circumstances: Two months previously my friend Gillian had slept with my boyfriend Len. I remember when she told me about it, I felt I had been kicked in the stomach, I was so upset. How could she do such a thing? Why? Soon afterwards she had gone to work as a receptionist for six months in another town. I had withdrawn from her and cut off.

"*The Dream: Gillian is sealed in a coffin. She forces open the coffin lid and sits up, rigid, pale and set. She is angry because of me having too much—an indoor bathroom and so many pairs of shoes.*

"The Meaning: After the dream I realised that she had slept with Len because she was jealous of me. I think she felt I was getting more than my share of the goodies at the time, sexually and otherwise. She didn't want to be written off (in the coffin): she wanted her anger to be seen and to make a mark. Funnily enough, I felt better about it all after the dream: I felt it had not been a mindless action or one she had done in spite of it hurting me. I felt it was actually to do with me, directed at me. It was all still very hurtful.''

This woman would need to check with her friend Gillian to be sure that the dream's insight was correct, but what she has been offered is a possible explanation for her friend's apparently inexplicable behaviour.

This example again highlights the importance of what happens between women—an area which has been hard for male therapists and theorists to tackle. The world of psychotherapy and the ''new age'' culture are no better equipped than the rest of our society to accept and understand women's relationships, from sexual love to close friendships to bitter emnity, with many ambivalent feelings in between. While our culture as a whole has devalued relationships between women, some feminist writers have been tempted to go the other way and idealise them. It is an area where it can be particularly painful to acknowledge negative feelings, but part of taking those relationships seriously is acknowledging and dealing with difficulties in them. Envy is a thorny but important issue in women's friendships, and here again dreams can help.

One woman sent the following dream:

"I am talking to S. and tell her that in the fall my son won't be in the playgroup any longer, so the group must find a replacement for him. She becomes very angry, says we've been dishonest . . . I argue with her . . . she remains angry.

"Now we are still talking in the same spot, somewhere inside. S. is sitting on the floor in front of me when someone comes in. The visitor is a man who comes over to S., greets her warmly and presents her with an astonishing assortment of cakes and fancy pastries. Some of the cakes are opium or hashish-filled, the man is S.'s lover and the whole feeling is very Middle Eastern, very exotic, Arabian-nights-like. S. becomes very soft and romantic, though she does not seem to

*be paying much attention to her lover. We eat the cakes; I
become high and continue eating without becoming full or
sick.''*

This woman comments: ''I'm working out an argument with
a friend—and think the Middle Eastern lover represents her
muse. (She is a poet.) Am I jealous?''

This interesting dream raises the issue of what women
envy each other for. The stereotype is that we compete for
men, but this dream suggests that a man can be a symbol of
other issues. Here the anger between the women is accepted
and in the open, while the jealousy or envy is tentative and
the overall mood of the last part of the dream seems lyrical.

Freud explained much of women's psychology in terms of
a concept of penis envy. Later Melanie Klein, who brought
many new ideas to the psychoanalytic tradition, suggested
that children were envious of their mother's breasts and that
this was more significant. Because there is inevitably frustration as well as enjoyment for the child around feeding—
since the breast is not always available—Klein suggested
that the child turns away from the mother and her breasts,
and looks instead to the father's penis as an object of satisfaction. The child is excluded when the parents are totally
absorbed in each other, and this is most clearly the case during sexual intercourse. The child is therefore furious when
the parents have sex and can also, according to Klein, think
that the mother is taking and keeping the father's penis inside
her body during sex. The result is feelings of hatred and envy
towards both parents, but particularly towards the mother;
the breast is what the child most wants, and cannot bear
continually wanting because she cannot always have it. The
child's strongest hating and envying impulses are therefore
directed towards the mother, and these feelings can become
a deep-seated pattern which manifests itself in all close relationships the child goes on to have with other women
throughout her life.

Envy is an important topic which tends to become invisible and needs to be looked at squarely; Melanie Klein's theory can be useful in this. However, she gives it a universal status which would reduce all children's development to a uniform pattern. She does not allow for the impact of different environments, different parenting, different issues: the child is locked inescapably into this primary pattern of envy of the breast. Again we have the implication that such feelings in dreams are intrinsic, preordained. I am reminded of the popular assumption in our misogynist culture that women are *naturally* spiteful and "catty." In both cases women's feelings are described as inevitable when they could equally well be understood as social in origin.

As Marie Maguire points out in *Living with the Sphinx*, feminists have taken a different view. They "have often expressed the hope that envious and competitive feelings would prove to be a product of capitalism and patriarchy, and would become less intense or even disappear completely as women developed more open and co-operative relationships with each other." This view would see Klein's scenario as specific to certain situations and societies rather than intrinsic and universal. Marie Maguire questions Klein's theory that the child is innately aggressive. She suggests that envy comes from a history of frustration or deprivation early in life, which lowers the child's self-esteem and leads her to compare herself with others. Such feelings may contribute a lot to the envy that often arises between women friends. It is exaggerated by the values of our society where women—faced with discrimination and encouraged to believe we are not good enough—end up competing with other women for the attributes of power and validation in a male world, whether these are attention, admiration, jobs, men or status. According to this view, the envy arises from deprivation, from a deep "hunger" for something we do not have (notice how many cakes the dreamer on page 128 can eat without feeling full or sick, suggesting a great need waiting to be filled). The difference of this approach is that instead of feeling stuck in something universal or archetypal, we may feel encouraged to try to make changes, for example to look at our needs more closely in the present and try to fill some of that hunger inside.

Being envious is uncomfortable, and increases the very feelings of self-hatred and low self-esteem which may have caused the envy in the first place. You feel bad, so you feel envious, so you feel even worse about yourself for being envious. Marie Maguire describes the self-hatred this triggered in the dreams of one of her clients:

"In one woman's nightmare, this unconscious persecutory aspect of herself was represented by a sweet young girl transformed by envy into a rotting, grimacing witch, with ragged clothes, stringy hair and a foul, poisonous smell, who lurked, snarling, behind a partition, waiting to attack."

While an analytic therapist might encourage this woman to bring the "witch" into the session to find out more about her, someone working on the dream at home or in a self-help group could use another approach such as Gestalt. Either way the woman would be helped to "own" the witch as part of herself and find out what the witch needs. Rather than seeing such feelings as inevitable, and the witch-figure as "archetypal," a woman-centred approach might look at the specific experiences, in family and society, which can prompt such feelings and such dreams in women. What do we envy? What does that tell us about what we need in our lives? When we feel empowered to pursue our own goals in adult life, we are perhaps less likely to turn bitter feelings against ourselves and others like us. Sometimes, also, to fully understand their charge, we need to look for the roots of those feelings in early childhood—which involves coming to terms with the past.

Reading and Notes

Dodd, Jenny, "A Mothers' Dream Group," Montague Ullman and Claire Limmer (eds.), *The Variety of Dream Experience*, Continuum, New York, 1989.

Fromm, E. *The Sane Society*, Holt, Rinehart and Winston, New York, 1955.

Gay Flames, "Gay Liberation Meets the Shrinks," Pamphlet 6, published by Gay Flames, Box 410, Old Chelsea Station, New York, NY 10011, undated.

Goodison, Lucy, *Moving Heaven and Earth: Sexuality, Spirituality and Social Change*, Thorsons SF, San Francisco, 1992.

Jung, Carl G. (ed.) *Man and His Symbols*, Doubleday, New York, 1969.

Klein, Melanie, *The Psycho-analysis of Children*, translator Alix Strachey, The Hogarth Press and the Institute of Psychoanalysis, London, 1980.

Maguire, Marie, "Casting the evil eye—women and envy," Sheila Ernst and Marie Maguire (eds.), *Living with the Sphinx*, The Women's Press, London, 1987, pp. 117, 138.

O'Connor, Noreen and Joanna Ryan, *Wild Desires and Mistaken Identities: Lesbianism and Psychoanalysis*, Columbia University Press, New York, 1994.

Ullman, Montague, "Dreams and Society," Montague Ullman and Claire Limmer (eds.), *The Variety of Dream Experience*, Continuum, New York, 1989.

6
Coming to Terms with the Past

One of the gifts of dreams is that they carry our past into consciousness so that we can come to terms with it. Dreams remind us of what we were too young to remember, and what we have needed to forget. Often these memories awake painful feelings which were locked into the unconscious, and sometimes those painful feelings need to be explored and expressed in the present in order to come to peace with the past.

Here is an example in which a therapist was able to pick out two words from a dream which provided a key to a lost childhood experience. Carol Jeffrey wrote in *Self and Society* about a woman client recounting a dream that began: *"I contracted a fatal illness and was in the hospital. I seemed to be about three years old."* The woman then gave a 20–minute-long account of her cage-like cot in the dream, the doctors and nurses around, her mother crying, and herself feeling very unhappy and frightened. As she listened to the dream, Carol Jeffrey noted a strange reaction in herself: although she heard the whole account, she remained emotionally stuck at the first two words *"I contracted"*. This is typical of good dreamwork: a small or even missing part can be revealed as very important, and an intuitive response like this is always worth checking out with the dreamer. Carol Jeffrey asked the woman what happened to her when she was three years old. The woman then exploded into agonised crying which lasted almost as long as telling the dream. When she finally calmed down enough to talk, and had been reassured, the dreamer said that when she was three her baby sister died and she believed that she was to blame. When the sister was born she had told her parents to "Take that away, I don't like it," and had tried to get the baby out of the cot. As a result she was punished and made to feel bad. She then began to get ill and became very shut up inside herself, guarding every action she made: "I didn't grow much either and I've always been small and thin ..." Carol Jeffrey pointed out to her: "That was when you *contracted* and shut up your energies inside a cage, and you have never been able to 'uncontract' or expand and move freely into life."

The therapist commented that before this dream, nothing had ever connected the dreamer's problems to that early and painful event in her life: "It happened while she was largely 'unconscious' at age three, and so the whole damaging complex had become encapsulated until the dream rang the bell and she recovered the memory. The work on this 'contraction' (the contracting process of her illness and also the contract which she then made with herself to curtail her energies and imprison her vitality) led her eventually to greater freedom and a more healthy life." An interesting point about this dreamwork is that the therapist was helpful through honestly noticing her own reactions. We sometimes imagine that helping a person with their dream means applying a theory or telling them about themselves. But this can be inaccurate and intrusive. In this case Carol Jeffrey's own reaction helped her to put her finger on a crucial issue.

REPRESSION AND REICH

The theme of sibling rivalry is one which recurs in women's dreams. Rage, jealousy—sometimes even murderous hatred—

about sisters or brothers, and the accompanying feelings of
guilt about these forbidden emotions, can be painful to uncover. What is interesting in the example above is the understanding that when those feelings were punished and
suppressed in the three-year-old girl, her whole body was
affected. She "contracted" into herself, and her body development was cramped at the same time as her self-
expression. It was Wilhelm Reich who first put forward a
clear theory about this process. He suggested that when the
expression of feeling is repressed in a child, this is accompanied by a tightening in the muscles which, as the child
grows up, becomes habitual. Discouraged from crying, a
child will tense her jaw and back; forbidden to hit, her arms
and shoulders will get used to being held in tightly. Feeling
bad about herself and her self-expression, she will shrink into
herself both emotionally and physically. Reich's theory was
of energy flow through the body which is restricted or
blocked at various places as a result of this kind of conditioning. Only through finding the tensions, and releasing the
feelings locked behind them, can we unblock the energy flow
and start to free ourselves from the childhood restrictions.
This expression—through the unlocked flow of tears—was
triggered directly by the dreamwork in the example above.

Some Reichian therapists work on breathing patterns and
apply pressure to tense parts of the body to help release painful memories. For a layperson the best thing is to be patient
and attentive to the dreamer, and not to push her into any
emotional release for which she is not ready. If the dreamer
is crying, angry, or overwhelmed by an old memory, make
sure that she keeps her feet on the ground and her eyes open
so that she is steadied by maintaining contact with present
reality.

Even if they are not expressed in an emotional way, acknowledging difficult feelings like jealousy, grief, loss, fear,
rage and envy can help to heal them. Just bringing the unconscious into consciousness is a way of coming to terms

with the past. The person who pioneered this approach, and who introduced the whole idea of the "unconsious" into our vocabulary, was the founder of psychoanalysis, Sigmund Freud.

FREUD ON THE FAMILY

Many critics have pointed out the shortcomings of Freud's theories, particularly in relation to women. But he created the momentum for the whole modern movement of dream-work, and it is useful to be aware of his strengths as well as his weaknesses. So here is a brief example of his method at work. It is from one of his patients, a man whose father had died several years earlier. From a small and innocuous snippet, Freud tracks down a hidden meaning: that the man had actually wished his father dead. In the dream

"His father was dead but had been exhumed and looked bad. He had been living since then and the dreamer was doing all he could to prevent him noticing it."

Typically, Freud starts the dream exploration by using "free-association." In this case the dreamer made the association that after his father's funeral he had a bad toothache. He told Freud that following the Jewish doctrine, "If thy tooth offend thee, pluck it out!" he had wanted to take the tooth out immediately, until his dentist gave him something for it and told him to wait three days to have it removed. Continuing his free associations, the dreamer linked "taking out" the tooth with the "taking out" of his exhumed dead father's body in the dream. He also cited the popular interpretation of losing a tooth as losing a member of the family. The dreamer then launched into talking about his father's long and expensive illness prior to death, and how he himself had, in obedience to Jewish law, conscientiously paid the bills without wishing the whole business over. Here Freud made a link between the wish to "take out" the tooth and a repressed wish to "take out" his father by a speedy death that would put an end to his painful and costly life:

> I do not doubt that this was really his attitude towards his father during his tedious illness and that his boastful assurances of his filial piety were meant to distract him from these memories.

Freud suggests that these unconscious hostile impulses towards his father may have originated in childhood, perhaps linked to the father forbidding him sexual activity. "He looked bad" in the dream account is then linked by Freud to the after-effects of masturbation, as was the phrase about the dreamer trying to "prevent him noticing it." Freud concludes with the reminder that "we must always interpret what are called 'dreams with a dental stimulus' as relating to masturbation and the dreaded punishment for it."

Here we clearly see Freud's method at work. He disregards the apparent meaning of the dream and uses the patient's associations—combined with a belief in the fixed meaning of certain symbols (such as teeth linking to masturbation)—to track down its childhood roots. Freud was attracted to find the "deepest and chronologically most remote" of the hidden thoughts and wishes behind a dream. Even anxiety-dreams were linked to wishes—they were seen as a reaction to repressed wishes becoming too powerful. Freud contrasted the "uninhibited shamelessness and immorality of the tendencies openly exhibited in some dreams' with the more civilised behaviour of waking social life. He believed that to disguise these unconscious and unacceptable thoughts, the dream uses various processes such as "condensation" (summarising a lot into one symbol) and "displacement" (shifting meaning or feeling from one element to another), so as to throw the conscious mind off the track.

Freud's approach is helpful with many dreams. But compare his patient's dream with the following dream account by Alison Leonard. From a man's dream about his dead father being exhumed, we move to a woman's dream about her dead mother, also rising from her coffin:

"For many years I had a recurring dream about my mother: *I was in a strange house—I was being shown round it—and after seeing a few rooms I realised that in one room, just off vision on the left hand side (it was always the left hand side) was an open coffin. Slowly, the body in the coffin rose to a sitting position. I knew that it was Mother, and she wasn't in fact dead. I felt 'Oh God, that charade's got to start all over again', and I knew that it was my job to go and warn my brother and sister that they'd better get ready to start 'all that over again.'*

"My mother had, in life, dominated the family by her illnesses, and by requiring us to be perfect as people and as her children. We played up to this, on the whole, fearing that if we didn't, she would die. My feeling when she died was entirely of relief, with not a twinge of guilt. But many years after her death I began to work on my anger against her, and was aware of a context of reincarnation, or at any rate of the existence of some kind of spiritual other world. I began to feel that she had passed beyond the kind of ignorance that led her to treat her children as she did, and that now she was in some way wiser. I was left, though, with this dream, which showed that I was still bound by her as child to hysterically dominant mother. My insights hadn't filtered through.

"After having one of these recurrent dreams I went to see a friend who said, 'You can talk to your dreams, you know.' I asked how, and she said, 'Say what you feel to the person in the dream.' So, as I drove back through the narrow Welsh lanes (rather dangerously!) I turned my head to the left and said to Mother: 'It's all right. You're dead and I'm alive. You're where you are and can get on with that, and I'm where I am and I'm going to get on with it. All this stuff about coffins and carrying on the charade is old stuff, irrelevant. Let's just let it go and forget it.'

"I haven't had the dream again since then. I've had other, pleasanter dreams about Mother. For instance, there was one where *my sister and I were chopping carrots and celery in preparation for a big party. After a while of chopping and chatting, my sister suddenly said, 'Oh! We were supposed to go and see Mother!' I said, 'She won't mind. She'll realise that we're busy getting ready for the party. It's all right.' And I could picture her enjoying thinking of us being busy and forget about her.*"

Notice the differences from Freud's example of the man with the toothache. Here the dreamer frankly acknowledges difficult feelings towards her mother both in the dream and in real life: no cloak-and-dagger stuff here, no need for complex detective work to track those feelings down. Is this because greater emotional honesty is possible in the late twentieth century, partly due to the influence of Freud's work? Which in turn has made his theory of dream concealment less relevant and calls for a corresponding change of method? Freud suggests that children have direct, undisguised dreams, and thus implies that disguising dream messages is something learned rather than innate, and is in some situations not necessary. It is interesting that the end result of Freud's dreamwork, the negative feelings towards the parent, is the starting point of Alison Leonard's dreamwork and she goes on from there. Is this also a reflection of the greater emotional honesty within women's culture since the rebirth of the women's movement in the 1960s and 1970s? Whatever the reason, it would seem to call for a different approach to the dream.

Another difference in the two accounts lies in the use made of the dream. Within psychoanalysis and psychodynamic therapy, the dream is taken as a communication from the patient to the analyst, and the interpretation offered by the analyst is part of the dance of intense interaction between the two on the path to healing. For example, the patient would be expected to redirect some of the negative feelings for the parent onto the analyst—a process called transference—and they would be worked through in that relationship.

Outside psychoanalysis and psychodynamic therapy, it is not possible to work on dreams with that particular focus. However, there is also a greater freedom. The dreamer is not restricted to looking at dreams only on an emotional wavelength. In her dream Alison Leonard sees her feelings about her dead mother in a broader context, where she can imagine her mother living on in some form freed from the attitudes and behaviour that bound her in life. With a friend's help, the dream is used as a basis for moving on and reaching some kind of resolution transcending the conflicts present during her mother's lifetime. Perhaps we sometimes need to sit and sweat with the uncomfortable emotions carried by a dream. At other times, perhaps we need to have a good look at them and then open the window so that the fresh air can move things round and change the atmosphere. I do not believe there is one single right way.

SEEING CHILDHOOD AS IT REALLY WAS

Many people look at their childhood through rose-tinted spectacles, picturing it as a perfect and idyllic period, and not wanting to acknowledge the reality of it. Freud's interpretations of his patients' dreams tended to identify unacknowledged, unpleasant, aspects of the past, to which they often expressed resistance. When working alone with a dream, it can be very tempting to twist the meaning to something we want. As Nan Zimmerman puts it in *The Variety of Dream Experience*, "Our dreams are honest. Unfortunately our waking selves do not always bring spontaneous honesty to work on the dream." This is where it is very useful to have another person there to put forward—respectfully—the interpretation we may be avoiding. She gives the following example of a dream she had:

"I dream of walking down a dark path. I see a storybook cottage with warm light flowing from the windows. A light snow falls. I peek into a window and see my family as it was when I was eight. Two children and their parents sit around a large oak table having supper. They laugh and eat, the epitome of 'family.' I am sad and long to be inside."

On waking she is full of nostalgia and dissatisfaction with her present life. However, after friends give her their feedback on the dream, she realises that she is sentimentalising her past in order to remain a child, locked out of her own home. Her childhood was not so wonderful; she is using an idyllic myth of what never happened to avoid facing adult responsibilities for lacks in her life in the present. The dream shows that by keeping her nose pressed against the window of the past, she escapes thinking about changes she needs to make to her "dark path" now. She points out that this debunking of the dream came from talking to others, who commented on it without bullying her. Nan Zimmerman suggests that in a caring dream group, members will be sensitive about causing the dreamer pain, and a dreamer will take responsibility to follow through on difficult truths made evident in a dream—even if they take some time to assimilate.

Perhaps the key element is the spirit in which an unpalatable interpretation is offered, and how far the relationship or situation allows the dreamer to respond. Some of Freud's case histories, and some examples of bad psychoanalytic practice, show us a psychotherapist using his professional position to impose an interpretation on an unwilling dreamer. A dream group can similarly use its concerted authority to put pressure on a dreamer to accept its views. A crucial factor seems to be that the dreamer has the right to reject interpretations that do not feel appropriate. Winifred Rushforth wrote in *Self and Society* that a group facilitator should stimulate interest in a dream presented to the group, and try to clarify its details, ''but still with reserve and respect for the dreamer's defences. I found myself recently using a good Scots word in this connection—'speir' or 'speer.' Don't speer too hard at this point, don't press your questions beyond the dream.'' And when it comes to interpreting dreams in the group:

> Quite often a spontaneous interpretation is presented immediately either by the dreamer or by one of the group. This must be accepted but not allowed to block further work on the dream. All dreams have great possibilities in their message. ''Tread lightly for you tread on my dreams.'' So we keep a gentle touch and are aware that we need not squeeze the last drop out of any dream.

One way of starting clearly to gauge the impact on us of our parents and upbringing has been developed by Akhter Ahsen. He calls it ''prolucid dreaming'' and—as described in his book of that name—it involves reliving a dream while bearing your parents in mind, each in turn, to see what effect that has on your feelings in the dream. The dreamer follows a clear sequence: first s/he recalls a dream, and then gives a conscious interpretation of the dream. S/he then thinks of her mother and keeps her mother in mind while going through the experience of the dream again. Then s/he does the same thinking of her father and keeping him in mind. The results are very interesting. A woman who dreamt that she was being chased, and started flying to get away, found that when she kept her mother in mind she felt like a dead weight and could not get off the ground: "the person has caught me . . . It is her, my mother." When she has her father as a filter, she finds he can fly with her and she feels happy. Another woman, 33 years old, dreamt that

a spider bit her hand, and her head blew up and off and got infected. The doctors said they could do nothing, except for one who was encouraging. She saw white blood cells starting to take over and make it better, and the nightmare ended on a note of hope.

Her conscious interpretation found no precise meaning except that she was surprised at the hopeful ending. When she relived the dream keeping her mother in mind, she found that her mother was standing with the doctors, talking, confusing her, making things worse: "It feels like she is the infection." With the father filter, she felt that her father was tugging at her by an invisible rope between their two minds; she got an irritation in her throat, then finally managed to cut the rope and felt better as the white blood cells healed her. After this experience, the dreamer had expanded her understanding of the dream and gained a sense that "There is something in my mind which is stronger than my parents." She described how her father tried to guide her in everything: "I need to tell him to save his breath and let me live my own life."

Ahsen comments that in most dreamers one parent at least is found capable of providing support, and that here the father was the most serious hurdle to the dreamer's independence. His experiential work challenges some of the fixed models which have been proposed for parent/child—and particularly mother/child—relationships.

MALE THEORIES, OUR DREAMS AND OUR MOTHERS

As critics have pointed out, traditional psychoanalysis was very much oriented towards the male experience. Freud's most widely known theory is that of the "Oedipus complex," a pattern of behaviour whereby the male child, like Oedipus in the Greek myth, is sexually attracted towards his mother and hostile to his father, who is seen as a rival. (In the myth, Oedipus accidentally kills his father.) In reaction to such male bias, women working within the Freudian tradition have successfully drawn attention to the female child's experience and the primacy of the mother in her early life. The result is that the focus of psychoanalysis, as Janet Sayers puts it:

> has shifted from the past and individual issues concerning patriarchal power, repression, resistance, knowledge, sex and castration, to the present and interpersonal issues concerning maternal care and its vicissitudes—identification, idealization and envy, deprivation and loss, love and hate, introjection and projection. (*Mothering Psychoanalysis*)

While women practitioners have radically influenced Freud's legacy, it is perhaps surprising that his younger colleague Jung has been so little challenged, especially since his theories about motherhood are in some ways hard to swallow.

Jung believed that a mother or a mother symbol in a dream is a reflection of a fixed supernatural mother figure, the "mother archetype"—which he describes in *The Archetypes and the Collective Unconscious* as the "prototype or primordial image of the mother that is pre-existent and supraordinate to all the phenomena in which the 'maternal' is manifest." In other words, real mothers in our dreams are in some way a reflection of a prior and primordial image of motherhood. This primordial image is powerful but limiting and rather sinister.

Jung, like Freud, was mostly concerned with the experience of the male child, and in this context the mother archetype can emerge in dreams and myth through symbols of a dark container or vessel which traps the son or solar hero. In *Symbols of Transformation* he refers to the mother's "voracious maw" and "the womb of death," like the whale enclosing Jonah. One whole chapter of that book is called "The Battle for Deliverance from the Mother." Elsewhere Jung writes about the "paternal principle, the Logos, which eternally struggles to extricate itself from the primal warmth and primal darkness of the maternal womb; in a word, from unconsciousness." In presenting this scenario, rather than identifying social pressures which may make it crucial for a boy to reject the world of the mother in order to play the "masculine" role required of him, Jung gives the process of separation from the mother the glamour of a mythic struggle for survival. It is surprising to me that many thoughtful and self-aware women have embraced Jung's theories and definition of female roles so warmly: conscious women embracing the stereotype of the unconscious female.

Jung suggests in *The Archetypes and the Collective Unconscious* that these archetypes are "definite forms in the psyche which seem to be present always and everywhere." He scoured the myths of distant and ancient peoples to find proof for his theory; but his case is by no means watertight. In the field I know about myself, prehistoric Greece and Greek myths, the evidence in no way proves that his view of mothers and motherhood was held throughout history. As I describe in *Moving Heaven and Earth*, I could find no firm evidence for a "Mother-Goddess" in early Greece: there are many female figures from the earliest times but very few clear representations of mother and child until the Late Bronze Age; other aspects of female activity seem to be emphasised instead. Again, there is nothing to suggest that women represented the dark, the moon or the unconscious, or indeed that this early culture created the same divisions between light and dark, conscious and unconscious as we do. Evidence suggests that early in the Bronze Age the sun was a female symbol, and women were not exclusively associated with Earth until the Early Iron Age—by which time a patri-archal culture had developed which saw women as second-class citizens. In the field of myth one can find uniformity if one looks for it, but what impresses me is the *diversity* be-tween different cultures and the dramatic changes that reli-gious and mythic symbols can undergo over time as societies change.

Perhaps Jung has confused women's role in his contem-porary society, and the way that is reflected in the society's dreams, with a universal "essence" of women. Jung himself does not rise above the prejudices of his culture. His nor-mally generous writings are marred by a certain misogyny. Although he describes the power and fascination of the "fe-male" moon, the dark, the primitive and the unconscious, he clearly sees them as inferior to the sun and the light.

Jung admits feeling that the "mother–daughter experi-ence . . . is alien to man and shuts him out," and it is this relationship between mother and daughter which male the-orists have found hardest to understand. Unlike a boy, a girl grows up to identify with her mother who is seen by our society as an inferior being; this is not something she is meant to escape from—as Jung's solar heroes do—but grow into. So while our mothers may play difficult roles in our dreams, we can understand it in a different way. Modern feminist writers on therapy have acknowledged the frequent tensions in the mother-daughter relationship in a culture where mothers often have low self-esteem and little social recognition, and were not themselves well-mothered because the same was true of the previous generation. The experience is perhaps not so much one of a trap as of a gap, as many women find that the identities they have built to cope with the world "were constructed around a lack of certain basic experiences, those of symbiosis with the mother and of de-velopment through a series of psychological phases neces-sary to the establishment of a separate identity" (as Sheila Ernst puts it in *Living with the Sphinx*). So while Jung's solar heroes make an epic escape from the "Terrible Mother," women are perhaps more aware of the social reality behind dream symbols. In *In Our Experience*, Pam Trevithick describes running workshops with working-class women who were "sad for our mother's losses—for her loss of spirit and hope for life, for the joys that weren't shared, the skills and effort that went unnoticed, the emptiness that went unnourished, the love that wasn't returned, the views that weren't respected, the sacrifice that wasn't appreciated, the emotions that were ignored or mocked, the loneliness that consumed her and all the work that went unpaid."

Seeing the mother as a timeless symbol of the unconscious does not acknowledge this reality, nor does it provide any model or possibility of escape from her under-role. Mythic constructs seem to be useful when they grow out of and illuminate lived experience, but not if they obscure it, or seem to glorify an unacceptable social reality.

Whatever his own personal blind spots, Jung's theory of the archetypes has been taken up by writers like Erich Neumann (*The Great Mother*), and many women have linked the "Earth-Mother" archetype to their belief in an ancient "Great Goddess" who validates their present sense of female identity. Jung's spiritual interests and his positive attitude towards dream insights have contributed to the growth of a dream-conscious women's culture in recent decades.

OURSELVES, OUR DREAMS AND OUR MOTHERS

The following example seems to show a dreamer who has fruitfully drawn on the spiritual aspects of Jung's legacy without embracing the notion of the "mother archetype":

"I had this dream a few years ago, the night after I had been to a particularly exciting lecture by Starhawk. She had 250 people, including men though mainly women, chanting an ancient Babylonian chant where 'the Goddess praises her vulva'—quite mind-boggling!—and performing a spiral dance. It was a most powerful assertion of femaleness at not just a physical, political or emotional level, but at a cosmic spiritual level too.

"That night I dreamed that I was visiting my mother's house, which was also where I spent my adolescence, with some builders who wanted to buy it, knock it down and incorporate it into the flats they were building next door. They pointed out to me, and my mother, and an old woman who was there too, a huge gap all along the eaves on the east side, and that there was not, and never had been, a north wall. I was both amazed and relieved: if there had never been a north wall, no wonder I had always felt cold in that house! But now it was falling away on the east as well—it was alarmingly unsafe, and my mother would have to move out. She would hate to move, and I wondered what I could do to help her.

"I woke up with some anxiety, but an overwhelming feeling of relief: at last I understood WHY I had always been so cold in that house. I was vindicated . . .

"This dream is powerful at many levels. The most obvious seemed to me at the time that my mother was beginning to face death—her house seemed a symbol of her body, her life on earth. At the time I registered this, and then, like the rest of the family, buried it. No one would or could talk about it when I tried to raise it—and I am so used to being silenced in my family that I didn't try that hard. In the event, my mother didn't give serious cause for concern until a year later, when she dramatically lost weight and developed a headache. Over that summer, it was decided that she would move out of the house and go and live with my sister in Yorkshire, miles away. But on the night she was due to leave, she collapsed very suddenly and died.

"So the dream was prophetic in a number of concrete

ways: my mother *did* have to move out of the house—though not because of the house; it *was* bought up by the builder next door, who *did* convert it into flats; I *did* try to help her move house, but found it difficult to do so in a way she could accept. She did die.

"But the dream has other levels too . . . For me the north is about grounding, nurturance, endurance, darkness, the element earth—in short, symbolically, my mother's body, which I had always felt was somehow forbidden, withheld from me. In my therapy I later came to realise that the words from the Church of England service about renouncing 'the world, the flesh and the Devil' were for me about my mother's body. In other words, the 'north wall' of my mother's house in the dream somehow stood for her physical presence—warm, nurturing, sustaining—which in an important sense had never really been there in my early life. This was difficult to grasp, as it happened quite subtly—most people saw my mother as she saw herself, as warm, generous, affectionate: it has been very hard and painful for me to acknowledge just how rejected and un-nurtured I felt. The dream makes my situation crystal clear: and it is very striking that I had this dream just after the experience of the lecture, where I had felt warm, sustained and nurtured both by the spiral dance and by Starhawk's cosmic assertion of femaleness.

"My mother's withholding of her body from me, and her accompanying rejection of my female body too as I grew up, is for me very much associated with her religious beliefs. It was as if the Church's assertion of the divinity of fatherhood sanctioned the subordination of motherhood and women, and the rejection of daughters.

"As I look back on it now, although I did not do very much with the dream except think about it from time to time, it did mark the beginning of my mourning for my mother. But the dream at another level is also about separation: in the dream as in real life I do not live in her house any more."

Notice here the many and varied insights which emerge after the dream. It would be hard to see this symbol as a "disguise" in the Freudian sense; rather it seems that the many varied comments which the dream is making could *only* be embodied in that particular symbol. It is not something which could be "translated"; rather it stands in itself. Jung in *Symbols of Transformation* quotes the alchemists' saying "for those who have the symbol the passage is easy," and this account suggests that this particular symbol of the house provided understanding and sustenance through a period of major change—the death of a mother.

Perhaps also in the background lies some influence from Jung's positive emphasis on being able to move forward. Jung criticised Freud's theory of neurosis for encouraging the patient to feel that the cause of his neurosis "lies in the remote past. In reality the neurosis is manufactured anew every day . . ." Jung emphasised the power of symbols to effect transformation in the present. This dreamer can draw out the themes of separating from her mother, making changes and moving forward.

What is different, however, from a Jungian approach is that there is no fixed attitude about a "mother archetype" or "female essence." The dream illuminates a specific experience of a specific mother and is valued as such. The dreamer acknowledges gaps in her mothering and their effect on her (the missing wall); but there is no symbolism of being trapped. This is not a dream about Jonah trapped in a whale. It is a dream about a very different experience of mothering, one which the dreamer relates to social pressures on her mother rather than to a universal or essential definition of motherhood.

Perhaps it has been hard for male theorists to see the mother as anything but "other," and therefore as in some way dangerous and mystical. According to Freud she can in the child's eyes be incomplete and castrated because of her lack of a penis. According to Jung she is a devouring monster holding back her children who have to escape her to survive. She is also described as a magical being who holds the power of the unconscious. At the same time there coexists for Freud and Jung an image of the idealised "perfect" mother. All of these views seem to have more to do with male mythology than with women's real lives. Whether feared, decried, dramatised, or idealised, women's actual experience is denied.

Perhaps the hardest—and most important—thing for us to do as women is to look our mother's experience in the eye and see if we can accept it. This is what Cosi Fabian, a Briton living in San Francisco, does in this dream, which she calls "Reconciliation with Dead Mother":

"Circumstances: One element of my reclamation of the ancient ritual of menstruation is to retreat for three days. Honouring this 'time of dreams and visions' I make a particular effort (!) to sleep, particularly valuing the half-light state of dozing . . .

"The day before this dream I had for the first time used my mother's and grandmother's name—Fabian—as my own professional name.. Part of the first workshop given under this 'new' name was a call for honouring our foremothers, understanding their 'dysfunctions' in the context of their times, and praising their domestic crafts as true—if distorted—creativity of a 'fine arts' calibre.

"Background: Overwhelmed by grief, alcoholism and impending blindness, my mother died a suicide twelve years ago, three years after we last spent time together upon the death of my father. Both her, and my, alcoholism was denied by family, doctors. We shared low self-esteem and a sense of failure engendered unknowingly by my father. Denial and distance (I've lived in San Francisco for over 20 years) meant that no resolution was possible in life.

"My own severe but untreated Post-Traumatic Stress Disorder resulting from an air disaster in 1972 contributed to the psychic chaos.

"This was the dream:

"*I am in a Moroccan-type bazaar, which is somehow enclosed in an airplane cabin. My father comes around the corner behind me, to my left, and says, 'It's your mother. . . .*'

"*His tone of voice bespeaks the tacit 'she's drunk again.*' (Remember: her alcoholism was never acknowledged in life. It was called 'neuralgia', 'depression'. Valium, Mandrax and Cortizone were over-prescribed.)

"*We move to another section of the bazaar/plane. My mother is crawling on the floor, trying to look out of the floor-level small windows. She starts to move towards me. I squat down, gently but* FIRMLY *moving my father aside, behind me. I have a child's-eye perspective of Father—all shoes and trousers. This is the 'father' pushed aside.*

"*I sit cross-legged and my mother, relaxed on the floor, lays her head in my lap. Conscious in the dream of the supra-real situation, I wonder which version of my mother has come to me. Will she look old and sad and sick? Or young and clear?*

"*She is both, and neither: her hair is long, wavy, like in photographs before the War, before I was born. But it isn't the near-black of her youth—it's no-colour, opalescent. As is her skin. Her face is without age: smooth like white glass but somehow still holding her full lifespan.*

"*An officious stewardess comes fussing over and says disapprovingly: 'What's going on here?'*

"*I look down at my mother, at the restful smile on her timeless, semi-iridescent face.*

"*'It's all right. She's just drunk.*'

"*It's as if I'd said, 'It's okay, she's just got a bad cold.' In the dream I am astonished at the heretofore unknown acceptance and compassion in my voice.*

"*I sit there, oblivious of father and plane and officials, cradling her smiling face in my lap.*

"*We are at peace.*

"Within a month I was able to visit England, land of my sorrows, for the first time since my mother's death—the ghosts and confusion and hurt and guilt laid to rest.

"My first day back in the familiar Suffolk countryside turned out to be Mothering Sunday.

"I cried sweet tears."

Reading and Notes

Ahsen, Akhter, *Prolucid Dreaming*, Brandon House, New York, 1992, pp. 35, 41–2.

Ernst, Sheila, "Can a Daughter Be a Woman? Women's Identity and Psychological Separation," Sheila Ernst and Marie Maguire (eds.), *Living with the Sphinx*, The Women's Press, London, 1987, p. 74.

Freud, Sigmund, *Introductory Lectures on Psychoanalysis*, The Pelican Freud Library Vol 1, translator J. Strachey, Penguin Books, Harmondsworth, 1974, pp. 223–6 (father and tooth dream), 157–67 (children's dreams). Published in the U.S. by W. W. Norton, New York, 1976.

Freud, Sigmund, *Introductory Lectures on Psychoanalysis*, The Pelican Freud Libary Vol 2, translator J. Strachey, Penguin Books, Harmondsworth, 1973, pp. 49–50 (condensation and displacement). Published in the U.S. by W. W. Norton, New York, 1976.

Goodison, Lucy, *Moving Heaven and Earth: Sexuality, Spirituality and Social Change*, Thorsons SF, San Francisco, 1992.

Jeffrey, Carol, "Using Dreams in Therapy," *Self and Soci-*

ety, Vol IX, 3, May/June 1981 ("Dreams" issue), published by Self and Society, 39 Blenkarne Road, London SW11 6HZ, p. 102.

Jung, Carl G., *The Archetypes and the Collective Unconscious*, translator R. F. C. Hull, Princeton University Press, Princeton, NJ, 1967, pp. 75 (prototype of mother), 96 (paternal principle), 42 (forms in psyche), 203 (mother-daughter experience) [Vol IX, Part 1 of *Collected Works*].

Jung, Carl G., *Symbols of Transformation*, translator R. F. C. Hull, Princeton University Press, Princeton, NJ, 1967, pp. 347–8 (womb of death), 298ff (deliverance from mother), 442 (symbol makes passage easy), 420–1 (neurosis manufactured anew) [Vol v of *Collected Works*].

Neumann, Erich, *The Great Mother: An Analysis of the Archetype*, translator R. Mannheim, Princeton University Press, Princeton, NJ, 1964.

Reich, Wilhelm, *Character Analysis*, Noonday Press (Farrar, Straus & Giroux), New York, 1972 (first published Orgone Institute Press, 1949). For descriptions and developments of Reich's work, see also Alexander Lowen, *Bioenergetics*, Coventure, London, 1976 and David Boadella (ed.) *In the Wake of Reich*, Coventure, London, 1976.

Rushforth, Winifred, "The Analytic Dream Group," *Self and Society*, Vol IX, 3, May/June 1981, ("Dreams" issue), published by Self and Society, 39 Blenkarne Road, London SW11 6HZ, p. 132.

Sayers, Janet, *Mothering Psychoanalysis: Helene Deutsch, Karen Horney, Anna Freud and Melanie Klein*, W. W. Norton, New York, 1991, p. 3.

Trevithick, Pam, "Unconsciousness Raising with Working-class Women," Sue Krzowski and Pat Land (eds.), *In Our Experience: Workshops at the Women's Therapy Centre*, The Women's Press, London, 1988, p. 77.

Zimmerman, Nan, "After the Dream Is Over," Montague Ullman and Claire Limmer (eds.), *The Variety of Dream Experience*, Continuum, New York, 1989, pp. 45–6.

7

Understanding Society: Problem-Solving, Work and Politics

"All I wrote from a middle-of-the-night dream was the phrase: '*I lay down my boxing gloves forever.*' I knew what it was about, though. I had just come quite clear the day before that I would never again drive like a man. I live in the city and drivers are very competitive, men feeling personally either puffed up or insulted by their 'winning or losing' in little traffic battles. I have my ego to protect, too! I never liked to let anybody cut in front of me, got very protective about my space, pushing like men—and feeling exhausted by all this battle attitude. I drove enough in traffic that I decided I didn't have this kind of emotional and physical energy to spare. At some point I just realised that this was men's way of being in the world and I didn't feel comfortable with it. When I dreamt the phrase 'I lay down my boxing gloves forever' it just confirmed from my deep consciousness the rightness of my decision to drive like a woman—calmly, peacefully, not wasting my energy on ego games."

This snatch of a dream-phrase from Marti Matthews, and accompanying thoughts about driving in Chicago traffic, touch on a question about dreams which this book has not yet fully discussed: how much can they—or should they— be used to grapple with social issues? Or with economic, moral, intellectual and political dilemmas? How much can they help us with issues about work, economic power, justice and politics?

The mainstream of male theory has emphasised the dream's connection with our inner life: the unconscious, re- pressed memories and energies, the 'underworld.' Most of the dream theories mentioned so far in this book connect dreams to emotions, relationships, the internal landscape. James Hillman has suggested that by bringing them into the day world at all we are in danger of abusing and distorting them; he rejects as an inappropriate "humanism" the notion that dreams can be a reflection of a message for human af- fairs.

Women's experiences seem to say differently. In this book there are many examples of dreams which seem to be offer- ing an active comment on social issues. We can perhaps un- derstand why it is that—apart from the work of Montague Ullman and Nan Zimmerman—this aspect of dreams has been largely ignored. Since Freud, dreams have been brought into the province of psychotherapy, and it is not surprising that the white male professional theorists of that province have been slow to notice dream comments on social injustice, inequality between the sexes, and the interaction between social problems and the inner life. It is perhaps also not sur- prising that those working in the field of psychotherapy tend to absorb all experience into that framework, so that every- thing is explained in psychological terms, dreams included— just as sociologists tend to see everything in sociological terms, and scientists in scientific terms. It has been a contri- bution of women to challenge the way knowledge has thus been partitioned up into rival world views, and to suggest that experience rarely fits neatly into any one of those compartments.

Another reason why dreams get set apart from daily life is that they fall on the other side of our culture's exaggerated division between "conscious" and "unconscious," day and night, logic and fantasy, thought and feeling. Dreams themselves do not seem to observe such distinctions, and range freely from the mundane to the sublime, but it challenges a basic tenet of our culture to suggest that dreams can not only imagine but also think. Just how effectively they can think has been shown by some recent experiments with the problem-solving abilities of dreams.

DREAMS AND PROBLEM-SOLVING

Morton Schatzman, an American psychiatrist now working as a psychotherapist in Britain, published the following puzzle in *The Sunday Times* and *New Scientist*:

> What is curious about the sentence, *Show this bold Prussian that praises slaughter, slaughter brings rout?*

As part of a series of tests of the problem-solving capacities of dreams, he invited readers to find the solution to this—and other—puzzles in their dreams. He has explained that he deliberately chose to set brain twisters rather than serious problems so that there should be one simple correct answer and his results would be clear as to whether the dream contained it. His results emphasised the versatility of dreams and their willingness to engage with any questions presented to them. His findings suggested a living mechanism which can harness not only the imagination but also the intellect, to tackle not just emotional but also theoretical problems.

One of the responses he received was the following account from a young woman A-level student:

"Last night, for about 15 minutes, I studied the sentence, but could not solve the problem. I went to sleep thinking about it. About 4 A.M. I woke with a dream.

"*In the dream, I was waiting for someone in an empty room. I was rather anxious, as I had an appointment for which I was late. A woman, presumably the 'someone,' arrived, and I handed her a slip of paper. (I think the slip had this problem printed on it.) She read the paper and started to laugh. I couldn't see what was funny, especially as a battle had just started outside. I demanded to know what was going on, but she just shrugged her shoulders, saying, 'Oh, the Prussians are coming.' I said, 'Surely, it's the Persians.' We argued about this, until I remembered I was late and I ran out into the battle.*

"*The battle, however, disappeared as I ran towards a small terraced house. Inside, a group of people were sitting around a table. They looked at me, and all except a very fierce balding man started to laugh. The man shouted for quiet, and told me to stop hanging around in doorways. I couldn't move, however, as my left leg was missing. All I could say was, 'My leg hurts.'*

"*Someone helped me to a chair, and a girl sitting opposite suggested that I might feel better if I took my head off. I was grateful for this suggestion, but my head wouldn't come off. The fierce man shook his head and said, 'Too many vowels, too many letters.' My head started to float away—and I woke up.*

"I don't usually wake up in the middle of the night. Possibly I woke up because my leg had become entangled in the bedclothes and was hurting. As I wrote down the dream, I tried to find some significance in the arrangement of the vowels, vowels being almost the last thing mentioned in the dream. Failing in this, I gave up and went back to sleep . . .

"I re-read the dream this afternoon, and it struck me that perhaps I should remove the first letter (head?) of each word to form the sentence, 'How his old Russian hat raises laughter, laughter rings out.' I wondered briefly if there was another solution, but it seemed very unlikely that by chance one sentence should be formed from another in such a way." (from *New Scientist*, my italics)

I have quoted this account at length because it seems to offer much insight into the way dreams can solve problems. The solution was the "correct" one, and it is intriguing to try to understand how it was solved and how it was communicated to the dreamer. By the time the dream started, it seems that some part of her already knew the answer. Most people are familiar with the idea that the unconscious mind can hold information to which the conscious mind has no access. Schatzman cites the example of the nineteenth-century French researcher Alfred Maury who was puzzling, when awake, where the French town "Mussidan" was. Soon after, in a dream, he met someone from Mussidan and asked him. The man said it was the main town of an area in the Dordogne. On waking Maury consulted an atlas and found this information correct. The implication is that there is a mechanism present which can store "forgotten" information, and can process new information or problems so as to come up with answers.

The way the solution to the "Prussians" brain teaser was communicated suggested to Schatzman that the part of the mind which knows the answer is playing "hide-and-seek" with the dreamer. Perhaps it is more a question of that faculty using a different language, so that the answer is conveyed several times in different ways: via signposts (the handing over of the slip of paper); drama (the slaughter and laughter); and metaphorical clues (the suggestion she take her head off). What strikes me is the playful quality of the communication, and also the fact that some of the clues are not quite right:

only the second phrase of "Too many vowels, too many letters" is actually true for solving the problem. There are also false trails, like the hurting leg which apparently had more to do with twisted bedclothes than answering the problem. Seeing the indirect, hit-and-miss style the dream uses to communicate such a precise and specific answer, one realises how great the chances are of mis-communication, mis-remembering or mis-understanding on the part of the dreamer when more important issues are at stake. Schatzman points out that sometimes we may be in the position of radio hams uncertain whether what we are hearing is an important message or simply static.

The classic examples that are usually cited to show dreams solving intellectual problems are the case of the geologist Agassiz who had a dream about fossilised fish, and the organic chemist Kékulé who had a dream solving a long-standing problem about the molecular structure of benzene. The invention of the sewing machine by Elias Howe also apparently arose out of a dream image. Such problem-solving feats are consistent with the theories of the French psychologist Jean Piaget, who rejected Freud's sharp distinction between rational and symbolic thought. Instead Piaget's research led him to believe that there is a continuity between dream symbols and the symbols that are used in waking life, for example by children playing and adults daydreaming. He saw these symbols not as a result of neurosis—as in psychoanalysis—but as the sign of a healthy individual processing their experience. Past experiences are assimilated to present ones in order to progress our emotional and intellectual development, and he suggested that even when we think we are at our most lucidly "intellectual" there are unconscious symbolising faculties at work. While the experiences of people like Agassiz and Kékulé could be dismissed as "chance," Schatzman's experiments suggest a purposefulness in those unconscious faculties.

Schatzman's inquiries also throw light on the way dreams

choose symbols for use. One of the responses to his teaser was from a woman who had watched two films before bed on the night she solved the problem. One film featured Herbert Lom as Attila the Hun, and the other starred Clint Eastwood. In her dream, after Eastwood quotes the teaser almost word for word at Lom/Attila, the latter responds by raging, *"I am not Prussian, but Russian,"* thus giving the crucial clue about removing the first letter of the words. The dream has evidently used characters and settings fresh-sown in the unconscious in order to dramatise the solution. Interesting too are the time factors involved: the A-level student did not recognise the proffered solution until the afternoon after her dream. The Lom/Eastwood dreamer woke with the thought "Take the 's' off slaughter" and had to go downstairs to check *The Sunday Times* because "For a week I hadn't thought about the problem and had forgotten the precise sentence in the problem, yet—and this is quite exciting—I still found the key to a solution." All of these elements give food for thought about our interpretation of more important dreams: does a dream sometimes simply repeat the same message in different forms? Do we sufficiently acknowledge the pacing of dreams, in combination with our conscious mind, in gradually reaching answers to problems? The gentle persistence of these dreams in offering solutions to the dreamer makes it tempting to think of a motivated and personified force at work. Schatzman says that problem-solving dreams remind him of the elves in the Grimm's fairy tale, who work through the night to make shoes for the poor shoemaker and his wife while they are asleep.

Psychotherapist Jenner Roth has developed a similar idea in her concept of a "dream team" busy at work on our behalf:

"From childhood on I was curious and fascinated by the genesis of dreams. Why? Where? How? When? Ultimately

I answered these questions (at least to my own satisfaction) through my concept of the 'dream team.'

"The 'dream team' is made up of many tiny, little people who live inside my head and carefully watch for all the things I miss and might need or want to know. They look out through my eyes and hear through my ears. They are also aware of my feelings, both gross and some so subtle I am not consciously aware of them.

"They are very friendly and happy creatures. They are busy and smiley. For some reason they wear hats. They are there for the sole purpose of caring for me by watching, sifting through the material and producing dreams for me . . . They are very loving and caring, extremely intelligent and have the most marvellous sense of humour.

"They will act to inform me or to help me clear out stress or answer puzzles or make decisions. I find them to be persistent and if I do not listen to them or understand them they will repeat the dreams until I do. They have even put in subtitles and voice-overs when I am at my most obtuse."

However we visualise or symbolise the dream-making force at work in cases like this—and it is certainly human as on some level it is part of our biology—the evidence for its intelligence and information-processing capacity is convincing. Rather than thinking of something misty and primordial, we perhaps need to recognise that we are dealing with something dynamic, up-to-the-minute, and very present in our current concerns and calculations. As such, it is unlikely to be out of its depth in the discussion of our working life or social and political issues.

DREAMS ABOUT WORK

Dream insights are good at pointing out hypocrisy, inauthenticity, pressure, suppression, resentment and helplessness.

A place where many people come up against those issues is at work, and often the unequal and hierarchical relationships of the workplace are the subject of fierce criticism in dreams. Jenny Dodd, in *The Variety of Dream Experience*, quotes a woman who, after a humiliating harangue from her boss, dreamt about her hated school headmistress, a strict disciplinarian. The dreamer was apparently helped by the comparison: "The feelings of powerlessness, helplessness, and revenge were paralleled. The links thus made freed the dreamer from responding on an infantile level. They enabled her to remain clear and levelheaded in the present situation and not allow herself to be further manipulated or humiliated."

Many women may recognise this experience of humiliation at work. Many may also be familiar with the strain of being in a job where as a woman they have to try harder than men in order to be recognised or taken seriously. Years ago, after leaving my first job working for the BBC, I myself had a dream in which I was:

"dancing on my knees along the sea front in Algiers for BBC Television, to a musical accompaniment. It was one long tracking shot, shot from behind me."

The image still captures for me the sense of discomfited and self-diminishing "performance" which that job called for simply because of the nature of the institution.

These thoughtful dreams can comment on many different aspects of our involvement with the world of work. Another important issue for many women is the difficulty of finding a place and an identity in that world at all, in the face of childcare demands as well as our own and others' expectations. In the following dream, Mary Winegarden shows her feelings and thoughts about re-entering the world of work when she had small children:

"I am swimming, in what feels like the ocean (there are waves) but actually is a very, very large tank, an oval tank, rather like a skating rink, except that we are swimming around and around, rather than skating. I feel a powerful current underneath, which impels us forward quite rapidly; in fact I find it impossible to swim in the reverse direction. I can only continue swimming in the same direction, around and around. A. and W. (women friends) are swimming with me, and at some point one of them . . . points towards an ocean liner kind of thing (a large ship) and then grabs on to the prow and suggests that I do likewise. She explains that it's easier to hold on to the ship's prow and get carried along, rather than swimming on your own. To me, the ship looks too large and menacing, too overpowering. I choose to continue swimming on my own."

Mary Winegarden comments that this dream "reflects my anguish about my lack of a work identity—a 'real' identity in the world. The boys were both little (seven months and three years) and while I was mothering full time, G. was working very intensely with the Circus. I feel trapped ('I can only continue swimming in the same direction, around and around') doing all the mundane household chores. The two women are both circus performers (both without children at this point), who suggest that I come work with the Circus, too, but I don't want this, even if it is 'easier to hold on to the ship's prow and get carried along.' I feel I must define my own identity—the ship is 'too overpowering.'

"The water imagery is always powerful for me—as I love swimming, love being in the water. But here the pleasure seems diminished—perhaps my love for the kids and joy in mothering is also diminished by the frustrations I feel. (The 'powerful current underneath' could represent strong creative desires which I couldn't act on—couldn't 'reverse direction.')"

This dream expresses common feelings of frustration at the difficulty—often impossibility—of combining the demands of mothering with the need to express ourselves through work in the world.

DREAMS AS SOCIAL CRITICISM

Working with Ullman's approach to dreams, John Wikse sees dreams functioning as a form of "social intelligence." He gives the simple example of how he was standing one day with an academic colleague when a student approached and told the colleague a dream she had had about him:

he was standing at the blackboard trying to hammer a nail into it, but kept missing the nail.

The colleague laughed and admitted that he sometimes talked "around" a topic, rather than getting to the point. Because of the humour of the dream, its comment could be shared constructively with the person it was aimed at; but the dreamer's unconscious is actually making an incisive criticism of the quality of her superior's lecturing. Wikse stresses the role of the dream as a source of social information and insight, and uses the term "critical imagination" to describe the way that dreams can challenge the distortions of perception generated in unequal relationships, "wherever there are age, class, race, sex, or other invidious divisions among people that correspond to actual power imbalances." Thus in the student-teacher relationship, as in a worker-manager relationship, people learn in daily life to communicate in ways that will not rock the boat; but the dream is not bound by any such considerations.

Wikse also gives the more complex example of a woman who dreams that:

she scolds her daughter for spending too much money on stationery. Her husband asks if she is going to complain about it. She finds the manager, and says she is a long-time customer. He offers her a Barbie Doll, but she tells him that she is too old for dolls and asks for her money back.

Writing about this dream in *The Variety of Dream Experience*, Wikse sees it as reflecting a growing awareness in the dreamer of a "social-sexual identification" through a cluster of relationships: being angry at her daughter; being seen by her husband as complaining; being a passive customer for whom life is managed by others. Her resentment as a "long-time" customer who has bought into the system but is not getting satisfaction, is coming to the surface in the dream: "The question involves genuine satisfaction and maturation . . . The Barbie Doll is both a personal and a social metaphor. It points to . . . the patterns of satisfaction that are expected to compensate for being treated, as an adult woman, like a little girl. This social image integrates a set of tensions around familial, economic, and sexual identity. It illuminates the interconnections." He sees the dream as a signpost of the dreamer's move towards rejecting this "Barbie Doll" identity.

Since dreams have this strong critical faculty, which can be humorous and—as in the case of the Barbie Doll dream—sometimes quite subtle and sharp, it is a shame that books about dreams in the West have rarely discussed politics, and books about politics never mention dreams. Even within the women's movement in the West, it tends to be only those feminists who are interested in "new age," neo-pagan, or "Goddess" issues who would take dreams seriously; and they are often working within a ready-made vocabulary— whether Jungian or other—rather than exploring with an open mind the links between dreams, society, and the struggle for social justice. This seems to be yet another symptom of those patriarchal splits which tell us that we are *either* practical, down-to-earth and political *or* spiritual, dreamy and airy-fairy. Montague Ullman suggests that by marginalising dreams to "therapy" and laboratory research, our society is actively protecting itself against the penetrating criticism which the freer dream mind is capable of making: "It serves as a defensive manœuvre that protects society against the social truths that are apt to emerge if the social relevance were to be given its just due."

Wikse stresses how important it is to disentangle the threads of the social and personal relations which are often interwoven in dreams. He gives the example of a couple where the husband had recently lost his job:

the husband woke in the night lashing out, dreaming that he was being suffocated by the wife; she woke screaming and he told her the dream. She then dreamt that he was being suffocated by the God of economic power.

Wikse suggests that there is a dream communication happening between these two partners around the theme of suffocation. If the husband's anger at the wife is related to wider economic insecurities, he needs to learn to distinguish when his anger at her is "a compensation for the weight of a deeper powerlessness."

The fact that personal issues are involved does not invalidate the social factors present. Another woman dreamt that:

A day out in the country was spoilt by low-flying military planes. One of them landed; she shouted at the pilot about his murderous technology, and attacked him up against the wall.

To interpret this dream simply as an inner drama—the planes symbolising a friend or relative or a part of herself that the dreamer is in conflict with—is to miss the point that we are daily subjected to noise and other forms of pollution, and the helpless rage we feel at this is as much part of our inner life as any other emotion. It is not a question of "either/or." This woman who dreamt about the planes may well have difficulties with anger, or with invasiveness, or with letting herself relax and enjoy things. But the inner drama expresses itself through an external equivalent: the aeroplane. The private conflict expresses itself in the dream through finding a parallel in the dreamer's experience of the wider social reality. As Ullman has put it: "Some of these images are bi-directional; that is, they have something to say about the unsolved problems of society just as they do about the unsolved problems of the individual."

DREAMS AND POLITICAL ACTIVISM

For those who are politically active, there are also useful insights to be gained from dreams. A woman trade unionist dreamt:

she was behaving surreptitiously and being questioned at work and was then stopped as she left school on her bicycle.

She concludes that, "At work I feel like a naughty schoolgirl." In a society which tends to dismiss or ridicule opposition voices, this dream suggests that this woman felt infantilised by attitudes towards her activities.

Some dreams express the dreamer's own doubts:

"Outside there was an area of idyllic activity—trees and flowers and grass and children playing. Like an area of allotments. But on the hill-slope towering above us at a terrible angle were black-and-white camels. I couldn't stand it. Went to the man who ran the place, asking about the camels. He

*was alone in a wide bed. He said he was sick of left-wingers
who are too idealistic in wanting better things for the camels.
Their opposition to the right, he said, comes from a wrong
image of the kind of military discipline which runs an air-
port. They got this after the war, he said, and are left-wing
just for the sake of being left-wing: 'The camel, for example,
is not capable of that much. He is a bright camel, an intelligent rustic camel with rural origins. But it is sentimental
to champion his cause. . . . '*

*" 'How did you know,' I asked, 'that this camel was par-
ticularly bright?'*

" 'He was wielding pliers.' "

The dreamer comments: "At the time I was experiencing a
lot of pressure to be 'right-on' and politically correct. I didn't
have the confidence to express my doubts to my comrades.
So it seems a lot of the debate was banished to my subconscious."

This apparently frivolous dream from a politically concerned
woman seems to be making a serious effort to tackle some
concerns about lack of realism, over-idealism and an obses-
sion with new orthodoxies on the left. The criticism is mainly
from an intellectual viewpoint. In other cases a dream can
present an emotional challenge, commenting on factors like
body experience and family history which may be influencing the dreamer's motivation to become active in oppositional politics:

*"In a quadrangle there is a big statue. Some students are
staging a demonstration against the man the statue is of; it
seems he used to work in the canteen at this place (Hampton
Court?). I support them but as a tourist I don't want to be
involved. They douse the quad with water, then throw shit at
the statue. I try to hide in an archway and am pissed off."*

This woman comments: "I was very active politically at the time and was upset at my reaction to the students' demo in the dream. I 'Gestalted' the roles of the students and the statue without much success or insight. Re-reading my journal a few years later, it jumped out at me that it's all about food, digestion and excreta: water, shit, being 'pissed-off,' the canteen. Did I link being politically active with 'making a mess,' throwing shit at authority? Part of me was doing it in real life, while part of me just wanted to run for shelter?"

These examples show that dreams can comment on points of political theory and practice, as well as on the emotional and personal motivations which can get woven into political activism. While some dreams reflect utopian ideals and celebrate revolutionary heroism, perhaps more interesting are dreams like these which are sceptical, questioning the dreamer's own conscious beliefs. They raise the issue about how oppositional political activity can be symbolised in a dominant culture which sees it either as glamorously heroic or as child-like "shit-stirring"—both of which views fail to acknowledge the many complex and mixed reasons which motivate people to question the values they were brought up with and challenge the status quo.

DREAMS ABOUT INEQUALITY BETWEEN THE SEXES

Some dreams feature a particular relationship but also carry insights about the social dimension of male/female relationships, commenting on gender inequalities or male violence. Take this dream, which the dreamer sees as touching on ageing, death and the relationship between the sexes:

"I'm walking through a hospital lobby. I think I am pushing a buggy. Suddenly I notice a very old couple, a man and a

woman. The woman is a patient, and is on a hospital bed (one on wheels). The man, her husband I assume, is pushing it. But suddenly he is lifting her by the lapels of her dressing-gown, and shaking her in a fury. She looks absolutely terrified. Then he drops her, stops shaking her and pushes her in the bed to another part of the lobby, where another elderly woman happens to be sitting on a chair. The sitting woman leans over to the woman in the bed to comfort her, and they both begin to cry. The man has his back to me and I cannot see his expression. The women both are absolutely overwhelmed with grief, their mouths open. I had felt unable to intervene (I was too shocked? in a hurry?), but I am deeply upset that a man can be that violent to a woman, even at that age and stage of their lives. I think I start to suck my thumb! My sister comes up and starts to talk to me—she has probably witnessed the incident too—but I am too upset to reply.''

The woman who had this dream commented: ''I worked on this dream in my dream group. That evening there was only me and Brenda (normally we get at least three out of the four members present). I acted the different voices, being the different people in it. I was the man and the woman who was his wife and I was the spectator who cried, and my sister. But it didn't feel like that was what it was about. I also talked about it to my counsellor and she thought that all the characters were parts of myself. At one point I could see that theory was arguable. The woman colluded in her own victimisation, and in the world I have been trusting in ways I shouldn't. So maybe that is a message and a warning. Also it could be part of me in that I have been bad at defending myself against myself—I torture myself mentally and give myself a hard time. But basically it feels the dream is about male violence to women.

''I had the dream a few months after my mother died and it is set in a hospital in Boston where she and my father had

worked at different times. I think it is saying something about
their apparently 'blissful' marriage. That sounds harsh but at
the end of the day my mother sacrificed herself a lot for my
father and that contributed to her death. It feels like a *real*
nightmare, a real experience in the world such as I have seen
and lived through (not so much physical violence, but emotional violence in my last relationship with a man). Some
dreams I do feel are very much like an internal dialogue and
others feel more like a reflection of reality. Of things about
reality that are frightening. This did feel more like that kind
of dream.

"This was all several months ago. Now I could work on
it all over again and get something different from it."

This example suggests the multi-levels that dreams can op-
erate on; this woman was able to acknowledge the different
possible levels of meaning of her dream and "hold" them
all as possibilities, while remaining clear that the main focus
of it for her was not the internal but the external and social.
The next dream, the last in this chapter, takes a thoughtful
look at the issues of sexual permissiveness. It features a male
lover who seems to be standing for a man the dreamer has
known as well as embodying certain values which she is
renouncing; and also symbolising a period of her own life
which (with some regret) she is leaving behind as she looks
to get her needs better met in the future.

*"I am staying in Paris and having a lovely time. I meet a
beautiful man and we have lots of sex together—very beautiful and tender and funny and lots of good talking. We are
lining up at counters and ordering and eating food together
and it feels very good and happy and temporary, but somehow I don't mind that and I'm aware my body seems okay
and I'm surprised by that and then I am somehow aware
that it's not the seventies but the nineties and I ask if it's all
right we've been having unprotected sex. The man says no,*

*he has AIDS. I run from the room and put my clothes on
and feel really sad and upset that somehow I have betrayed
my children and I will die and then I also feel really sad for
him as he is so beautiful and yet he is dying and I go back
into the hotel and find a woman there who is youngish but
very confident and reassuring. I talk to the woman. She
seems to be some kind of health worker and she says I won't
catch AIDS . . .*

*"The man turns almost inside out and sucks his own penis
and I see him like a child taking comfort in his own body
but I also don't like it. What he is doing is distasteful. But
he is dying and I am feeling sad."*

The woman who had this dream comments: "I had that
dream at a time of change when I felt I was being asked by
the man I was separating from to cling on to values of the
seventies, although this is now the nineties. Or, to put it more
personally, I was being pressured to react in ways I might
have been able to in the past, but cannot do now without
endangering my psychic health and survival. In the dream I
am torn between past and present . . . But I am also com-
forted and helped by the woman 'health worker.' She seems
to represent a part of myself that is calm, working for my
health, younger than I am in some ways but more knowing
in others.

"The beautiful man is a sad figure. Not only is he dying,
but he ends up giving comfort to himself that the 'I' of the
dream finds infantile and almost disgusting. He is living in
the past, and fatally threatened by that.

"Of course those seventies' values my ex-partner still
maintains can look, feel and taste good—as pleasure does.
But, in that consumerist way, they are not for me. The seventies' values in this dream were those of sexual libertari-
anism which seemed . . . to take away from women the right
to say no to sex . . . Sex was debased so that it became something with no more meaning than a meal . . . The nineties'

values which the 'I' in the dream was struggling to establish are those which say that sex *does* have a meaning beyond satisfaction of an appetite; that 'easy-going' or 'heart-free' sex is generally easy only for men; that there is no reason why a woman should have sex with a man simply because she is a woman and he believes she should take care of him/his appetites, etc. Moreover, nineties' values seem to me (the dreamer) to offer women more opportunity to ask: is this action truthful for me? will this action serve me and my inner life?—whatever the current mores may be.

"The beautiful pathetic man could also be seen as one aspect of my own inner masculine which has literally come full circle. Maybe once he allowed me to be wild, dashing, adventurous. But I have outgrown him—just as I had outgrown the 'real life' man who had been in my life up until the point I had this dream.

"Now there is no nourishment I can get from such a figure. And there is no nourishment I want to give him. There is nothing left for my inner dream figure but to suck on himself. It is such a harsh, discomforting image, but perhaps its very emptiness means that it can now be left behind . . . Any kind of death or termination in dreams seems to me to allow for new life, or a new perspective, when the grieving is done. And even more recent dreams suggest to me that, indeed, a much more gentle, steady and supportive aspect of the inner masculine is ready to be embraced—a 'gentle giant' who will work for my inner good rather than for external goals and synthetic pleasures."

Reading and Notes

Dodd, Jenny, ''A Mothers' Dream Group,'' Montague Ullman and Claire Limmer (eds.), *The Variety of Dream Experience*, Continuum, New York, 1989, pp. 40–41.

Hillman, James, *The Dream and the Underworld*, Harper and Row, New York, 1979.

Piaget, Jean, *Play, Dreams and Imitation in Childhood*, W. W. Norton, New York, 1962.

Schatzman, Morton, "Dreams and Problem Solving," *International Medicine*, Vol 4, 4, 1984, p. 8 (Mussidan dream).

Schatzman, Morton, "The Meaning of Dreaming," *New Scientist*, 25 December 1986/1 January 1987, pp. 36–9 (P/Russian dream problem). See also "What Do We Mean When We Say That Dreams Are Meaningful?—And Some Evidence That They Are," revision of a paper presented at sixth annual international conference of the Association for the Study of Dreams, London University, 28 July 1989, pp. 12–13, 15–17 (P/Russian dream problem).

Ullman, Montague and Nan Zimmerman, *Working with Dreams: Self-Understanding, Problem-Solving and Enriched Creativity through Dream Appreciation*, Crucible/Jeremy Tarcher, Los Angeles, 1989 (first published 1979).

Ullman, Montague, "Dreams and Society," Montague Ullman and Claire Limmer (eds.), *The Variety of Dream Experience*, Continuum, New York, 1989, p. 293.

Wikse, John, "Night Rule: Dreams as Social Intelligence," Montague Ullman and Claire Limmer (eds.), *The Variety of Dream Experience*, Continuum, New York, 1989, pp. 195, 199, 206, 204.

8

Dealing with Difficulties, Decisions, Transitions

"*I'm driving along a winding country road in my gold Renault car. It's a dark and colourless place. The road begins to wind more acutely... The bends are coming at me now more quickly and sharply and I'm just about keeping control; it's with great effort that I turn the steering wheel. Then suddenly I'm off the road over the cliff and drowned in the car. I'm dead.*

"*In the next part of my dream I find myself looking down over the cliff at my car floating in the water. I'm alive and I'm wet. I realise my friend had revived me. (She must have been with me in the car, she's also wet.) Everything's okay.*"

This dreamer, Sonia Keizs, comments: "I was in the process of making a change of career... making a commitment to doing what I love to do, to practise homeopathy to help people. I had to give up my teaching job... I felt anxious and uncertain about losing my income. But for me there was no turning back. I had to act on what I believed and trusted... The dream strongly highlighted for me the death of... that

other life, all the things that stood for—nine-to-five depend-
ence, restrictions, etc. Its passing away was not without resistance. I tried hard to keep that old career on the road.
However, it had to go, I had to let go.

"The result is quite wonderful. In my dream I was helped,
I was okay. And so it has been in reality. I have been without
a regular large income and I have managed. What I have
gained is a faith and trust in the benevolence of life. A sort
of rebirth. I have freedom and autonomy and I'm building
up a homeopathic practice and making a living, however
small."

This example reflects the kind of feelings we may have about
any major life transition, whether it is changing work, moving house, starting or ending a relationship, growing old,
getting pregnant, or re-assessing our whole life direction. We
cannot tell the outcome in advance. In all these processes
dreams may be able to help, whether in working through
feelings of doubt, despair, fear and insecurity or in helping
us find hope or the way out of an impasse. The first step
may be in acknowledging a problem, and here dreams can
sometimes offer a gift in the form of a warning.

GETTING A WARNING

Here is the dream of a woman whose marriage was about to
break up. She eventually realises that her child drowning in
the dream represents her marriage which is going under:

*"I had this one about six months or a year before I left my
husband Phil. I was at a party being held by my cousin Alex
in the country. A lot of people were clustered around his
swimming pool which was at the front of his house, including
my then 19-year-old brother Jonathan and a few friends of*

mine from work. Phil was there sitting by the edge of the pool. It wasn't sunny. I think I had arrived late and I went over to greet people by the pool when I noticed that my son Abe (then 18 in real life) was a baby of six months and was lying facedown at the bottom of this pool wearing a turquoise babygro which I used to have when I was married to my first husband (who I left when Abe was two). I don't know why I couldn't jump in to save him myself but I asked Phil to save him and he was too busy brushing his hair (something he used to do in real life when we were late for an evening out with friends) and said very casually: 'Yes, in a minute when I've finished brushing my hair.' No one else was taking it seriously either and I was desperate. I offered my little brother money if he would jump in and save him but he wouldn't, and a group of people nearby laughed—partly at me because I was by now slapping myself in the head like a Turkish mourner—and partly at the situation. Someone said something like: 'I don't know, young people today won't do anything unless they're paid enough for it.' Then Phil (or Jonathan, my brother) did go in and he told me that he couldn't save him because his babygro was stuck on the draining grill down there. I think I woke up then."

This woman comments: "I told this to my analyst but we didn't really do anything with it. It was only later that I realised that Abe represented our marriage and his drowning was my concern about its demise which I didn't think Phil was taking very seriously. My little brother once witnessed one of our terrible rows and burst into tears when he thought Phil and I were going to split up, so I assume he was there as a clue that this dream was about a possible breakup. I think we were at my cousin's because my cousin is very fond of Phil and also because my cousin and his second wife went through a bad patch when he was going through a workaholic phase (which Phil was also going through at the time of the dream). Water is always a symbol of emotions in my dreams.

When I first went into analysis I had lots of dreams about terrifying creatures coming out of the water and harming me . . . it's interesting that Abe was an emblem of the marriage since he is the thing I care for more than anything else in the world which may be a clue to how much I cared about the marriage (which I don't think I was consciously aware of at the time).''

Without becoming paranoid, it is worth listening to dreams to see if they may be alerting us to a crisis on its way. Sometimes part of us is unconsciously aware of a situation running into trouble, and if we become consciously aware in time, we have the choice to dive in and save it.

UNDERSTANDING OUR FEAR

Sometimes nameless fears may grip us during waking hours or in the night. Here again a dream often carries the information we need to understand the source of that fear, so that we can do our best to deal with it. In the Irish psychotherapy journal *Inside Out*, Inger Nolan gives the example of ''Mary,'' an office worker in her fifties who had been in individual therapy for some time. One of her problems was that she felt a choking, paralysing fear when other people got angry, even when their anger was not directed towards her. She dreamt:

''She was curling up behind some bushes. There were loud and hostile people on the other side of the bushes.''

With the symbol of the curled-up body position, the dream is offering a clue which Inger Nolan notices and uses in ''Mary's'' dreamwork:

"When she told this dream she emphasised the awkward body position. I suggested she take the same position as in the dream, in order to explore further what it meant for her. As she curled up behind a chair in the therapy room, a vivid childhood memory suddenly appeared: Mary was silently witnessing a violent fight between her parents. Through focusing on the body in this way, Mary was able to re-experience the intense fear she felt in relation to her parents' arguing. This work led to other important memories she had forgotten. Gradually she found a healthier way of breathing and reacting to frightening situations."

When the source of our fear is in the past, we are not always able to read a dream clearly, and sometimes what we glean is not so much an answer as a hint which later dreams may enlarge on. Here is a fear dream of my own, which my peer dream group thought might reflect a memory of fears during birth:

"I am lying sunbathing on a very large barge. Suddenly a storm whips up and I realise the boat is loose; it starts travelling very fast through the crowded harbour, out of control. It is huge and I fear a major disaster if it hits something, for example a little blue mini floating ahead. Miraculously, it reaches the quayside without damaging anything and I can get off, although there is some problem about getting my baggage off with me."

When I shared this dream in the group, I suggested it related to my fear of being "too much" and causing damage if my energy really lets loose; arriving at the quayside I recognised a familiar feeling of having somehow "got away with it" accompanied by a sense of amazement and relief. The group, however, commented that this large boat travelling fast through water suggested to them the birth process, and they asked if that rang any bells for me. I said I did not have

much information about my birth, except that it was fast—
which would fit with the dream. If it was also headlong, that
might have been the beginning of a lifelong pattern. We
agreed to keep an open mind.

The above dreams point to causes of fear in past events.
Others show the dreamer the inner turmoil stirred up by a
present situation of difficulty or insecurity. Here is the recurrent nightmare of a woman from Barbados who was living
in the UK without official papers and was afraid of being
deported:

*"I find myself in the dream in a place in Barbados. I pass
this specific place in the dream, it's got this really deep drop.
You are walking on a grassy sort of land and then you come
to this drop. I've fallen off this drop once but I've never
reached the bottom of it. It's like a daze—going into noth-
ingness. It's got the feeling of being in Barbados and it's
also got the feeling of being in England.*

*"I've never gotten to the bottom of this dream. I think it
has connections with my situation here in England at the
moment: I'm betwixt and between and I don't know where I
stand."*

This woman connects her dream to the pressures and fear
caused by the threat of deportation. In this case she is aware
of her anxiety, but with its symbol of a precipitous, bottom-
less drop which is and isn't both Barbados and England, it
is showing her the dimensions of the threat posed to her root
situation and core questions of home and security. What can
she do? In a difficult world, dreams can sometimes help by
teaching us to live with discomfort, by showing us a lifeline,
or by helping us prepare for change and transition.

LIVING WITH DISCOMFORT

Sometimes my bathroom mirror shows me a tired early
morning face etched harshly by bright sunlight, disconcerting

to recognise and yet clearly my face—or one view of it. Similarly dreams sometimes offer reflections of life which are painful to get along with. One woman writes about a recurrent dream as if it were an old friend that she accepts and accommodates, although she has experienced it as discomforting:

"A dream I've had ever since I can remember, establishes an apparently dispiriting spectacle of myself in different social situations in which something is expected of me and from which there is no possibility of immediate escape. Everyone is having a good time; I am not . . . The scene shifts in response to changing events; so I might be at school, at work, at a party—but always I am the same, and so are the other people. I've known all these people but not at the same time; yet here they all are—sensible, appealing and adept, and all of them in the right place at the right time. Someone usually observes this somewhere along the line, although it's not necessary, so emphatically is the figure that's me in the dream on the margins, on the edge, of these enviable arrangements. This figure has no clear definitions: she can neither see clearly, nor can she be seen—because no one is looking at her."

This woman comments: "Waking from this dream has not been as dispiriting as might be expected. Whenever I start something new, it's accompanied by a new version of the dream. Sometimes I've become bored and frustrated enough to deploy techniques to deal with it, to put a stop to it, to stop myself dreaming it. But I've soon come to miss it, and I'm always pleased to see it when it comes back. Or rather, I can welcome a reminder that a dream is not to be taken literally unless it insists, and that since this is *my* dream, I can brush it against the grain in any direction that I wish.

"The techniques I used to deploy against it (appropriate military metaphor—this dream had to be dealt with as a threat from elsewhere) included concentrating, before falling asleep, on not having that dream, gazing at a candle to drive it away, and working hard during waking hours at not feeling like an outsider—as though there could be nothing interesting or exciting about not joining in. Arriving at liking the dream, and accepting it as some kind of part of my life, coincided I think with recognising both sides of the experience of feeling different.''

This woman's last comment about her dream reminds me of seeing Toni Morrison in a television interview talking about being an outsider. She commented that, growing up black in America, she was inevitably an outsider to the mainstream culture; then she described how she came to recognise this as a strength and a richness, as she both knew the mainstream culture, and had her own black culture, and had an interesting perspective on both. This woman's dream reminds me too of reading in Erving Goffman's study of ''Gender Advertisements'' that in adverts women are statistically more likely than men to be placed at the edge of the picture, half-hidden behind something, or with eyes averted. Goffman suggests that such framing reflects social positions and status. With or without the significant additional fact of belonging to an ethnic minority, women live with the daily experience of being marginalised, and this woman has found her own way of living with it.

Sometimes it requires courage to acknowledge that a dream is unresolved, and just sit with it. This involves trusting that the difficult issues it reflects will get sorted out in due course, without pushing things. Here is an example from Elinor McDonald, whose dream is set in her native Australia:

"I had an aerial view of a convent in the bush. My sister and I went to live there and be nuns. I couldn't hack the lifestyle and so I escaped and married a French king from

*the 16th or 17th century... My sister stayed at the convent
and became a bishop.*

*"I knew I wouldn't get my head chopped off because it
wasn't the right time of year. I lived in a red brick suburban
house... This dream was like a series of slides. I didn't ever
see any of the people involved although I knew they were
right beside me."*

Elinor McDonald describes this dream as odd and confusing.
When she worked on the dream, she asked the people (her
sister and the king) what they were doing in the dream:

"My sister sang 'Que Sera Sera' for me... I feel that by
singing this song she represents someone who has got their
life together and has time to tell me about mine... In the
dream she is settled—she has her plan. It feels odd to write
that because usually I am the one with settled plans and she
is the one without direction...

"The king said he had personal problems of his own and
that was why I was safe... When I picture him, he looks
like one of the Stuart kings with the long curly wig and the
silly spaniels. He had no real presence in the dream. I feel
distanced from everything when I try and think of what he
means to me. As a result I wish I could leave him out...
The whole thing felt unresolved."

Presented with a dream like this, a psychotherapist could
draw out several themes and might offer a number of interpretations. S/he might draw out themes of wildness/nature
(the convent in the bush); no sex/sex and intimacy (the convent versus marrying the French king), decadent sex (the wig
and silly spaniels); competition with her sister (can she accept her sister's wise song?); and violence (the danger of
decapitation). S/he might also talk about the distancing
mechanisms throughout the dream (the static images, not seeing the people involved). However, it is not clear how helpful

such interpretations would be to the dreamer. She herself comments that: "This dream is confronting me with things that I don't want to (or find very hard to) think about. Things like trust and giving a bit of myself without feeling that I am losing control. Control is very important at the moment." So it seems that the dream is giving the dreamer just enough insight into her predicament. The fact that not all of the dream is brutally clear may be a valuable mechanism for coping with the dreamer's situation. If the dream is indeed about trust, sex and intimacy, perhaps the dreamer and the dream know how far she can go in bringing such issues forward. It could be important for a therapist not to force her to look too closely at areas which are vague in such dreams, but to help the dreamer regain some sense of control through having her dream heard, working on it in her own way, and drawing her own conclusions. "Que Sera Sera" is about trusting what will happen. So perhaps her unconscious is working through the issues in a way which we cannot hope to understand, and perhaps she is taking her own time in closing the distance on these important themes in her life.

FINDING A LIFELINE

Sometimes a dream not only presents a problem, but draws attention to a personal resource which could help to solve it. Here is an example which seems to be using one of the most time-honoured of teaching methods: parable. It offers a resolution to a difficult situation by showing a possible pattern of reaction to a parallel situation. As the dreamer puts it:

"The following is an example of a dream that revealed that I could react differently to a conflict that normally I would have found extremely painful and humiliating.

"I had had my hair cut short and my partner's reaction

was quite extreme. He had always told me that he liked my hair long but I was in the middle of a middle-aged crisis where nothing looked good anymore. I didn't like my hair and I longed to cut it short. I had had it done on impulse in the hairdresser's and my partner felt that I had completely ignored his wishes and desires. He didn't like it and he thought it made me less attractive. I felt furious and misunderstood. It was my hair and anyway couldn't he see that I was struggling with getting older. Telling me I looked less attractive was, I felt, horribly insensitive. We rowed and I stormed off to sleep alone.

"I dreamed that I saw an old friend. In reality this friend and I had lost touch because she no longer wanted to keep contact. I had no idea why this had happened and I felt too hurt and humiliated to ever ask why she didn't want to contact me. I suspect that I was terrified that maybe she would say something that would reveal that I was a terrible person. In the dream we met in the street and to my surprise I asked quite simply, 'Why haven't you rung?' This was the dream.

"When I woke I felt curiously cheerful and at peace. I had gone to bed feeling persecuted and enraged. The dream indicated that somewhere I had taken on board the possibility that I wasn't so terrible. I had the freedom to ask a question and hear an answer. If I had upset her—and in some way I must have done—that didn't mean I was bad or that I had done something unforgivable. The cheerful feeling extended to my partner and I was able to look at him in a more charitable light. He didn't like what I had done, but it didn't mean that I had done anything that was so terrible. I didn't have to feel crushed by his reactions. This I might know intellectually but it was very nice to have it verified in a dream."

As well as teaching about a problem with a partner through a problem with a friend which had provoked similar feelings of self-doubt and persecution, this dream offered a resource:

it indicated "that somewhere I had taken on board the possibility that I wasn't so terrible." An important message and a source of succour at a time when this woman needed it.

When a dream offers a path of hope like this, it is something which the dreamer can keep with her in the day to help her cope. In the example that opens this chapter, the dreamer survives drowning to stand, wet, on the clifftop with her friend; again, this image of herself alive on the clifftop might be a picture she could hold in mind to steady her through the uncertain process of transition. Sometimes a friend or therapist can be helpful in identifying the element of hope in a dream which the dreamer herself has overlooked. In the next example, from *Gestalt Therapy Verbatim*, Fritz Perls works with a woman called Linda who has a dream:

of a lake drying up, with porpoises who are dying out and cannot reproduce. She thinks in the dream that when all the water dries up, some kind of treasure may be revealed, but all she finds is an old licence plate.

Speaking as the old licence plate, Linda says she is outdated, useless, of no value, and due for the rubbish heap. She is describing the feelings that many woman have in our culture as they go through the transition from youth to age. Fritz Perls is uncharacteristically gentle. When she plays the lake, Linda says she is soaking into the earth and dying; but she realises that even in the lake bed, flowers can take root, and new life can grow from her:

"I can paint—I can create—I can create beauty. I can no longer reproduce, I'm like the porpoise . . . but . . . I can play a part in something . . ."

Perls points to a contrast: on the surface there is an artefact (the licence plate representing the artificial person) but when Linda goes deeper she finds the apparent death is actually fertility. She realises she does not need a licence or permission to keep on growing in her life. Perls encourages her: "You don't have to be useless, if you are organismically creative, which means if you are involved."

The porpoises seem to represent the ageing of Linda's female reproductive functions, without which women can be made to feel they are for the scrap heap. The water seems to represent her life force, her hope and her creativity. Perls works without a rule book and is able to draw out the existential message without "interpreting." In this way Linda is enabled to own the strengths inherent in her dream, and to find beneath its dried-up symbolism fresh sources of life.

PREPARING FOR LIFE TRANSITIONS: PREGNANCY

Bearing children is one of life's big transitions. Women's dreams at that time illustrate how dreams can interact with such transitions. While the physical body prepares to give birth, a parallel process seems to go on in the dream world. Dreams during pregnancy suggest that women are adjusting to their changing body as well as anticipating the birth itself and childcare demands. Perhaps the process of preparation starts even before conception. Mary Winegarden had the following dreams four and three months respectively before the conception of her first child:

"I'm in New Orleans for the Mardi Gras and I'm at Mass. Among many people, we seem to be moving slowly forwards towards the altar (to Communion?).

"Two old ladies just ahead of me engage in conversation, which, after a few opening greetings and such, goes something like this: 'Did you know that elephants get very randy around Easter-time?' 'Yes, everybody gets randier in the

*spring, you know, and then we'll be seeing lots of babies
come Christmas . . . '*

*"They are very smiley, all-knowing and benevolently
winking. Then of course they ask me if I have any kids and
I say no, and am relieved that they don't ask whether I'm
married. I remain polite and friendly and they are just like
any other nice and nosy old ladies.*

*"Then it turns out that we are moving in a line towards
Communion, which seems to involve a sip of wine and a
healthy kiss on the lips! A middle-aged man comes up to my
friend (looks like Susan from high school) and gives her wine
and tries to kiss her and she's confused about what to do.
It's funny because it's such a awkward kiss. It seems that
once you've been given Communion, you are then supposed
to go and do likewise, so lots of people are walking around
kissing each other. I worry about spreading my sore throat.*

*"This leads to another dream about little boys . . . which
has gone . . ."*

In the second dream:

*"P. from Arkansas is here and is about to deliver her third
baby. She's left R., because he's beaten her and is an al-
coholic. At one point it seems that her labour has begun, so
S. and I are trying to help her, which involves a mysterious
dark, egg-like substance which we keep tasting (and it's
good) until I realise that it's almost gone and P. really needs
it.*

*"Then P. gets up; her labour hasn't started. I realise she's
completely unprepared for the birth and I, very composed,
start posing alternatives: Vanni, the midwife, San Francisco
General Hospital, etc. Whom should I call? I don't remember
much of what happened after that, except that . . . I do remember very clearly the intense tastiness of the egg-like
stuff."*

The festival atmosphere, the talk about randy elephants, babies, the Communion kiss and the egg-like substance are all very suggestive, and Mary Winegarden comments that:

"I see both dreams clearly as a preparation for conception: my unconscious readying itself for conceiving my first baby, quite in tune with whatever my body was doing. I was also working on a videotape documentary about midwives and the second dream reflects some of that practical knowledge."

The richness and physicality of the symbolism in these two dreams belies the rather monochrome version of motherhood which seems to have dominated dream theory. For Jung the notion of the "Mother Archetype" suggests a standard mythic template where the Mother represents unconscious as opposed to conscious, possessiveness as opposed to freedom, containment as opposed to development. In contrast the imagery of these dreams—with their smiling, winking, drinking, kissing and tasting—is dynamic, personal, creative, idiosyncratic, and very sensual.

Dreams seem to underline physical processes that are taking place. In *Women Dreaming*, Brenda Mallon notes that women in her survey dreamt at ovulation time of "small, delicate objects." One woman, Kate, dreamt of:

"cut-glass jewels; tiny, multi-coloured cubes in my hand . . . I took off some green alabaster scarab earrings only to find that one of them had cracked into four pieces . . ."

Brenda Mallon points out that the fertilised egg divides first into two, then four, and describes how Kate's dream continues with journeys and tunnels, suggesting the egg's movement through the Fallopian tubes. Like whiffs of steam escaping under the lid of a boiling saucepan, such examples give us a glimpse of a process cooking away in the dream world which is absorbing and registering body events.

What of women's attitudes and feelings about being pregnant? Dreams suggest that there can be many ambivalent feelings to be aired in the safety of the night. Here is an example from the journal of a woman three months pregnant:

"We go to a castle. There is a big vat of 'tadpoles', they look more like lizards with big heads with a mauve pattern. They bite me, first once, then a second time, on the wrist, it won't let go, I have to hit it to get it off, no one will help me. Later a man fights me. I go to punch him, I hit the wall by my bed with my hand and wake myself up."

This woman comments: "My thoughts were that the lizards were like sperm. I have been 'bitten' and they have taken hold—in my womb, where the baby is growing. Talking to my friend she said it can be hard to accept that a man gave me the baby. It means he went inside, had the power to fertilise and leave something growing in my body. I have been well and truly 'had'. Feeling helpless about the way my body has been taken over, I express my anger by hitting the wall. I am thrilled to be pregnant, but also feel some anger about the tiredness, morning sickness, etc., and about feeling suddenly immobilised."

The following dream from pregnancy again shows the theme of adjusting to a changed body image, and perhaps also to the effect of the hormones (the "powerful drug") on thinking and behaviour:

"Had a terrible and weird dream last night. We (the women?) were carried off and kept somewhere in a house . . . We can't get out. I am very aware of the effects of the drug they have given me which incapacitates me. I stand in front of the mirror in my mother's bedroom, my image is all blurred and wrong. I keep saying, 'If only I could concen-

trate hard enough, I could make it come right,' but the drug is too powerful . . . They are carting some of us off in a truck. 'They' seem to be 'the Mothers'. Their plan is very controlling but it gradually turns out that it might be benevolent at base.''

Sometimes the dreams of pregnancy reflect a new sense of connection with the female line of inheritance through our mothers, which is not always easy. The dream above carries a slightly sinister sense of ''the Mothers'' as well as a taking-stock in the dreamer's mother's bedroom.

Acknowledging issues that need to be worked through is not to deny the many dreams expressing a sheer physical delight in pregnancy, as in this woman's dream:

''One of these nights I dream about horses. Me being with the horse (riding in line?) feels like me being with the baby— the same closeness and sense of being completely in tune with another living creature, a strong animal physical bond, it is wonderful . . .''

Dreams can also reflect on the decision not to have a child.

Here is a poem from Stef Pixner's *Sawdust and White Spirit*:

> ''The right train''
>
> ''We walked by the canal
>   and the sun was eerie:
>   'What kind of a tree is that?'
>   'The warehouses are derelict'
>   'I can still change my mind.'
>
> ''It took no time at all
>
> ''The anaesthetist joked
>   when he couldn't find the vein

and when I woke
high as a kite
I fell in love with the Finnish nurse
whose moon face shone above me

"I felt like a baby myself

"learning the world
for the first time.
Even the strip lighting
and the paint cracking
across the ceiling

"You sat by the bed with plums
talking about your childhood
and we played 'I spy'

"After the abortion
I got my brain back
colours had interest again
I stopped eating tomatoes
and my breasts
relaxed
But sometimes
I dream
that I've missed the right train

"To go back one stop
I must first go to Tadzikistan
and though no one's information
can be trusted
I go on asking strangers
how to get back

"like I go on walking with you
by the seed-covered
weedy canal;
'What kind of a tree is that?'

'The warehouses are derelict'
'I can still change my mind.' ''

DREAM JOURNEYS

Many dreams about change, decision and transition use the symbol of travelling. Again, various interpretations have been put forward. Some claim that the ''journey within'' follows an archetypal pattern, following the steps of the ''hero'' who is called to adventure, receives supernatural aid, crosses certain thresholds, gets stuck, initiated, tempted, faces trials and finally returns. Such mythological blueprints might help some people, providing a structure for their experience. However, my own sense of the pleasure of myth lies very much in the richness and diversity of the elements and the story lines, so that different myths resonate with different people at different points in their lives. I am hesitant to reduce myths to standard patterns. I would prefer to start with an experience and then see whether there was a myth that fitted and illuminated it, rather than the other way round.

Some writers have also suggested that the individual symbols of journeys have a fixed meaning. Freud set the tone with his suggestion that departure represents dying. Jung includes ''earth, the woods, the sea or any still waters'' in his list of ''things arousing devotion or feelings of awe'' which can be symbols of the ''mother archetype.'' Water is often taken as a female symbol, representing the uterine ''Mother.'' Again, there are limitations to this kind of fixed symbolism. In the case of water, for example, it can be useful to recall that men also produce a whole series of different fluids and that all human beings, both male and female, are composed of approximately 60 percent water. The variety of different dream contexts in which water appears in this chapter alone would encourage us to keep an open mind.

Various suggestions have also been made about the symbolism of different forms of transport in travelling dreams, so that bicycling is said to indicate adolescence, a night sea journey the "death of the ego," a car represents sexual drives, and so on. While some of these may reflect associations that are common in our culture—and so may be relevant at times—it is worth starting without assumptions and exploring the dreamer's own associations first. The most helpful approach may be to ask questions such as: Who is in charge of the vehicle? Who is providing the power? Is the dreamer heading where she wants to go? Is she lost? Is she going too fast? Too slow? Is she burdened? Is there anything unusual about the vehicle? Is there any problem about it? How does the dreamer feel about that mode of travel? Does she have any specific associations, e.g. that her mother always rode a bicycle? And then to ask questions which relate that symbolism to the dreamer's life: In what ways is your life out of control? Do you know where you are going? What prevents you from taking charge of things? What burdens you? How do you feel about the friend whose car you borrowed in the dream?

Literal translations are not necessarily helpful, and as always a flexible approach can give surprising results. Sometimes when you listen carefully, the journey itself is not what calls most clearly for attention. Here is an example:

A woman had a long and complicated dream in which she was travelling in America, lost her sister, had no money, hitched a lift in a mini-bus, then found herself alone in a lorry with a boy who drove the vehicle into a cliff-top house and was almost out the other side when she shouted to him to stop. "The cab of the lorry was hanging out through a smashed window overhanging the drop. He said 'But I thought you wanted to die.' I said 'No, I don't want to die,

I don't want to die.' He lifted me out from the lorry and into the house for safety. The lorry was left hanging stuck.''

A long anecdotal dream like this could leave a friend or dream group puzzling. But one of them might just hone in on the repeated line ''I don't want to die,'' which is very striking. Is living or dying an issue in the dreamer's life? Was there a time recently when she was debating that issue? Through all the confusion, that one line stands out as a clear statement, and starting from there might lead to the heart of the dream's issues.

At other times, the way the dream is told might give a key: ''I find it hard to follow the plot but I am struck by your excitement as you tell it''; ''You seem bored and confused as you tell it—is boredom around a lot for you?''; ''I noticed you changed your body posture completely when you got to the bus stop in the dream.'' Recreating a dream body posture helped Mary make an important connection with her past in an example given earlier in this chapter.

Another useful approach can be to use a Gestalt technique where the dreamer speaks in sentences starting ''Life is . . .'' in order to describe the dream. She should stick to that format, and see whether any of the statements ring true about her present situation and experience. For example, the dreamer with the hitchhiking adventure opposite might find herself saying: ''Life is . . . an empty road with no direction''; ''Life is . . . being alone with no money''; ''Life is . . . losing my sister''; ''Life is . . . a crowded mini-bus driving me somewhere I don't know.'' This technique works for other dreams as well as ''journey'' ones. It can be useful for describing a dream's background (''Life is a fairground,''''Life is a desert''), drawing out interesting elements which might otherwise be overlooked, and reflecting the dreamer's feelings about her day-to-day existence.

MAKING DECISIONS

"When I think about the dream I have this very vivid image of a little car going up a cliff—a very precarious journey—and then going along the edge of the cliff. But it got to a safe place."

The woman who had this dream worked on it in her dream group and describes it as one of the deciding factors in going ahead with her pregnancy. Thinking about it over ten years later, she remembers clearly how the decision emerged:

"When I started work on it in the group I didn't realise it was about my pregnancy. We worked on it in a Gestalt way—me 'being' the car, the driver, the passenger, etc. I think I was driving. It became apparent that it was about my pregnancy. It was about whether it would be a safe journey to make or whether it was too hazardous or whether it would end up somewhere safe. It became clear that the dream was more or less saying 'Go ahead! This is a good direction to take.' I remember being quite surprised. It was very simple but very powerful and it was a big factor in the end in my deciding. I was heading in that direction anyway but somehow tapping into my unconscious, and working on it in the group of women that I trusted, made it seem very clear that it was the right thing to do.

"I had gone through all sorts of vaccillations about it. My heart was always quite clearly wanting to, but I was not completely sure. My son is now a teenager. The dream was right: it has been great to have him.

"Working on the dream with this group of women was also in a way like giving birth: we gave birth to this interpretation which helped me to give birth. It was like being in the hands of wise midwives."

We might all wish to have such assistance to midwife a major life decision. Unfortunately, dreams do not always speak so clearly and their help with decisions cannot be forced. It seems significant that this woman had no idea at first what her dream was about and was surprised by what she found. This is a sign that she was allowing something to come forward in its own time, and listening open-mindedly. Sometimes when we are faced with a decision, we become so preoccupied with the mechanics of making a choice, so locked into the "either/or" dilemma of the external options, that we are no longer open to the experience and understanding inside us which could inform that choice. When we become aware of the internal feelings, body sensations, hopes, fantasies and fears we are experiencing, a decision often "makes itself," from the inside out. So while dreams cannot be hijacked or interrogated to make decisions for us, the more aware we are of every aspect of our situation—including listening to dreams—the more likely we are to find the direction we need.

Some of these issues are illuminated in the following example. Psychotherapist Ann de Boursac worked with part of one of her own dreams in which:

she had lost her way outside a market town. None of the names on the signposts meant anything to her. She heard a flute playing, liked it and followed the sound, and so came to a fork in the road. There was an upper road on the left where a woman was standing playing the flute, and a lower road on the right with a woman who was probably a rider. She was attracted to the fluteplayer, who seemed to represent her healing work, and asked the way. The fluteplayer said she could go along her road, but the place she would get to was about twelve miles away. The dreamer decided that was too far and it might not be the right place when she got there, and so she decided to follow a hunch of her own.

Ann de Boursac worked on this dream three times. The first time was in a professional Gestalt group: she worked on the last part of the dream in which she asked for advice and then ignored it. She looked at that as a pattern in her life, and gained some useful insights. However, she felt there was more to find in the dream. She worked on it a second time a few days later in her leaderless dream group. Other group members suggested that she visualise taking the fluteplayer's path. At first this felt good to her, but then it fizzled out and she started to feel lost again. The group commented on this response. The third time she worked on the dream alone at home. She visualised coming back to the fork a third time. This time she went to meet the rider on the lower path and imagined a dialogue with her. The rider said, "You don't even know I'm here. You don't take any notice of me." The rider said that she had plenty of horses and they could all go together—the rider and the fluteplayer together—on the upper road and could get there with no problem. She became aware of the rider as a part of herself—a more physical, grounded part—which she did not always use to the full in following her life's path. Gradually she realised that the dream was about recognising the importance of the bottom half of her body, and the crucial role it could play in her healing work through its grounding, stamina and practical energy. The fluteplayer's path was the right path, but she needed her whole self on it to get where she was going.

This is a clear example of what can be gained by returning to a dream again and again. Ann de Boursac saw this one as a paradigm of her life, in its symbol of being at a fork and not deciding again and again. She quoted Fritz Perls' belief that if you really worked with one dream to the point where you had learnt all its lessons, you would be a completely cured and healthy person. This was one of those dreams; she said that she kept going back to the dream and it kept telling her things about herself.

Reading and Notes

Goffman, Erving, "Gender Advertisements," *Studies in the Anthropology of Visual Communication*, Vol 3, 2, Fall 1976, published by Society for the Anthropology of Visual Communication, Washington, D.C., pp. 128–30, 132–7, 140–44.

Jung, Carl G., *The Archetypes and the Collective Unconscious*, translator R. F. C. Hull, Princeton University Press, Princeton, NJ, 1967, p. 81 [Vol IX, Part 1 of *Collected Works*].

Mallon, Brenda, *Women Dreaming*, Fontana/Collins, London, 1987, pp. 56–7.

Nolan, Inger, "Working Creatively with Dreams," *Inside Out*, 12, Spring 1993, published by Inside Out, 23 Lower Albert Road, Glenageary, Co., Dublin, p. 13.

Perls, Fritz S., *Gestalt Therapy Verbatim*, Bantam Books, Toronto, New York, London, 1969, pp. 85–7 (Linda), 288–9 (brief example of "Life is . . .").

Pixner, Stef, *Sawdust and White Spirit*, Virago Press, London, 1985, pp. 62–3.

9
Making Friends with Myths, Monsters and "Spirits"

One of the gifts of dreams is that they bring us closer to a world of "magic," where we can converse with mythological creatures, feel a sense of awe, and see the dead walk. In touching this world, I will look for a path between superstition and cynicism, and approach with an open, demystifying attitude, to discover what such dreams may have to offer.

USING MYTHOLOGY

Dreams with mythological elements often shimmer as we wake, with an aura of extra significance. There can be a strong urge to find someone to state with confidence what those symbols mean. Jung is one of the writers who have responded with definitions which carry weight because they seem to have the backing of history and anthropology. Using waking visions or visualisations as well as dreams, he fits mythological symbols to his theory of the universal "archetypes," so that a figure or object in a dream may be identified with an archetype such as the "earth mother," "hero," "witch," "self," "animus," "anima" or "shadow." For example, in *Memories, Dreams and Reflections*, he describes a waking vision in which:

he follows a steep descent and, near the slope of a rock, sees a white-bearded old man with a beautiful young girl. They introduce themselves as Elijah and Salome.

Here Jung interprets these figures as the archetypes of the "wise old man" and the female "anima": "Salome is an anima figure. She is blind because she does not see the meaning of things. Elijah is the figure of the wise old prophet and represents the factor of intelligence and knowledge; Salome, the erotic element."

The gender typecasting here is disconcerting. The following dream of Jung's is even more problematic:

"I was with an unknown, brown-skinned man, a savage, in a lonely, rocky mountain landscape. It was before dawn. Then I heard Siegfried's horn sounding over the mountains and I knew that we had to kill him. We were armed with rifles and lay in wait for him ... Siegfried appeared high up on the crest of the mountain, in the first ray of the rising sun ... we shot at him, and he plunged down, struck dead." At the end of the dream there is a sense of remorse, but rain dissolves all traces of the dead.

Jung identifies the hero Siegfried with his own identity and his "heroic idealism" which—like Germany in World War II—wanted to achieve through imposing "will." He sees the black man as "an embodiment of the primitive shadow" and the rain as representing the dissolving of tension between consciousness (Siegfried) and the unconscious (the black man).

What leaps out from this dream and its interpretation is its racism: not only the use of the word "savage" associated with the "brown-skinned man," but also the linking of that figure with the "primitive shadow."

Many people have found Jung's approach to myth seductive, but before using it with our dreams I feel we need to be aware that there is a sleight of hand going on. Jung interprets the symbols of his own dreams and those of his patients, and then claims that such interpretations hold a universal truth. In these two examples he symbolises the primitive unconscious as a black man, idealism as a male European, blind eroticism as female, and wisdom as a bearded old man. Is such symbolism really archetypal for all time, or just stereotypical of attitudes to race and gender in Western society?

Jung's researches were wide-ranging, but he tended to look where he chose and find what he wanted to find to confirm his theories. He left us a legacy of writers—men and women—who follow in his footsteps, and tend to see the past as a fund of mythological moulds into which the present can be fitted. This can be inspiring, but we need to be aware that we are using the past rather than listening to it. I read, for example, that there are four different "female archetypes": the "Earth Mother," the "Hetaira," the "Amazon" and the "Medium" (in Annie Wilson's *The Wise Virgin*). These names have a historical—even a glamorous—ring to them. But in fact they are an apparently random selection of various roles and symbols assigned to women by the male-oriented culture of classical Greece, male fantasies which split women up as *either* "maternal" *or* "sexy" *or* "active in the world" *or* "sensitively mysterious." It is not clear how helpful such typecasting could be to women now—any more than it was then. When "archetypes" like these are portrayed as timeless and inevitable, there is little sense of women's possibility to visualise entirely new roles and symbols. At the same time, using such labels with your dream

symbols can divert you from looking as closely as you might
at the individual details of the dream and what it might be
saying about your life now: so that neither past nor present
is really listened to.

Some of the symbolic "archetypes" have been in circulation so long that it is hard to question them. The "Earth
Mother," for example, is according to Jung "always
chthonic" (i.e. of the underworld), associated with the moon,
"heavy with destiny" and linked to "the dark side of the
human psyche"; the symbol reappears in ecological circles
as "Gaia." However, evidence suggests that in the Aegean
Bronze Age both woman and womb were linked with the
sun, and in the early myth of Demeter and Persephone it is
actually a male figure, Hades, who represents the underworld. Tom Chetwynd's *A Dictionary of Symbols* tell us that
Icarus represents man's life "skimming between sun and
sea—that is, between male conscious Ego and feminine unconscious emotion." But if the sun was originally female in
Greek culture and was linked to the creative force of the
belly, the male Ego is sunk. It seems hard for people to
acknowledge that the process of perception is an active one,
and that we interpret what we see in the natural world in the
light of our own social experience.

Most of our inherited symbols are derived from male culture. One of the most famous dream symbols from writings
of the medieval period is the Holy Grail, the blood-filled
chalice which the Knights of the Round Table seek so ear-
nestly. Like most vessels, the Grail is taken as a female symbol and has been adopted with enthusiasm by many
twentieth-century women as a positive emblem of the feminine, of earth, nature, nourishment and intuition. In tune with
other "new age" writers, Annie Wilson describes it as "food
for the soul, a bowl of inspiration and symbolically the object
of all man's aspirations . . . A cup or vessel is a symbol of
the feminine." This quote could not be more explicit about
the way women are seen as food and inspiration for men,

and as the object of male aspirations, rather than being fed ourselves to fulfil our own aspirations. This is not surprising since the legend was written up by a man (Sir Thomas Malory) and is mainly concerned with the warlike doings of a group of men and their preoccupation with this mysterious and elusive female receptacle of desire. The Grail was a male fantasy about women. Far from being timeless, the myth and its symbols are the product of their time, class and gender.

My own research (published in *Death, Women and the Sun* and—more accessibly—in *Moving Heaven and Earth*) suggests that the Greek myths too were a moveable feast. Their symbolism changed drastically over the centuries they were in formation, and also varied from place to place with many different versions. They seem to reflect the social shifts and tensions in Greek society during that time—especially as regards the position of women. In his article "Law, Custom and Myth," the classicist John Gould acknowledged that in Greek myth "male attitudes to women . . . are marked by tension, anxiety and fear." Are these shifting and unfriendly sands a good basis on which to construct "archetypes" of the possibilities open to women now? If myths are stories told in a particular time and place for particular reasons, are they useful as general rules? They can give us ideas, but they should not override a dreamer's own sense of what a particular dream symbol stands for.

Here is an example of the use of a myth in just such an empowered way. Beata Bishop in *Caduceus* described two dreams which she related to a serious illness of hers. One dream featured an orchard added on to her garden: in it the neglected trees were covered with moss, which turned into *"large colourful creatures, insects or crabs—parasites which suck the life-blood of the tree."* She recorded but ignored the dream (and commented in retrospect that such a dream would now prompt a thorough health check). A few months later came another dream in which she was standing in bright sunshine on the deck of an ancient Greek ship with the Homeric hero Odysseus and his companions: *"all of them tall, bearded, godlike heroes. Odysseus made us stand between two concentric wooden circles, supported on waist-high legs. We were to face inward, he instructed us, and hold on to the inner circle when the storm came. That way we would come to no harm."* Two years later Beata Bishop became ill with cancer, and at the same time her best apple tree developed a canker on its trunk which eventually killed it: "But I managed to 'hold on to the inner circle' and recovered." Here the wily survivor Odysseus was experienced as an appropriate symbol to give guidance through the coming "storm" of her illness; the mythological scene is understood in terms of the needs and issues of a current situation rather than the other way round.

WITCHES AND DEMONS IN DREAMS

In Western culture people often dream about witches and demons. This is perhaps not surprising considering how thoroughly we have all imbibed Christian imagery even if we are not Christians. The question is how we understand such symbols. Some people take them on board in a religious sense—for example as manifestations of external forces of "evil." Others have offered personal, psychological and social explanations which account for them in a rather different way.

One scheme for understanding such dream symbolism in psychological terms is put forward by Alexander Lowen, who developed the ideas of Wilhelm Reich and is perhaps best known for his work on bio-energetics. In *The Betrayal of the Body* he suggests that the symbol of the demon is made up of the individual's repressed sexuality and repressed rage. The devil, he suggests, is symbolically located in the bowels of the earth and the bowels of the individual: the flames of hell are associated with the flames of sexual passion. The ghoul represents the infant living off others: made to feel that its demands are too great, it starts to feel monstrous. A dream on this topic may be a throwback to the early years of the individual's life and to feelings from that time. The monster, he suggests, has a heart of gold: all its negative aspects are on the outside, while inside is an innocent child. The demon is the reverse with sweetness and light on the outside. The "witch" symbol, he believes, crops up when a female has absorbed a male identity and punishes her "female" body.

Another approach is to see these symbols in a social context: understanding witches, for example, as women who were misjudged by patriarchy, and trying to set the record straight both in the history books and in our dream symbolism. Interpretations like Lowen's are turned around when a woman actively befriends the "witch" in herself and her female body. It is a challenging step, to rehabilitate a symbol as discredited as the "witch"—charred by a terrible history of persecution and worse in countless folk tales. However, since the resurgence of the women's movement in the sixties and seventies this is exactly what many women have set out to do, embracing a tradition in which women were seen as non-conformist, sexual, spiritual and powerful. This can be an illuminating approach to dream witches, although there is no continuous tradition of witchcraft from medieval times, and the modern version ("Wicca") is essentially a re-creation. It can feed the imagination but need not limit it. Thus Anne Wade does not use the framework of received religious tradition but takes a free, inventive approach in her work on a dream about a troupe of Quaker witches:

"I dreamt I was sitting in a pavement cafe with a group of ordinary Quaker women with whom I felt very safe and at ease. Suddenly the street was full of Quaker witches, all in black, grim and fierce, marching past, rank after rank. I felt

*distraught and very frightened, but everyone else accepted it
as normal.*

"There followed a series of dreams and waking visualisations about the Quaker witches. It was up to me to make
friends with them and find out what they were offering me.

"I was working at the time on being more open, less defensive, and worrying how to cope with the resultant vulnerability if someone tried to exploit this. There was a series
of episodes in waking reality in which I would find myself
thinking about the witches and imagining them rallying
round me and defending me, helping me with this difficulty.
They were totally, utterly, on my side. This was a shattering,
wonderful experience which disrupted some of my basic assumptions about life. They were grimly caring, still wild and
fierce but completely accepting of all that I was, determined
to protect and defend me and never again to allow anyone
to hurt me as I had been hurt as a child. They were so angry
at the way that child had been abused—they gave me great
strength and confidence in myself. Gradually they learnt
about love and trust.

"In Quaker meeting one day I found they were no longer
around me. I had absorbed most of them back into myself,
leaving a circle of flying buttresses supporting me. The meditating and dreams continued for a few weeks as I assimilated
these ideas and learned to use them."

She stresses the importance of not letting such symbols become fixed, and of not getting drawn into the world of metaphor away from daily living, but rather "being able to use
the insights in ordinary life, and keeping the images flowing
and fluid, letting go of them when I've used them, not holding on to them. They are not the reality—they are only one
way of expressing one aspect of it."

MONSTERS AND NIGHTMARES

Nightmares have not been the same since the spread of ideas
about Gestalt methods and Senoi practices. The Gestalt belief

that "everything in the dream is you" includes nightmare monsters. By acting out such elements, the theory suggests, you can re-own your own denied power which has turned against you. The nightmare then loses its fear. Another way of "disarming" nightmare figures is to move towards them, using techniques which have been attributed to the Senoi tribe. This exercise of choice and control in a dream usually breaks the hold of fear, and horrors run away or are defused. It is surely empowering to reclaim our own energies that are threatening from within, and beneficial to shed unnecessary fears; but sometimes there may be a danger of making our dreams bland, developing an illusory "omnipotence" which colonises even our nighttime experience, and denying real and appropriate fears. As Jenner Roth points out, even "un-pleasant" dreams can be serving a useful function: "I be-lieve all dreams if followed through with commitment can give us information to help us be clear and more congruent in our life. Nightmares and unpleasant dreams are a way of trying to exorcise stresses and pains and difficulties."

Let's look at some examples of what this dilemma about nightmares means in practice. How, for example, should the following dream about a ghost be taken?

"In my dream I come to a low-set basement window, like the flat of a therapist whose groups I have started attending. I look in and see very strange things—a giant eye, debris. Then I am inside and a ghost appears . . . in a little chair, a bit like R.'s pushchair . . . It is small and grey and female with big sockets for eyes. I am terrified. I keep shouting at it to go away. It doesn't. I keep saying, 'You don't exist! You don't exist!' In the end I have to stamp on it, trample all over it with my feet, and at last it vanishes. There is someone there watching, with me, standing there all through this."

In this case the dreamer clearly identifies the "ghost" as a part of herself: "Although this dream was really frightening and spooky—like a real ghost—when I worked on it I did see that the ghost was something to do with me. The clue is in the setting—the flat where I had started to do some therapy and was looking at my 'skeletons in the cupboard' for the first time. The ghost is both old and young . . . I see it as my hurt infant female side which 'haunts' me despite my frantic efforts to deny it. The pushchair points to childhood. I suppose it is encouraging that there is someone there watching with me—perhaps a part of me who can watch this desperate tussle without getting involved . . ."

With ghost and ghoul dreams, it is sometimes hard to hold on to this distinction between what is "in here" and what is "out there." Sometimes they may also involve other people. Here's an example:

"I dreamt that Dracula came into my bedroom at night. But I knew it was a dream and he could not hurt me."

This woman comments: "I realised later that 'Dracula' was an ex-boyfriend who had been hanging around me in an unhealthy way. He had been coming into my bed for the wrong reasons—all taking and no giving. It was not good even for him. I realised the relationship had become abusive. But also that I wasn't in love with him any more, so he couldn't hurt me now."

Rather than representing anything "supernatural," Dracula is here a very apt symbol for a draining relationship. Some apparitions, however, are disconcertingly articulate and independent-spirited. In *International Medicine*, Morton Schatzman cites the case history of Ruth, a young married woman with three children who came to his psychotherapy consulting room with the unusual problem that she was being persecuted by an apparition of her father, sometimes threatening violence. The father was actually still alive and had treated her violently when she was a child. A few weeks after the psychotherapy sessions started, she dreamt of her father shouting and menacing her. Frightened, she called out in her dream to Dr. Schatzman, who appeared. Her account of the dream, written soon after waking, starts as follows:

" 'What are you doing here?' my father says to Dr. Schatzman.

" 'I was invited,' Dr. Schatzman says, 'which is more than I can say for you.'

" 'Your psychiatrist is as crazy as you are,' my father says to me, 'because he's seeing me and talking to me now.' "

The apparition challenges the dream Schatzman to get rid of him, but Schatzman replies that they're not through with him yet. He tells the apparition that it is only there because Ruth allows it, that it can't harm anyone and is only a creation of Ruth's unconscious mind, an outlet for feelings she is not aware of. Ruth's account continues:

" 'No, that's not true,' I say to Dr. Schatzman. 'I don't think or feel the terrible things which he says I do. Those feelings couldn't be mine.'

" 'Are you sure?' Dr. Schatzman replies. 'Maybe the feelings he shows are feelings of yours that you don't think are allowed.' "

Of this dream account the real-life Schatzman comments that it seems almost too good to be true. The young woman regarded it as a turning point for her, and was very pleased that she had found the resources to deal with this major problem. Although she had used a "Schatzman" character to help her, she recognised that it was she herself who had resolved as well as created the whole drama. This is another example of using an ally from waking life to rout night enemies. There are people who would suggest that dramas like these reflect an actual exchange of energies between sleeping bodies, but this is not the interpretation favoured by either the young woman or Morton Schatzman in this example.

In other cases the explanations "It's a part of myself" or "It's a creation of my imagination" are not adequate. In *Lost in Translation* Eva Hoffman describes a recurrent dream which she experienced growing up as a Jew in Poland after World War II. She saw "*a tiny old woman—a wizened Baba Yaga, half grandmother, half witch, wearing a black kerchief and sitting shriveled and hunched on a tiny bench.*" The little old woman was way down in the courtyard of the flats where Eva Hoffman lived, a long, long way down, and looked up at her with "wise, malicious eyes. Perhaps, though, I am her. Perhaps I have been on the earth a long, long time and that's why I understand the look in her eyes. Perhaps this childish disguise is just a dream. Perhaps I am being dreamt by a Baba Yaga who has been here since the beginning of time and I am seeing from inside her ancient frame . . ." The image used is the folktale figure Baba Yaga, but the child Eva's preoccupations were about family members lost in the Holocaust, in particular her mother's sister. She described feeling as if her mother herself were "breakable," "as if she had been snatched from death only provisionally, and might be claimed by it at any moment. The ocean of death is so enormous, and life such a tenuous continent." There would be little point advancing with a "dream ally" to vanquish this Baba Yaga, because she represents a terrible piece of history which happened and cannot be banished; and death itself cannot be vanquished.

The "human potential" movement in psychotherapy sometimes seems to encourage individuals to feel that with the right "positive" attitude they can do anything. It also sometimes seems to suggest that all night experiences can be assimilated into human terms, as irrational fears or projections. But there are accounts of experiences which are not easily reducible to those terms. It is an idiosyncratic feature of Western society that people who give accounts of interactions with a spirit world are generally assumed to be suffering from an over-fertile imagination, eccentricity or mental disturbance.

TALKING TO SPIRITS?

In our culture the idea of contact with the dead is regarded as fantastic. But—marginalised from the mainstream—such experiences persist in creeping in round the edges. Without official recognition, they sometimes find a vocabulary within the realm of literature. A poem by the Portuguese poet Sophia de Mello Breyner Andresen describes the visits of "The Dead Men":

> Quietly at our side the dead
> Drink the exaltation of our life.
> Only the shadow following the wake of our gestures
> feels them pass
> when lightly
> they come in the night
> to seek our remains.
>
> They pass through rooms where we abandon
>   ourselves,
> Wrap themselves in the movements we trace
> Repeat the words we have said,
> And bending over our sleep
> they drink our dreams
> like milk.
>
> Intangible, without weight or contour
> They warm themselves with the heat of our blood.
> Smile at the images we live
> And weep for us out of sight,
> For they already know to where we are going.
> *(The Penguin Book of Women Poets)*

Are such thoughts fantastical? When we dream about the
dead, are we imagining them? Are dreams about our dear
departed simply a way of working out unresolved internal
conflicts about our relationship with them? Nan Zimmerman
writes in *The Variety of Dream Experience* of the resentment
she felt about her father's high expectations and the pressure
they inflicted. In her childhood she was sure that expressing
her anger would destroy him or banish her. On his death she
felt intense sorrow, guilt and anger. Several years later she
had a dream in which

she was furious with her father. He was behaving in a dis-
tancing, patronising way, and she lost control, screaming at
him all her pent-up grievances. When she stopped, petrified
in anticipation of her father's response, "My father looked
at me and smiled. It was a smile of complete acceptance.
There was no defensiveness, no condemnation, no hurt. An
avalanche of grief rushed over me. And I awoke."

On waking, Nan Zimmerman felt certain that her father could
accept her in a way he could not have done when alive, and
comments that this short dream "transformed his death into
a simple grief and a great appreciation of his love for me."
She comments that the issue is not whether the dead person
is actually communicating, or whether the dream image is a
projection. What is important is that such a lifelike encounter
can help the dreamer to make a real change.

   In some cases, however, the interaction with the dead is
such that the presence seems to have an autonomous existence and sometimes information to impart. One woman
wrote to me with an account of how her grandmother had
foreseen her own death in a dream. Shortly before her
death, the grandmother told a neighbour about a dream
where

"she had seen her husband (who had been dead for 20 years) and he had told her not to worry, because soon they would be together again.

"A few days later she dropped her key in the road on the way back from church, bent down to pick it up and was knocked down and killed by a passing car. The neighbour later told the dream to my mother, and she often repeated the story to me."

In many other societies, this kind of visitation is acknowledged and has its place within a coherent world view. To give just one example, Kilton Stewart in his unfortunately titled *Pygmies and Dream Giants* describes a community in the Philippines where "whenever someone died, his children dreamed of him repeatedly until the funeral feast." Stewart found that in cultures where such a visit from a dead parent was not expected, as in the USA, people either did not report such dreams or found them terrifying or depressing. Here, however, the dream of the parent was expected and accepted as part of the normal course of events; as long as the children were prepared to do what the deceased parent requested, such a dream would arouse no sense of guilt. Stewart is tempted to turn this practice into a psychotherapeutic principle: "Perhaps I had discovered a law: to help people to make a healthy adjustment to the shock of death, teach them to expect dream visitations from their dead loved ones." However, it is clear that for the people he is describing, such visitations are regarded not as a healing fiction but as an objective fact.

Within the same culture shamans and people undergoing treatment by shamans regularly had dreams featuring a spirit guide and other powerful dream characters who communicated with, and helped, the dreamer. The spirit sometimes talked through the patient or was seen by the patient in trance states, as well as appearing in dreams. Stewart gives a detailed example of one man, Pana, who had a dream of a man who looked like his father but had the head of a horse with a mane hanging over his face. This dream character or "dwindi" had picked Pana up in dreams and carried him through the air, showing him where game could be found. Later it had visited while Pana was awake and:

"he had gone off with it alone into the jungle on some very successful hunts. His wife had seen the dwindi one night when it called for him. To break the spell, she had rubbed her naked buttocks all over her husband's body. After that the dwindi had come no more. Pana had beaten his wife for using this magic to scare it away, but his spirit friend never returned."

Such accounts abound from traditional cultures. Are such peoples ignorant and credulous, or is Western culture perhaps dismissing a whole area of human experience because it does not have the means to understand it? Can all night experiences be assimilated into human terms, as irrational fears or projections? After the death of her daughter, during a period of intense grief, novelist Rosamond Lehmann had a series of experiences of which she has left unusually graphic accounts. In *The Swan in the Evening* she describes how one night she became aware of her father, who had died many years previously, standing beside her bed as if anxious to communicate with her:

"He looked as I remembered him in his middle years; and the heart-wrung concern for me I sensed in him caused me to try, wordlessly, to reassure him; also to thank him for this desperate effort to come back on my account. I knew what it was costing him . . ."

Rosamond Lehmann describes how she felt a pang "like homesickness" when he was not there any more, but also relief for her father's sake. She makes it clear that her father had not "materialised" as such, and that it was an inner event:

"Needless to say, at that time I had never heard of the subtle or the etheric or the resurrection body; or of astral projection; or of the scientific likelihood that countless forms, worlds within worlds of them, are invisible simply because they are travelling on different energy levels, or at different vibratory rates; and because our physical eyes are designed as instruments of limitation."

How have other women experienced those different energy levels, those "worlds within worlds"? Is there—apart from superstition and mysticism—any vocabulary or model of understanding which can provide a coherent framework for such experiences? This is the work of the next chapter.

Reading and Notes

Andresen, Sophia de Mello Breyner, "The Dead Men," translator Allan Francovich, *The Penguin Book of Women Poets*, Viking Penguin, New York, 1984, p. 242.

Bishop, Beata, "The Bridge of Dreams," *Caduceus*, Spring 1992, published by Caduceus, 38 Russell Terrace, Leamington Spa, Warwickshire CV31 1HE, p. 9.

Chetwynd, Tom, *A Dictionary of Symbols*, Thorsons SF, San Francisco, 1994.

Goodison, Lucy, *Death, Women and the Sun: Symbolism of Regeneration in Early Aegean Religion*, Institute of Classical Studies, London, 1989.

Goodison, Lucy, *Moving Heaven and Earth: Sexuality, Spirituality and Social Change*, Thorsons SF, San Francisco, 1992.

Gould, John, "Law, Custom and Myth: Aspects of the Social Position of Women in Classical Athens," *Journal of Hellenic Studies*, 100, 1980, pp. 57–8.

Hoffman, Eva, *Lost in Translation: A Life in a New Language*, Viking Penguin, New York, 1990.

Jung, Carl G., *Memories, Dreams, Reflections*, Random House, New York, 1989.

Lehmann, Rosamond, *The Swan in the Evening*, Virago Press, London, 1982, pp. 110–111.

Lowen, Alexander, *The Betrayal of the Body*, Macmillan, New York, 1969, pp. 10–16, 128–44.

Schatzman, Morton, "Dreams and Problem Solving," *International Medicine*, Vol 4, 4, 1984, pp. 7–8.

Senoi: see, most accessibly, Patricia Garfield, *Creative Dreaming*, Futura, London, 1974, pp. 80–117. To get closer to the source, see Kilton Stewart, "Dream Theory in Malaya," C. Tart (ed.), *Altered States of Consciousness*, John Wiley, Chichester, 1969. The Senoi were apparently first found by Herbert Noone in the 1930s, but his notes are lost, and doubts have been cast on the authenticity of surviving reports; see Ann Faraday and John Wren Lewis in *Dream Network Bulletin*, Vol 3–4, March-April 1984, published by Dream Network Bulletin, 487 4th Street, Brooklyn, New York 11215.

Stewart, Kilton, *Pygmies and Dream Giants*, Victor Gollancz, London, 1955, pp. 44–5, 54, 91.

Wilson, Annie, *The Wise Virgin*, Turnstone, London, 1979, pp. 183, 186.

Zimmerman, Nan, "After the Dream Is Over," Montague Ullman and Claire Limmer (eds.), *The Variety of Dream Experience*, Continuum, New York, 1989.

10
Exploring the Unknown

Some dreams open a door onto experiences which defy our sense of what is rationally possible, and yet intersect with waking life in a way that makes it hard to dismiss them as "just dreams." Many people have had dreams which they describe as "weird" or "supernatural." What do such experiences mean? Are they simply sensational or can they be helpful and healing? The examples that women record range from the curious to the frightening:

"My husband and I woke up and told each other we had both just been dreaming about his best friend in America. We thought this was quite weird but when we went downstairs we found on the doormat the second letter my husband had ever received from him in his life."

"From very early childhood I had repetitive spinning dreams. I would be doing something . . . and all of a sudden I would begin spinning uncontrollably. I always hated those dreams, the wild force of them was so frightening, and I felt so helpless. I spent the whole time trying to keep a finger or toe in contact with the ground, to keep from flying away and losing myself utterly . . . Finally, I asked my parents what to

*do about it. Being good holistic Californians, they advised
me to let go and see where it took me. Maybe, they said, I
could travel to interesting places. So the next time . . . (I
slipped down onto a frozen lake, where I began to spin with
the momentum) I let go. And I woke up immediately, and
never had another one again."*

"I remember having a dream as a child (about age six or
seven) that *Frankenstein was chasing me. Finally I realised
that this did not have to continue, so I shouted 'Help!' and
found a spray bottle in my hand, which I proceeded to spray
him with until he was all evaporated.*"

*"I dream I am soaring through the air—cold wind rushing
past. Then I think 'I'm flying—where shall I fly?' I come
down by a house on a little knoll with an altar and a picture
of the devil on it. I grab the picture and tear it in half then
shoot up into the air using all my power to get away safely.
Then I wake up in bed and turn the light on. I'm still dreaming. I seem to be in my childhood bedroom. I have the torn
picture in my hands. Then I really wake up, very shaken,
without the picture. I can't get back to sleep and I have a
stiff neck which lasts for a month after this. Scary."*

"There has been one very startling dream which was definitely premonitory, one which I dreamed the day before my
brother M. died. He had been ill with cancer, but had recently
had an apparent recovery. We had expected his death months
before; we were not expecting it when it occurred. But a
dream warned me. This is exactly what I wrote down immediately upon waking:

" '1:30 A.M. December 5.

" '*Long dream in which I seemed to be M., fulfilling ritual
obligations. Everything is hazy now except the feeling of
vomiting endless amounts of bile, waking exhausted and*

*empty, unable to get back to sleep. When I closed my eyes,
vivid pictures of blood splattered everywhere. I was shaking.'*
  "My brother died the next day."

What is happening in these accounts? Can we really communicate with other people and see the future? What is going
on when we dream we are flying, or "wake up" in a dream?
While some people dismiss such experiences, others seem to
relish and cultivate a sense of "mystery" about them. Instead
I will try to approach them like any other experience, to be
noticed and made sense of as far as possible—no more and
no less mysterious than any other aspect of life.

TELEPATHY

"Recently I met someone for the first time (in real life) who
had dreamt about me a week before meeting me . . ."

Such experiences are reported between two individuals and
between members of a group. Gaie Houston was struck by
discovering the overlap between dreams when they are told
within a closed community:

  I have lived in a group for some weeks, in which a
  Californian Indian instituted daily dream meetings. The
  overlap of focus in our dreams was exciting, even if
  unsurprising. What was more uncanny was the likeness
  of imagery in these nocturnal poems. And a conse-
  quence of the sharing was, for me, a shift in consciousness, as I let myself be aware that the unconscious mind
  of many other, apparently disparate, people was probably composing my dreams as well as their own." *(Self
  and Society)*

Such experiences have prompted some writers to suggest that sleep, which we think of as something private, is in fact a very social dimension of our existence. Henry Wilberg hints at "a truly socialist level of the psyche in which personal identity is neither merely 'private property' nor some impersonal 'archetype'."

If such sleep communication happens, I feel the important questions are: How does it work? And what is the purpose? There is a limited interest in pursuing the "paranormal" for its own sake. Spiritual traditions suggest that—like any form of communication—it can be used to co-operate, influence, interfere with, or help each other.

In the "Seth" books, Jane Roberts suggests that we make plans with other people in our sleep, that large mass events are actually planned together by all involved, and the conscious experience of those events is a trying out of ideas planned. Nigel Hamilton, a psychotherapist who is also a representative of the Sufi Order of the West, coins the term "co-dreaming" to describe the way that "your psyche and the psyche of the other person are sharing the same dream realm, . . . During our relationships with other people (marriage partners, children, neighbours, client-therapist relationships, etc.) we often find ourselves tapping into other people's dream worlds or psyches, without realizing it." He points out the problems this creates in dream interpretation since part of your dream may belong to someone else. He suggests that without being aware of it we can become influenced or even obsessed by other people, alive or dead; dreamers may need help to use their active imaginations to release themselves from this influence (for example, by visualising the other psyche separating and moving on to its natural destination). With commitment and awareness, however, he believes "it is possible to learn to become conscious while you are dreaming and therefore communicate with and even help the psyche of the other person, as well as your own."

Is this what is happening here?

"I dreamt I was ill in bed and my friend E.—who I have not seen for ages—came to visit me. I was very happy and strengthened to see her, and got a very good feeling from her. In the morning I felt as if I had actually seen her and it had done me a power of good."

Denise Linn in *Pocketful of Dreams* calls this "night healing." She suggests that many ordinary people may be involved in such activity without being consciously aware of it. She devotes a chapter to the issue and stresses that for those who undertake it actively—meditating before sleep to focus on the person they wish to help—it is important to follow the same guidelines concerning respect, compassion and non-interference that apply to any other healing work.

Jenner Roth also stresses the social nature of dreaming and believes that "When we have an especially vivid dream about someone we know, it is important to share that with them—we sometimes get information for others in our own dreams."

She distinguishes those dreams which seem realistic and are simply reminding us of things we have absorbed but not consciously registered during the day, such as a forgotten appointment, from the prescient dream which "usually has realistic people, locations and events but in a way that we can't make 'sense' of. It is often amusing or bizarre and has a quality of 'known-ness' to us. These dreams do not usually demand interpretation but leave us feeling bemused until the event dreamt about actually occurs. Typical prescient dreams are of receiving a letter or a telephone call from someone . . ."

Again, it seems important to scrutinise our experience carefully. Can we be confident about distinguishing a genuine premonition from a dream which mirrors our own personal hopes and fears about the future?

PROPHETIC DREAMS

"I had split up from my lover and desperately wanted to get back together.

"*I dreamt about a plate we had in our kitchen, which we had bought together. In the dream it was broken and could not be mended. As I woke up, I had a phrase in my mind: 'Too late, too late, says the broken plate.'*

"I took the dream as 'higher knowledge' that the relationship was irreparably broken. But a few months later we got back together and have been together ever since. The dream was wrong."

Was the dream wrong? Or was it presenting a possibility which this woman needed to face? Or did she misinterpret it? Perhaps there is again a danger here of fetishising dreams. From seeing all dreams as vain imaginings to seeing all dreams as wise visions is not such a big jump. Both attitudes set dreams apart. Perhaps we could imagine the sleeping mind more like the waking mind: it sometimes picks up messages from others, but it sometimes mis-hears; it sometimes has a dazzling intuition about what is likely to happen, and it sometimes misjudges. How do we know which is which? Perhaps, as during the day, it depends on how genuinely receptive the psyche is, and whether incoming information is touching on blind spots in us.

An example of this process is given in *Inside Out*. Therapist Hank O'Mahony writes about "Nora," a widow who had recently re-married. In her dream she walks into a kitchen and sees two people arguing:

"He's saying she doesn't love him, that she's too busy and is never available when he wants her. She looks at him, she seems very angry. She begins to speak but stops, turns around and walks away. 'I now recognize the couple—they

*are very close friends of mine. Then I wake up feeling scared
and breathing very badly.' ''*

Nora feared the dream might be predicting an imminent crisis
for her friends. The therapist asks Nora to breathe more fully
and suggests that she acts the roles of the two people in the
dream. Doing so, she rapidly realises that the threatening
conflict concerns not her friends' but her own marriage. It
touches on an urgent and unresolved issue about her own
independence and autonomy in relation to her husband. Hank
O'Mahony points out that in her dream Nora had projected
her worst fears about her new marriage and its future onto
her friends. After re-owning the projection, she could see
both their and her own situation more clearly. When we are
busy blanking out our own problems, we are not likely to
see other people's problems clearly, like static blocking incoming programmes on a radio receiver.

The other difficulty is that we have no vocabulary in Western culture for working with prescient dreams or for sifting
their messages. What seems to deter us is the barrier we place
between them and our daytime perceptions: the latter are
"real," while the dream perceptions are generally seen as
"unreal." Some other cultures seem to have a more flexible
attitude. Chilean-born novelist Isabel Allende described on
BBC Radio how her daughter had been seriously ill for a
year in a coma. During that time she felt that they could
communicate in dreams: "I could feel her in dreams. I could
talk to her in dreams. She would appear to me healthy or
sick, but I had a relationship with her when I was asleep."

When her daughter's death was imminent: "I knew a
month before because I couldn't dream, the dreams stopped.
She started to drift away. And because I couldn't feel her
spirit, I knew she was dying."

The difference for Isabel Allende was that she had not
been conditioned like most of us to dismiss such experiences:
"There was nothing spooky about it. I grew up with the idea

that there is another dimension of reality, a dimension of emotions and dreams and premonitions and the past, that was always . . . haunting you.''

What is this other dimension? Perhaps, rather than seeing it as something mystical, we can see it as something physical: as the exercise of physical faculties which in Western culture are denied; as the use of a part of our body which our society ignores, but which other cultures call the ''energy body.''

THE ENERGY BODY

In her autobiographical *The Swan in the Evening*, Rosamond Lehmann describes an experience she had while grieving the death of her daughter Sally. Resting during the afternoon, she suddenly heard a high-pitched vibration like a harp-string. Then: ''. . . a sort of convulsion or alarum struck me in the heart centre, followed by a violent tugging sensation in this region. As if attached to an invisible kite string that was pulling me out, out, upwards, upwards, I began to be forcibly ejected from the centre of my body.''

She felt tears down her face, and her eardrums being ''shaken,'' her sense of sound becoming very acute, and then: ''I was drifting and floating now . . . but where, and for how long? There is no way of telling. Perhaps for only a few seconds of earth time.''

Notice how important the senses are throughout this passage. This kind of event has often been described as an ''out-of-body'' experience, but there is definitely a body to which it is happening. Various spiritual disciplines propose the existence of another body, an ''energy body,'' an extension of the visible body which exists in and around it, is closely involved in all its activities, and can sometimes separate from it.

The Kahunas of Hawaii, for example, have passed on a

coherent theory about how such events happen. They were practitioners of a discipline which has been documented by Max Freedom Long in *The Secret Science Behind Miracles* and several other books, based on his reasearches in Hawaii earlier this century. At that time, after a hundred years of incursions by Christianity, the traditional knowledge was in danger of dying out. The powers of the Kahunas, which allegedly included fire-walking, prophecy and healing, were based on an understanding of the human being as having three spirits. Using a standard terminology of gradation between low and high, Long translates these three spirits as the "low self" or sub-conscious ("unihipili," which remembers and is the source of all emotions); the "middle self" or conscious ("uhane," the seat of reason); and the "high self" or superconscious ("aumakua," which has higher knowledge and a broader vision of past, present and future). This is not very different from some of the psychological theories we are familiar with in the West, such as the model of "id," "ego" and "superego." The difference is that in the Kahunas' system these are not theoretical but physical entities. Each resides in a "shadowy body" ("kino aka") existing around the visible physical body, and linked to it. Each uses waves of vital force of varying intensity ("mana," "mana mana" and "mana-loa," respectively) in its activities.

This view of the human being can accommodate experiences such as telepathy and "out-of-body" experiences. The shadowy body of the "low self" or sub-conscious uses mana (described by Long as a "low voltage electrical force") which can extend in a thread connecting to someone or something at a distance; along this thread thought forms can travel in telepathy. The process is described as follows: the "low self" or sub-conscious slips the control of the "middle self" (often in sleep) to project a "finger" of invisible shadowy substance and thus extends its sensory perceptions. In this way it makes observations of distant things or scenes, or contacts absent people from whom a telepathic or mind-reading impression is to be gained. It then brings back thought forms of the impressions, which may appear in dreams. Such thought forms usually travel following an older thread which already connects it to the distant people or things. This description is consistent with accounts given by some Western psychics of sending out a "white beam" to make telepathic contact.

As for the experiences of "flying" and "travelling," the Kahunas' framework again provides a vocabulary for understanding these activities without any mystery. The often-recorded sensation of moving "out of the body" tends at first to inspire Westerners with alarm. Denise Linn describes her first experience, which started when she woke at 3 A.M. aware of a strange rocking, floating sensation:

"The ceiling which is normally six to seven feet above my bed was now only inches from my body. I was weightless . . . What was happening? I couldn't quite understand why I was hovering so near the ceiling. Was it a dream? No, I was fully conscious . . . I rolled over gently, noticing my bed was below . . . with me in it! The terror of observing my own body was so frightening that I immediately zoomed back into my body with a harsh jolt. The shock was so profound that it took a long time before I ventured out again."

In *Pocketful of Dreams* she describes how she gradually became more confident. At first she stayed close to home, travelling through the rooms of her house, and noticing that she often found herself in a different time frame—daylight instead of evening—as if she were in an arena outside the normal space/time continuum. Gradually she ventured into flying, low at first, then higher and farther.

The Kahunas' system understands this experience as happening at times when the two lower spirits (sub-conscious and "middle self") travel away from the physical body in their shadowy bodies, sometimes to a great distance, while a connecting thread of shadow material maintains the link between the shadow bodies and the physical body.

The "high self" is also connected at all times to the physical body by a thread of the "aka" or "shadowy body stuff." Although messages about the future are received *via* the sub-conscious or "low self," they are believed to come from the "high self" which can see certain elements of the future. The "high self" could be called on for knowledge and guidance, and also for assistance. In this way the Kahunas were believed to be able to help an individual mould his life ahead. Long points out that in the same way help could be enlisted to work for a better future for society as a whole.

"ASTRAL" BEINGS

While such disciplines as the Kahunas' locate "psychic" experiences within a coherent theory, and may bring hundreds of years of tradition and practice to back it up, this whole field remains alien to the mainstream of Western culture. Our world view faces even greater problems accommodating the thought that some of these sleep communications seem to be not with the living at all, but with the dead—or worse. Much of the difficulty lies with our division between the "rational," i.e. the small island of experience which we think we can explain, and the "irrational," which is used to describe everything foreign to that. The "irrational" is a whole world of experiences with its own geography, topography and ethnology, which we can learn about. I shall try to chart such experiences with an open mind.

While "out of her body," as described earlier, Rosamond Lehmann met the daughter whose death she was grieving, and experienced an intense communion with her. Her account is articulate:

"Now I was with Sally. She was behind my left shoulder, leaning on it . . ." After a brief conversation about Sally's husband, *"Sally and I remained together, wordlessly communicating. More than anything, it was like laughing together, as we always did laugh . . . There was no light, no colour, no external scenic feature: only close embrace, profound and happy communion; also the strongest possible impression of her individuality."*

Rosamond Lehmann then found herself back in her body, awake and cheerful, and for some time after this experience noticed changes in her perception, seeing the garden outside as shimmering, vibrating and incandescent, as if she were looking "through the surfaces of all things into the manifold iridescent rays which . . . composed the substances of all things."

This sensual language resonates with the Kahunas' belief that the "shadowy bodies" are physical although they are not visible. As regular users of electricity, radio and radar waves, we should have no problem in accepting the physical existence of something we cannot see and can only experience the effects of. For me the question is not so much "Can it happen?"—we have so very many well-attested accounts— but "What is the point?" of having or seeking such experiences.

Rosamond Lehmann's experience gave her intense pleasure and comfort; as a bereaved mother she was in especial circumstances. This is very different from interacting with spirits of the unknown dead, or seeking to have a long-term contact with the dead as guides or helpers. According to the Kahunas, contact with spirits of the dead is again made through the "low self." Unfortunately, contact may also be with the "low self" of the dead, who may know little more about the future—or anything else—than we do. Good spiritual teachers remind us that not all the dead are wise. There

can be a tendency to glamorise this kind of experience. Apart
from personal concerns like those besetting Rosamond Lehmann, what might be the motive for pursuing communication
with the dead? I am reminded of Confucius' maxim that if
you are unable to serve living people, how can you serve
spirits?

Alongside our society's dismissal of anything supernatural, there exists its pair: the credulous belief that anything
from that "other world" represents supernatural wisdom.
There can be a tendency to imagine that every dream which
is like a vision is visionary. For example, during her period
of intense grieving Rosamond Lehmann had other experiences. In one she describes

*hearing a thunderclap, then a disembodied voice which tells
her: "Fall on your knees, be flung down." She finds herself
hurled on the ground in a landscape of rocks and desert.
She is then helped to rise by a kneeling figure in pale robes—
"a holy Being, obviously at prayer" who has "the face of
a real person, though not one I had ever seen before." His
features are distinctive and he has a short beard. He looks
at her with eyes like burning coals and she wakes suddenly
in the middle of the night.*

Pondering the experience, she wonders if this was a vision
of a saint or of Jesus in the Garden of Gethsemane.

For many people such an experience would be enough to
prompt a conversion to Christianity. Others would explain it
by turning to a different belief system, such as that of the
Jungian archetypes. In *Journey of a Dream Animal* Kathleen
Jenks records a dream in which:

*an unknown man tried to rape her in her grandparents' bath-
room. She fled from the house and in the street met a child
who let her escape on his bicycle while he rode behind on
the fender. She describes him as having a hauntingly beau-*

*tiful face, and a sunniness and maturity about him. She is
also struck by his total trust in her. At the end of the dream,
after she has reached her uncle's house, the rapist catches
up and is not afraid of her uncle. The beautiful boy pulls a
gun and shoots the rapist dead.*

She woke in terror. Afterwards the image of the child stayed
in her memory and consoled her. She was particularly moved
by his trust: "The more I thought about the dream, the more
touching it became. My unconscious mind actually trusted
me to handle my flight from darkness to light." A few weeks
later she began reading Jung, and identified the boy as "the
archetypal 'child-saviour.' He was a symbol of ancient, ever-
young wisdom buried deeply within the psyche . . . a power
of healing and integration deep within me." With a shock
she identified the rapist as a man she was involved with, a
"spiritual rapist" whose "mental cruelty . . . long silences
were designed to ravish and plunder my spirit . . . And my
own psyche was sounding an urgent SOS." She saw the child
in the dream as wanting her to be free of this destructive
relationship, but comments that it was a long time in her life
before it achieved its goal.

Here the appearance of a particularly numinous dream figure—the boy who saves her—prompted in Kathleen Jenks
the interpretation that he represented not only "a power of
healing and integration" in her unconscious, but also the
"archetypal child-saviour" of Jungian theory. In this way,
special or divine-seeming agencies in our dreams are interpreted as divine personae in the mythic/religious belief system of the dreamer—whether Christian or Jungian—and
serve to validate that system. But there are other ways of
understanding such experiences. Similar to the Kahunas'
view that they happen through the "low self," esoteric teachers in the West suggest that visions and visionary figures
reach us through the medium of the "astral" level of the
energy field around the body. This "astral" level is involved

in the processing of emotional problems and blockages, and is affected by our imagination and cultural conditioning. That area is therefore imprinted with certain symbols of our belief system, which tend to mediate our night experiences. As a result many dream "visions" on the astral plane are simply mirrors of our own imaginings.

While the tendency of our culture is either to dismiss such experiences as fantastical or elevate them as divine, what is emerging is a geography, a way of understanding and gauging them: some of them consoling, some illuminating, some a waste of time. We do not have to embrace all the gifts our dreams offer. The Kahunas' system is consistent with a series of spiritual teachings which affirm that certain forces or energies "out there" do have an objective reality, and can be met in the altered states of dreaming; equally those teachings insist that those forces or entities are neither mystical nor divine. They are forms of energy, and human beings are at root energy, and when we shift our awareness onto the right wavelength, we can perceive them and interact with them. Usually, rather than perceiving them as energy, our sleeping self tends to clothe them in symbols (whether mystic, religious or simply surreal). But they feel different from the dreams which are a re-creation of a personal scenario or internal drama. Heather McDougal is clear about this distinction as she describes an unusual experience she had one afternoon:

"I had this dream while snoozing on the couch in my living room. It was one of those nap dreams where reality becomes different, and you're dreaming, but it's only a sort of half-sleep you're in, you're still aware of your surroundings somehow.

"I'm sitting on my couch in my living room, only it's different. The placement of the couch is slightly different, and there's a fireplace instead of a mantel with a heater. I feel a sort of torpor, an immovability. The light is even differ-

ent—more like the sort of light sunshine makes reflected onto the walls from water.

"Suddenly something large comes in the door behind the couch, and an enormous lion, coloured purple with faint designs across his flanks and shoulders, paces around the corner of the couch. His skin is extraordinarily smooth and supple, like some breeds of short-haired dogs can be, only much softer. I still can't move, caught in that space between dreaming and waking where the limbs are frozen and the voice doesn't work.

"The lion climbs up on the couch beside me, his bulk filling the remainder of its length, and proceeds to yawn and stretch and rub against me. At this point I seem to be able to move, and I tentatively reach out and stroke him. The response is quick and warm, and I find myself running my fingers through his mane and lying down next to him; we fall into an ecstasy of snuggling. This dissolves into sleep, and I wake a few minutes later."

Heather McDougal understands this experience as follows: "I always think of the lion as being a visitation more than anything else. He (definitely he) doesn't seem terribly symbolic. It feels more like somebody who visited me. It almost doesn't feel like a dream—more like a psychic type of thing, some entity. I didn't go anywhere or do anything, I was aware. I knew I was drowsing but it had changed, I was in a different state of the same place, almost like (I hesitate to say) another dimension. The place had changed but only because my perception had changed.

"It happens to me often that I get in a state of mind like I'm overcome with drowsiness. It usually happens in the afternoon. I find myself laying down in a patch of sunshine and just sort of drifting for a very short time, it's very like a trance. It comes over me . . . I can't avoid it. If I succumb to it I go into this incredibly deep state where I'm still aware and I have these incredibly brief deep dreams. It's not like I contact the spirit world, it's more like I get into another place where other people live—not ghosts or the dead. I think the lion was somebody who lived in that place. I associated him with my cat somehow, but she is female. She was there sleeping with me at the time. It almost felt like he was a creature who lived with me everyday and was around and knew me but I didn't usually live where he lived. He was just coming in to be affectionate because he knew me and he lived with me. He was very familiar. I woke up and I felt so loved and secretly pleased that I had this friend."

The most detailed model for understanding such experiences has been provided by Carlos Castaneda in the books which describe his apprenticeship in Mexico to a Yaqui Indian "Don Juan" to learn a native American tradition of "sorcery." Here again, there is nothing mystical—though much that is amazing. What many term "astral" experiences are understood here as the result of the manipulation of awareness. Parallel to the Kahunas' "shadowy bodies" around the physical body, in these teachings the human being is seen as having a "luminous cocoon" of energy around the physical body. There are innumerable filaments of energy moving within the cocoon, and myriad filaments of energy in the world outside the cocoon. Through a point on the outer rim of the cocoon called the "assemblage point," a tiny selection of the filaments outside are transmitted into the cocoon, and light up a very few of the filaments inside. The position of the "assemblage point" determines which filaments are selected to enter the cocoon and therefore how we perceive the world.

Don Juan teaches Castaneda that our social conditioning encourages the assemblage point to become fixed at a certain place so that there is a "consensual" version of perceived reality with which all members of society agree. However, in children the assemblage point is still mobile, and the sorcery training involves learning voluntarily to move the assemblage point so that different filaments enter the luminous cocoon and a different version of reality is perceived. When we are asleep, the assemblage point moves of its own accord, with the same result. As Heather McDougal described her experience—without having read Castaneda—"The place had changed but only because my perception had changed ... it's ... like I get into another place where other people live ..."

Don Juan teaches Castaneda to "fix" his assemblage point temporarily at the new positions he reaches in dreaming so as to have a sustained experience of different realities. He distinguishes between ordinary dreams which are our own fantasies or "phantom projections," and these ones where we tap into alternative realities and the elements we encounter are "energy-generating items" in their own right. While learning to maintain the shifts of awareness in his dreams to these parallel realities, Castaneda has unusual visions and meets entities. Some of them he is at first inclined to view in a religious sense, but Don Juan explains to him that they are just some of the many different energy formations—organic and inorganic—which exist in the universe, and which the normal fixation of our assemblage point in daily life does not permit us to perceive. Don Juan emphasises that life is energy, and a major part of Castaneda's sorcery training is learning to *see* the energy which gives shape to our recognisable world as well as to these other perceivable realities. Throughout his apprenticeship, Castaneda continually reverts to attempting to deny or dismiss the unusual experiences he is having, and Don Juan continually encourages him to honour his senses rather than the system of belief he was brought up with.

Don Juan teaches Castaneda that contact with occupants of those other realities can involve a fruitful exchange of energy and mutual enjoyment. But he also warns him that not all those occupants are friendly and some are dangerous; those other worlds can be as predatory and ruthless as our own. Another apprentice of Don Juan's, Florinda Donner, writes in *Shabono* about a dream where a friendly ghost, her sister, sought to draw her too far into the world of the dead. This frightening dream was up to a point a close replica of an event which took place when she was a child of five years: on a day outing, her family had stopped by a shallow river in a forest. Separating from the others, Florinda Donner's 15-year-old sister dared her to come wading in the river and squatted to show menstrual blood turning the water red between her feet. Florinda was bewildered and asked if she were hurt. Her sister stood up in silence and, smiling, beckoned Florinda to follow her. Florinda stayed in the water terrified as she watched her sister climb the opposite bank. The dream, which she had as an adult, followed the same sequence of events and:

"In my dream I experienced the same fear, but I told myself that now I was an adult there was nothing to be afraid of. I was about to follow my sister up the steep bank when I heard Juan Caridad's voice urging me to remain in the water. 'She is calling you from the land of the dead,' he said. 'Don't you remember that she is dead?'"

Florinda Donner records that however much she asked, Don Juan would not discuss how he managed to appear in her dreams or how he knew that her sister was dead.

In Castaneda's *The Art of Dreaming*, which summarises and clarifies many of the teachings of his earlier eight books, Castaneda has to be protected by Don Juan from being drawn into another world, and Don Juan is continually warning him not to become overly fascinated with or dependent on his meetings with the organic and inorganic beings who inhabit the other dimensions he explores. The aim of the apprenticeship is not to become preoccupied with the power that can be derived from entering other worlds, but to develop discipline and purpose so as to increase the amount of energy available and attain freedom. The dreaming practices are aimed at perfecting his "energy body" so that he has flexibility in his awareness. From learning to focus his attention on his hands and other features in his dreams, to examining everything in his dreams in great detail, to waking up voluntarily from one dream into another, to watching his sleeping body on the bed, to "seeing" the energy of real items in his dreams, to moving from one alternative reality to another, he learns to shift his assemblage point and hold it at new positions so as to control his awareness. At the same time working to achieve a clearance of emotional debris from the past, he develops an incredible clarity and facility in the operation of his "energy body." This kind of manipulation of awareness in dreams is not part of our vocabulary in the West, but the closest thing we have to it is what is known as "lucid dreaming."

LUCID DREAMING

"My mother once had a flying dream where she was really enjoying herself, flying all around and looking at everything, until all of a sudden she realized she had no idea how to land. So, using the theory that if you call for help in your dreams something will always appear, she shouted 'Help!' The next thing she knew two elephant legs descended from her midsection, and she was able to land safely."

Lucid dreaming is when a dreamer becomes aware "I am dreaming" and can change their behaviour in a dream accordingly. It is an experience which has fascinated many writers. In his introduction to Hervey de Saint-Denys' book on the subject, Morton Schatzman's list of sources includes Frederik Van Eeden, a Dutch physician who started studying his dreams in 1896 and coined the term "lucid dreams";

Peter Ouspensky, a Russian-born mystic who published a book in 1912; Mary Arnold-Foster from England who published in 1921; Oliver Fox, an English theosophist; J. H. M. Whiteman, a South African mathematician who published in 1961; and Castaneda. I would add Robert Monroe, who has published more recently, but prefer Oliver Fox's careful investigate approach. Recent research has discovered that it is possible for the dreamer to give physical signals to indicate that lucid dreaming is in progress.

Saint-Denys himself was a dedicated investigator of this phenomenon. For example, in one dream:

he found himself in an avenue of trees in a garden and was aware of dreaming. A flowering lilac branch appeared before him and he "thought of the various problems I wished to solve." He then investigated whether he could smell the lilac (he could) and then tackled the question whether it was "a stereotyped vision, the unalterable reproduction of a memory-image imprinted in the fibres of my brain"—in which case he would not be able to modify it. To test this out, he broke off the head of lilac flowers bit by bit and watched the cluster getting smaller just as it would in real life.

This was a dream researcher's approach to lucid dreaming. Other dreamers use the experience differently. The Senoi dreamers allegedly used this awareness to turn to confront any dream elements that were frightening them; it is one way to get out of a tight spot, as with the dreamer's shout for help above. Others have used the lucid state to experiment with different behaviour, and also to have sexual experiences.

Attitudes to lucid dreaming vary. Robin Shohet in *Dream Sharing* suspects that the desire to be lucid in a dream may be "an attempt to control the dream state before being receptive to the actual messages that can be learnt" and comments that "The main advantage as far as I can see (orgasms notwithstanding) is help with nightmares." Others have found it a source of joy. Oliver Fox described how at the onset of lucidity "Instantly the vividness of life increased a hundredfold . . . Never had I felt so absolutely well . . ." and Stephen LaBerge and Jayne Gackenbach in "Lucid Dreaming" suggest that it "is arguably one of the most remarkable states of consciousness a normal person is likely to experience." They point out that it encourages "our capacity to vividly create model universes that can provide a new perspective on our view of waking life and the physical universe" and that it facilitates "divergent thinking and the creative generation of ideas—brainstorming, as it were." It seems that our culture is nowhere near understanding its possibilities; LaBerge cites the story of Benjamin Franklin asked by a woman about the discovery of electricity, "What *use* is it?"—to which he replied, "What use, madam, is a newborn baby?" The same, perhaps, could be said of lucid dreaming. Perhaps too, like electricity, it is a resource that is in itself neutral and can be used for good or ill: sometimes manipulated, as Robin Shohet fears, and sometimes taken as an opportunity to use ourselves more fully and enhance life.

Research does suggest that lucid dreaming is prolonged by achieving a "balance between spontaneity and control, involvement and detachment, absorption and perspective," and that low self-esteem and inner conflicts may block it—suggesting that skills useful for lucid dreaming are useful for life in general. Castaneda's years of learning to use the lucid sleep state is seen as part of a process of shedding limiting habits, thoughts and emotions so as to be able to develop a new way of perceiving. Outside that tradition, many women have addressed similar issues in their dreams; the next chapter shows what some women feel they have learnt in this way about the meaning of life—and death.

Reading and Notes

Allende, Isabel, speaking to Sue Lawley on *Desert Island Discs*, BBC Radio 4, 12 September 1993.

Castaneda, Carlos, *The Art of Dreaming*, HarperCollins, New York, 1993. Castaneda's apprenticeship is also described in his eight earlier books; for teachings on the anatomy of the "energy body," see especially his *The Fire From Within*, Pocket Books, New York, 1991.

Donner, Florinda, *Shabono*, HarperCollins, San Francisco, 1992, pp. 176–7.

Fox, Oliver, *Astral Projection: A Record of Research*, Rider, London, 1939, p. 39 (also published by University Books, New Hyde Park, New York, 1962).

Hamilton, Nigel, "Exploring our Dreams," *Caduceus*, Spring 1992, published by Caduceus, 38 Russell Terrace, Leamington Spa, Warwickshire CV31 1HE, p. 11.

Houston, Gaie, "Just a Dream," *Self and Society*, Vol IX, 3, May/June 1981 ("Dreams" issue), published by Self and Society, 39 Blenkarne Road, London SW11 6HZ, p. 104.

Jenks, Kathleen, *Journey of a Dream Animal*, The Julian Press, New York, 1975, pp. 24–7.

LaBerge, Stephen, and Jayne Gackenbach, "Lucid Dreaming," Benjamin B. Wolman and Montague Ullman (eds.) *Handbook of States of Consciousness*, Van Nostrand Reinhold, New York, 1986, pp. 159, 193, 188.

Lehmann, Rosamond, *The Swan in the Evening*, Virago Press, London, 1982, pp. 111–14, 134–6.

Linn, Denise, *Pocketful of Dreams*, Piatkus, London, 1993, pp. 122, 131–141.

Long, Max Freedom, *The Secret Science Behind Miracles*, DeVorss, PO Box 550, Marina del Rey, California 90291, 1976, pp. 137–40, 155–7, 165–71, 176, 178, 184–5, 187–8 (first published 1948).

Lucid dreaming: see Keith M. T. Hearne, *Lucid Dreams: An Electrophysiological and Physiological Study*, Unpublished Ph.D thesis, University of Liverpool, 1978.

O'Mahony, Hank, "Becoming the Dream—A Gestalt Approach," *Inside Out*, 12, Spring 1993, published by Inside Out, 23 Lower Albert Road, Glenageary, Co., Dublin, pp. 4–6.

Roberts, Jane, *The Nature of Personal Reality*, a Seth Book, Prentice-Hall, New Jersey, 1974.

Saint-Denys, Hervey de, see under Schatzman.

Schatzman, Morton, "Introduction," Hervey de Saint-Denys, *Dreams and How to Guide Them*, translated by Nicholas Fry, Morton Schatzman (ed.), Gerald Duckworth, London, 1982, pp. 2, 11.

Shohet, Robin, *Dream Sharing: How to Enhance Your Understanding of Dreams by Group Sharing and Discussion*, Turnstone Press, Wellingborough, 1985, pp. 45, 74–5.

Wilberg, Henry P., "The Dream-Art Science of Waking Life; A New Kabbalah," *Self and Society*, Vol IX, 3, May/June 1981, ("Dreams" issue), published by Self and Society, 39 Blenkarne Road, London SW11 6HZ, p. 123.

11

Finding a Purpose in Life and Death

If some dreams are showing us the watch face of our life, others seem to show not only the cogs ticking inside, but sometimes even the watchmaker at work and the metal ore still in the ground. Such dreams extend the sense of what reality is. What can they teach us about the nature of things? Can they help us to locate a purpose in the process of living and dying? This chapter contains accounts from some women who feel that they can.

GLIMPSES OF "SOUL"?

"One of the most important dreams I have ever had was where I saw the colour of my soul:

"I was sleeping soundly when I heard the clap of hands. I thought my ears really heard it. The sound pulled my consciousness into my dreaming. I felt that someone was beside me, guiding me. I saw a circle in front of me. Then I saw another circle. 'No,' the guide said. 'That's not what you're seeing.' I looked again and I saw one circle that would change colours from one to the other. 'No,' said the guide

again. 'That's not what you're seeing! Look again.' I looked a third time and this time it seemed as if I were the one changing, not the circles. It was one circle with two dimensions, and somehow in one moment I could see one dimension and then in another moment I was able to see the other dimension. I was right. 'That's the colour of my soul,' I exclaimed as I saw the really intense dark orangish red (not reddish orange) circle, like a burning sunset. I knew I was right and was surprised at my own knowing. The guide confirmed my rightness.''

Thinking on waking about the other dimension of the circle, the dreamer Marti Matthews ''realised that the other colour must be 'my' colour—the colour of my personality, my conscious life, my persona, as Jungians say—the me as I live in the world.'' She regretted not noticing that colour in the dream, but found that when she shut her eyes and allowed herself ''the confidence that I do know the colour of myself,'' she saw it ''—a French or powder blue, soft light grey-blue. Then I was amazed at how much distance there was between the two colours! I saw the goal of my life—to bring this burning energy into some kind of control, some poise—quite a task!''

Marti Matthews had this dream after a series which seemed to be teaching about a long journey her soul had made prior to this life:

''I recognized the color of my soul because of previous dreams and intuitions where for some time I had been learning about my other lives ('reincarnations'). I had been amazed to learn about them: they all were lively to say the least, very far from my 'persona' or my self-image. In one I was a French Canadian lumberjack, beer-drinking, male chauvinist, crazy about dancing to fiddle music, bad tempered. In another I am a French gypsy woman who rather ruined her life having child after child by different men, but stubbornly refused to cave in to various pressures and to the end was a wild woman (not a good mother though!), etc., etc. I learned about these through combinations of dream-work, intuition work, and self-observation in ordinary life. I had always identified with my quiet persona, but by the time I had this dream about the colour of my soul, I knew there were parts of me deeply alive and deeply repressed by the persona I had inherited from my mother—shy, studious, kind. I'm glad for all I've learned from her, but now I feel that the orangish red is much more truly my self, it's the real me that's most deeply functioning most of the time, and my challenge is to blend my gentle persona with my deepest energy and through this marriage give birth to a strong and focused me.''

Reincarnation will be discussed more fully later. What particularly interests me here is the sense of her soul which this dream gives Marti Matthews, leaving the impression of a circle vibrating with a particular colour. This is strangely consistent with the teaching I have received that the ''soul'' level of the energy field is a wide circle or sphere around the body, and that it consists of certain colours representing the energy of your ''qualities.'' You may to a greater or lesser degree be able to draw these qualities in to the inner layers of the field and the physical body in order to express them in your life.

Other women have had an experience of ''soul'' which carries more a sense of moving out of this world into something beyond. Beata Bishop described such an experience in *Caduceus*:

"I was in outer space, in total, impenetrable darkness and, in the earthly sense of the word, I was dead, yet fully alive in every other sense. Somewhere in that deep darkness I was aware of the presence of God. And I asked the presence to let me shed everything that was unimportant and only keep

the essence. Upon this a tremendous wind arose which shook, tore and buffeted me, as if I had been a leaf in a gale. I could feel parts of me breaking off and floating away, going, going, gone into some black hole—but perhaps I was in the ultimate black hole?—until the wind suddenly ceased, and I felt at peace, whole, with my essence clear and undiminished.''

Beata Bishop hesitates between calling this a dream or a vision of the night, and comments that ''Words can only describe the sequence, not the overwhelming power of the experience. For me, it confirmed the illusory nature of physical death and the survival of the essence which I had long suspected. There was nothing left to fear.'' She compares her experience with a similar ''cosmic stripping-down experience'' which Jung describes in his autobiography.

There are other parallels to this experience of a vastness out there from which we come into this life and to which we may perhaps return. In the Castaneda books, the teachings of Don Juan distinguish between the ''tonal'' and the ''nagual.'' The ''tonal'' is the practical world of daily living, which embraces everything we know and do as human beings between birth and death, our abilities to judge, assess and witness, and everything we have a word for, including God. The ''nagual'' is the inconceivable, the immensity beyond for which there are no words, no names, no feelings and no knowledge. The teachings stress the importance of dealing with the tonal. In one passage in *Tales of Power* Don Juan uses the tabletop in a restaurant as symbol for the tonal; he stresses the need to work at keeping the table clean and tidy—only then is one in a fit state to face the nagual, which is everything around, beyond, above and below the table. Contacting the ''spiritual'' is not a question of escaping from mundane concerns, but of setting your everyday house in order as a means of acquiring the skills to deal with that other world. Human life is seen as a temporary condition when a few elements from the nagual are bonded together. The human being is seen as a "cluster" of elements from that world; on death they separate again and return into the immensity. This notion of the cluster is rather different from the monadic idea of the soul which prevails in the West. It finds a resonance in the following woman's dream:

"In some kind of portentous situation a man says to me, 'I feel like a mosaic'. There was lots more of the dream, but that is the only bit that stayed with me."

This woman wondered afterwards: "Does the concept of personhood as one unified monolithic centralised force/essence/soul reflect patriarchal thinking? As opposed to a mosaic, which is less centralized, less reductionist, more collective?"

I am intrigued by the way these different models turn our normal perspective inside out. We tend to think of the familiar world of everyday life as the centre of the universe with perhaps a little airy-fairy area called spirituality off somewhere in the margins. These teachings put it the other way, suggesting that the important thing is the immensity of spirit, from elements of which our world is temporarily glued together: it is our world which is the dream. When Alice wants to wake the Red King in *Through the Looking-Glass*, Tweedledum tells her:

> "If that there King was to wake . . . you'd go out—bang!—just like a candle! . . . it's no use *your* talking about waking him . . . when you're only one of the things in his dream. You know very well you're not real."
>   "I *am* real," said Alice, and began to cry.

Is the Red King part of Alice's dream? Or is Alice part of the Red King's dream? Do we dream of spirit? Or are we ourselves simply the dream creations of a larger force? These

questions cannot be answered. But we can find out how some
women have used the gifts of dreams to clarify their own
sense of what living and dying is about.

LIFE AS A LEARNING PROCESS

*"I am learning the violin from an old man but can't remem-
ber the time of the classes nor can I find time to practise. I
feel confused as to why I am there. I am surprised he remembers my name."*

This woman comments: "At the time of this dream I am
feeling very harassed and am guiltily neglecting my spiritual
practices. Yet, despite my neglect—'nor can I find time to
practise'—my wise old man remembers me.

"I found this a tender and consoling dream: that I am not
forgotten by my inner wisdom, even when I am too frag-
mented to make contact with it and draw from it."

This metaphor, of life—and spirituality—being about
teaching and learning, recurs in the following example:

*"In the dream I'm working on a camp and I'm cooking in
a big tent, on a gas cooker. I'm making some sort of sauce,
and it has some small bright green things in it, which might
be broccoli or sprouts, and a master cook is watching me. I
put the sauce on one side to cool and when I pick it up,
underneath from the pan is hanging something else, which
has grown from the pan."*

In a day off from her job teaching children, Jo Robinson
explored this dream on her own, using a mixture of visualisation, Gestalt, journal-writing and contemplation. Re-
entering the dream, she found it yielded a surprising number
of insights. One is about the sauce:

"I look in the pan. There is something green that has the liquid crushed out of it. It has become jelly, which has taken the shape of the pan . . . it's like taking a photo of a feeling . . . The colour now feels significant—it's deep lime green and transparent. The insight now is about how we as humans interact with nature; use it, change it, rob, pollute, harness, and work with it, thus changing and shaping the environment and leaving our shape in it, as though the environment is an enormous jelly which is shaped by our activities and yet we are shaped by the shape that is created."

Developing a Gestalt-type dialogue, she finds the master cook insisting that this mixture, which she thinks she has finished and put on one side, "can be melted down to become a different shape. It can be worked on again." As the mixture she says: "I am green. I am vibrant and full of energy. I am in a pan, being worked on with a wooden spoon and heat. I am going to change shape and flow and become more liquid, less definable, and then I will be stored . . . I can be 'brought back to life easily' if I take this form. I will become more able to change." The new growth underneath the pan has a similar message of change: "I look fragile and transitory and yet I'm deceptively powerful. I am growing." She concludes that "my dream is about . . . allowing myself to undergo fundamental changes to the very core of my being. That it is okay to break down structures (patterns). That I am learning to be my own teacher. The feeling now is that it is only ourselves who can teach ourselves, we have to contact the teacher within. All a 'teacher' can do is to enable a 'pupil' to access their own teacher."

Jo Robinson's themes are about gaining access to one's own authority as part of a process of personal change and regeneration. Sometimes these "teaching" dreams come at a time of great personal crisis, and their message is one of courage to survive and face life. The following woman's dream came at a time of devastation after the end of a relationship and gave her "hope and strength to believe I should go on."

At the start, the dreamer is walking down a wide strip of empty road with three elderly women who appear to be in their sixties. All is grey, then the dreamer sees some trees and she tells the women that it is time to go another way. One woman, with a bitter face, chicken skin on her upper arms, and wearing house slippers, crosses the road and tells the other women to follow her and ignore the dreamer. A second woman follows without question. The third woman whines about being taken care of. So the dreamer gives the woman some money; she takes it coldly, and then follows the others.

Through the trees the dreamer comes to some spiny bushes. She sees that the only way forward is to go through them. The bushes rip at her clothing and painfully tear her skin. Finally, she comes to a clearing where there is water rushing by. A group of women are being instructed by another woman about how to ride the water on body-boards. Moving to a shore, the dreamer sees that some of the group turn the experience into a contest. They are paddling so hard, the water is rough and choppy. Behind, the instructor and others paddle lightly and here the water remains blue, calm, and the dreamer notices the trees, the sunlight, the sounds.

The instructor is alerted to a change in the air and begins to paddle assuredly and swiftly with strong arms when suddenly a large wave comes from behind. Catching the wave, it takes her over the others (who get taken under) and she rides it into shore.

At the shore, everyone cheers for her and she is given a medal. The dreamer admires the woman. There is an aura of confidence and greatness about her, yet she is "average" in size, shape and looks. Suddenly the woman turns her attention to the dreamer and "with words both firm and gentle

says, 'And you will win, too. I know because I am the coun-
sellor.' She then bends closer and taking hold of the medal
around her neck shows that it is emblazoned with the holy
spirit.''

The dreamer, Mary Pikul, describes her waking: ''And then
I woke with a force that seemed to suck air like a vacuum.
It was about 5 A.M. and I got up and I remembered everything . . . I was not a very spiritual person at this time, but
there was no doubt in my mind that I had just received a
message—an answer to a prayer—from God, the omnipres-
ent source of all that is.''

Here the message of encouragement was powerful and clear,
but afterwards Mary Pikul struggled for several years to resolve for herself exactly what it meant in terms of her life.
She felt clear about the start of the dream:

''The old bitter woman who crosses the street, the passive
woman who follows her, and the manipulative woman . . .
were warnings to me and helped me from becoming bitter,
passive and/or manipulative after the loss of the relationship.
Turning away from them meant accepting that I needed to
make some changes in my life—with myself. Going through
the pain of realizing and accepting this is going through the
bushes. What now? The ride on the water is the time of self-
development. The difference between the two groups is about
living through life with either *trust, patience and persever-*
ance, or living life with *fear*. So it is that many women rush
into marriage, children, etc., feeling that this is the route to
happiness rather than developing oneself for the sake of oneself.''

But what was the meaning of the numinous phrase ''You
will win, too''? Encouraged by a dream dictionary, she believed for two years that this meant ''that my lover and I

would come back together again . . ." This gave her "a reason to live." In time, however, as she changed and grew, she herself became the reason to live ("I saw . . . living my life lovingly was its own reward . . .") and years later her understanding of that dream phrase was still evolving, while the dream remained an inspiration for her: "listening to one's inner leadings, without bending to pressure from others—this is how you win . . . Winners enjoy intimacy, expressing feelings of warmth, tenderness and closeness towards others. Winners enjoy sincere and genuine love."

In this teaching dream which carried a major life message and kept the dreamer going through two very difficult years, it is interesting that the usual symbol of a wise man is replaced by a wise woman. Described as very "average" in shape and looks, this female figure bides her time, surges to victory, wins a medal and has a very personal message for the dreamer. One wonders whether, in a society with different values, women might appear more often in dreams in this counselling role. The relationship between gender and spirituality can itself be questioned in these illuminating dreams, which seem to be turning over the broader issues of life, love, change and purpose. Here is an example from Marti Matthews:

The dream starts with a Buddhist holy man floating idyllically down river in a procession of boats ("It was dusk and everyone had lanterns"). Then it shifts to a scene away from the river where a naked Caucasian woman, who is giving a healing massage, is criticised by a monk for having made a mistake with her eighth husband. "She was devastated . . . It was as if they'd said she'd gotten off her spiritual path to enlightenment."

This prompts a dawning realisation for the dreamer in the dream that "the needs of women were different from the needs of men on their spiritual paths, that the spiritual development of men and women were opposite. What was right *for a woman was wrong for a man, and vice versa. These women were being very sensual here, naked, engaging in pleasure, and this was what they needed to learn and to grow in for their spiritual fulfillment.''*

In a closing scene so familiar that it would be funny if it were not distressing, the dreamer tries to get the attention of others in the dream to share this insight, but cannot because her husband will not stop talking out loud. ''Here was gigantic pain. I awakened, perplexed . . .''

This dream raises issues about gender differences, and about facing male chauvinism in a ''spiritual'' environment—an experience which may be familiar to some readers. Many spiritual teachings are uncomfortable with the topic of anger, and in a situation where daily life continues to confront us with social inequalities, racial prejudices and gender injustices, it remains a very real problem to find a response which combines appropriate anger with a ''spiritual'' perspective. Ten months later Marti Matthews had another dream, which resolves the issue as follows:

''I saw this young woman I've seen before in a dream—she's Tibetan, and a young female Dalai Lama. At one point she flew over us, she touched a man in passing, she was angry or annoyed with him (and perhaps with others) or hurt. But she immediately let go of her anger and smiled and said sincerely 'I love you' and flew on. She didn't fly constantly yet, but she could sometimes fly a little ways.

''A wise man had said to her 'Don't worry; you will make it to the end.' As she felt this slight hurt or anger flying over certain people, the words of this old Chinese man came to her again: 'Don't worry, you will make it to your end.'

''Then I had a sense of beyond her end, beyond anyone's end, when not only I have died but all those who touched my life including those who hurt me. They are so irrelevant, in the end. The purpose of one's life is so much larger, the

purpose of the life of this female Dalai Lama is much larger than little hurts. Her life belongs to the world. These people are irrelevant, in the end, they fade into the past and have such a small part of even that.

"She is me. (end of dream)"

This sense of setting personal emotions and problems in the context of something larger recurs in the following dream. If life is a school, who sets the lessons? What is the time-table? And what do we do at break time? Here we see emotional and gender conflicts set in the context of a kind of half-way house or "gap between lives" where such conflicts are seen as an educational process which can be commented on and transcended:

The dream starts at an all-night party in a house in Brixton. There is a scene with women in the cellar ("the atmosphere is intimate—like brothel scenes in Toulouse Lautrec paintings") which is interrupted by the arrival of large male figures on horses wielding whips "like the gorillas in the film The Planet of the Apes. *They . . . start picking people out of the crowd with a strange blue-speckled thing like a long mouth organ/wand. I am one of the people they point at. I am feeling "This has all happened before" . . . At the same time I feel "I don't want this. Enough." It's frightening, upsetting, I want to get out of it.*

The dreamer's shift of consciousness leads to a shift in the dream setting. The dream continues:

"I start saying, 'I don't want any more of this dream'—now I find myself addressing an auditorium of people like in a conference—reasonably full, not packed. I seem to be speaking through a sheet of glass. I am not sure if they can hear me but I carry on speaking: 'It has been useful, I've learnt a lot from it, but I don't want any more.' They seem to have

*heard me, because they start getting up from their seats and
going out.*

*"Among them is one man going out whom I know I have
to speak to—I seem to have some history/involvement with
him. I go up to him and take his arm: 'I just wanted to say
goodbye,' and reach to kiss his cheek. He turns half-
reluctantly—too busy—but when we make contact we are
glued together at a point in the belly. There is a mutual
recognition, he says (or I say?), 'I didn't realise, you're a
Pete.' Being a Pete (the name of an ex-lover I was very
attached to) I understand at once as meaning being of a
certain energy quality, maybe being part of the same group
soul . . . We are standing by a window glued together with
this stomach connection. I cannot leave."*

This dreamer comments: "I cannot understand what is going
on in this dream. My own personal issues (about closeness
with women, fearing male aggression) suddenly disappear
into a framework where the dream (my life?) is a kind of
educational theatre piece for an audience in some half-way
world between heaven and earth. I had been reading the
'Seth' books and this must have given me the 'group soul'
idea—although that kind of experience of inexplicable
'bonding' has happened to me in my everyday life."

The "Seth" books by Jane Roberts suggest that we all live
many lives, and choose to enter the world to gain experience
that will "teach" us. They also suggest that when in dreams
you meet someone who seems strangely familiar, this may
be another member of the same "group soul" to which a
number of souls belong. From such writings, and familiarity
with Buddhist teachings, the idea has become popular in
"new age" circles that we choose when we are born and to
whom. The trials and tribulations we experience in life are
therefore also to some extent "chosen" for their educational
value. Although it can be very irritating to be told by such

people that, for example, getting your car smashed up is something you have "chosen" as a learning experience, it can also in some contexts be a stimulating idea. In some circumstances it can provide a sense of perspective and purpose in dealing with painful life experiences like illness, abuse and injustice. It defuses self-pity, and can help us to respond to life's difficulties "actively like a warrior," as Don Juan puts it. For the dreamer above, the intimacy/aggression conflict is seen as an important lesson, and at the same time the "auditorium" scene gives some distance on it, perhaps signalling her ability not to get swallowed up in it. The "stomach bonding" with the man at the end perhaps suggests the possibility of a different quality of relationship.

These ideas of a "soul" dimension co-existing with, and giving a different perspective on, human problems have a historical counterpart in the native Australian tradition of the "Dreaming." When a child is conceived, this is apparently not seen as solely the result of the parents' lovemaking; rather it is believed that a spirit child, who already exists "in the Dreaming" has been waiting to be "dreamt" into the mother's womb. The spirit child, who chooses to enter a woman when seeing one to its liking, is a complete entity originating in the long-distant past. This individual spirit, which is part of the limitless reservoir of spirit emanating from the "Dreaming," is not blood-related to any human being, and takes responsibility for entering this life.

Such ideas affect our attitude to death, which in these belief systems is not the end of everything, but an interim period between lives; the out-of-life experience may even be far more pleasurable and rewarding than life itself. Accounts of near-death experiences have added to a literature which paints life as a hard option, a tough lesson, compared to death:

"It was not like a dream. I walked, I met people, I spoke to them and that all made complete sense. It's exactly as if it

happened five minutes ago . . . It was a heavenly experience and a blissful experience,"

said one woman interviewed on a BBC Television *Everyman* programme. Another woman interviewed on the same programme dreamt, while practically or clinically dead in hospital, that:

> *she was travelling down a long black tunnel which divided into two passages. One was light—this was death—and the other was darker and much harder, which she took and woke up to find she had given birth to a baby boy: "I felt very cheated as though the other route would have been so much nicer . . . so much more welcoming."*

DEATH AS A WAY TO FREEDOM?

Such ideas about the nature of life can affect our understanding of dreams about impending death. In *The Variety of Dream Experience*, Nan Zimmerman quotes two dreams which Gram Shriver had a few months before her death at the age of 94. Gram was a devout Christian and lived with her devoted daughter Lil.

"In the first dream Gram sees two feet surrounded in light. They are the feet of Jesus; she looks up and very much wants to see his face, but cannot. She feels sad because she has more to do."

"In the second dream she is in an aeroplane, then outside it, flying free, until Lil tells her to come down because she is upset and worried about her flying outside the plane.

Gram does not want to come down, but thinks she should do what her daughter wants, and lands in a haystack."

Nan Zimmerman suggests that Gram was ready to die. She was not frightened, and believed she would be united with God in a way not possible while she was alive. Gram's understanding of the first dream was "that she continued to live because there was spiritual work remaining for her to accomplish." When that issue was resolved, "Gram anticipated with exhilaration the freedom of physical death in her metaphor of flying free of the plane. Then, remembering her daughter's love and concern for her welfare, she was brought 'down to earth.' Gram was saying in her dream that she heard her daughter's earnest desire that she live." Afterwards, Lil talked to friends about the great loss Gram's death would be, and began to see it as an inevitable transition for them both. Gram planned her funeral and had her coffin made. The day after it was finished, Gram died. In this account, death is seen as a freedom from which loved ones may unwittingly detain us.

Penny Cloutte writes about coming to terms with the death of a close friend in a rather different way, through a dream which she had a few months later:

"My friend Liz died in the spring, of cancer. Just before she died she asked me to conduct her funeral, and I did. Three hundred people came. She was from South Africa and an ANC activist, and so there was a strong ANC input into her funeral. The singing, especially the wonderful African women's voices, helped very powerfully to get me through and make it bearable. The most painful part of my role had been to press the button which sent her coffin off into the furnace at the end of the ceremony.

"I had the dream of her in early June. I dreamt I was in Coram's Fields with a whole group of women and children, and bumped into Liz there, to my great surprise! She looked

happy and healthy and much younger than she had been even before she got ill, except for a squiggly white scar on her cheek. She was having a good time playing with the children, but broke off to come over and hug me, as pleased to see me as I was to see her! She seemed generally very happy. She told me that dying really wasn't so bad—the worst bit had been lying in her coffin in the Crematorium, hearing everyone being so sad and longing to be released. She thanked me for releasing her, gave me a hug and rushed off to resume playing with the children—she was having such a good time with them. I woke up feeling peaceful and reassured.

"I still feel tearful whenever I think of this dream—but happy tears. The message seems to be that Liz is happy now. Coram's Fields is a children's playground in Bloomsbury where I spent many happy hours with my daughter when she was little . . . It is a powerful symbol of child-centred living, with a sign on the gate saying no adults are admitted without accompanying children! I had met Liz there a couple of times with her children, but there had been hitches both times— once she had been told off by the attendant for allowing her six-year-old to play in the Under-5s' space. So Liz had missed out on the joys of this playground, literally. Symbolically she had missed out on playing spaces all her life: both as the child of demanding, academic parents, and as an adult committed to the struggle. Between political activities, her full-time job, and the demands of her family . . . she had no time or energy for pleasure or play. The dream suggests that she has found it now.

"I have often made fun of the notion of death as an escape from the troubles of this world to a better place, particularly as I grew up and away from the Victorian Christian notions of my family. Such a concept of death seemed to me a denial of the reality of loss. I embraced existentialism for what I saw as its cosmic courage in the face of the reality of death. I had been inclined to mock both the Christian notion—

'Mary Ann has gone to rest/Safe at last on Abraham's breast'—and the 'Joe Hill' version of denial popular on the left: 'Don't mourn—organize!' I was aware, before I had the dream, that I have as I grow older moved away from the existentialist world view and come to have more belief in and respect for spiritual values. This dream has underlined for me just how far I have moved!

"She had died on the Spring Equinox, at the dark of the moon, and in my diary the text for that week was: 'Day is a boat that will carry you to someplace new'. The dream seems to be saying the same thing: that after death we go to a different kind of space, where it is possible to get what we have lacked in this life. That the Universe has more kindness and meaning in it than my earlier beliefs allowed . . .

"The other part of the dream was a validation of my role in pressing that button; of how important the rites of separation are; that the dying and the dead need us to let go of them, so that life can go on. By letting go we do not lose them, as we fear, but make it possible for them to come back to us in a different way . . .

"This dream feels like a gift, an act of grace; a reward, even, for pressing that button."

Such dreams may not only help us come to terms with death by challenging our sense of it as purely negative; they sometimes also seem to suggest why a death happens and that the dying may even choose their time.

DO WE CHOOSE THE TIME OF OUR DEATH?

Marti Matthews' husband Tom died unexpectedly of a heart attack in 1987. Some time afterwards she wrote an account which pieced together experiences and suggestions that in some way—quite inconceivable in terms of our culture's attitudes—both she and her husband had known about his death in advance and even intended it. Looking through her dream journals from earlier in the year of his death, she was astounded to find this dream:

"Tom and I decide together to tear our house down."

About four years before Tom's death, they had experienced a "mid-life crisis." They had survived with a happier relationship in the end, but when Tom had wanted some form of "re-marriage" ceremony Marti had not wanted it. Despite her love for him and their family, she had felt socially pressured into their marriage originally, and still had unresolved feelings about the road not taken. In 1985 she had two dreams where they did re-marry, but woke both times with the reaction: "Why would I do that? I wouldn't marry Tom again . . ." She feels that this was a turning point in their life, a clarification of intention. Two days after one of those dreams, she dreamt that

". . . two whales were living in the watery basement of the houseboat we lived on. They seemed dangerous and unpredictable, because communication between our species was almost nil. I and our two children were up above when a disruption started below. One of the whales was upset. I attempted to keep the boat afloat while the fury of the whale increased. I hoped the children were old enough and strong enough to weather this.

"The meaning of these whales in our basement has always seemed right in front of my nose, yet I couldn't verbalise it. Now it finally seems clear—they were the subconscious minds or deeper consciousness or higher selves of Tom and me."

It was, Marti felt, the larger consciousness of both of them who had made the decision. On the night of Tom's death,

before she had heard about the death, a close friend of
Marti's had the following dream:

*"A tall, dark-haired man with a paunchy stomach [although
she didn't recognise Tom, these were his characteristics]
came to her kitchen door and tried to enter. Because he was
very angry, she was afraid of him, so she took a pair of
scissors and tried to stab him. However, she couldn't kill
him because he was already dead—and this was why he was
so angry!"*

Marti comments that when she heard this dream, she was
"both astounded and relieved; it confirmed my intuition that
Tom's ego-awareness was as shocked and distraught over
this event as I was, even though our higher selves or our
deeper consciousness had decided upon it." After Tom's
death she felt as if she had died too, and found some solace
in Seth's idea that we re-incarnate several times within one
lifetime, despite the apparent visible continuity; she tried not
to resist the new life she was being born into after Tom's
death. She was grateful for the rituals of mourning, which
helped her to separate, although the pain went on for much
longer. She tried to stay in touch with the rightness of the
event which partly "lies in the opportunity for me to feel
and use my own strength. And I know the same is true for
Tom. We had achieved happiness together, but perhaps we
had come to lean on each other too much." She also feels
that: "we will stay in touch with each other. In dreams, we
are frequently together—sometimes doing things, sometimes
just aware that the other is 'going off to a different school
and we'll meet later' [quote from a dream]."

Choosing the time of our death, meeting loved ones
"later," seeing life as a learning process, finding a spiritual
path, gaining a sense of "soul": such ideas are usually
placed in the realm of religion. What would it mean to place
them instead in the realm of the physical, to see them on a
continuum with the rest of our experience—emotional, in-

tellectual—and to find ways of including them in a process of self-healing? The next chapter looks at ways in which women have tried to do exactly that.

Reading and Notes

Bishop, Beata, "The Bridge of Dreams," *Caduceus*, Spring 1992, published by Caduceus, 38 Russell Terrace, Leamington Spa, Warwickshire CV31 1HE, pp. 8–9.

Castaneda, Carlos, *Tales of Power*, Pocket Books, New York, 1991, pp. 123ff.

Carroll, Lewis, *Through the Looking-Glass, and What Alice Found There*, Macmillan Children's Books, New York, 1980, p. 74 (first published 1872).

Life Before Death, television documentary shown on *Everyman* series, BBC1, 11 July 1993.

Matthews, Marti, "Death in a New Age," *Reality Change*, Vol 7, 3, pp. 20–25 (on her husband's death).

Native Australian "Dreaming": for an accessible introduction, see James G. Cowan, *The Elements of the Aborigine Tradition*, Element, Shaftesbury, Dorset, and Rockport, Massachusetts, 1992.

Roberts, Jane, *The Nature of Personal Reality*, a Seth Book, Prentice-Hall, New Jersey, 1974.

Zimmerman, Nan, "After the Dream Is Over," Montague Ullman and Claire Limmer (eds.), *The Variety of Dream Experience*, Continuum, New York, 1989.

12

Energy, Integration and Self-Healing

"*Just two nights ago I was dreaming that I'm in a bar sitting on one of these high chairs and drinking . . . Then my head starts to spin, feel dizzy. I told my friend I can't stand it any more being drunk. Everything started to spin around. I can't feel gravity, I'm up in the air. I was falling down from the high chair and as I fell down I was awake.*"

This woman had the above dream while she was living in London and her husband was stranded in their native country, Iran, without passport, work permit or permission to travel. She comments:

"My husband's situation needs me to be always aware of what's going on: maybe I can do something for him, maybe I can stop something bad happening. To keep him and our son going, and keep myself going—sometimes I think I just can't do it. This fainting means I'm trying to do something that my body can't cope with. If I just give up for a moment, I've lost.

"Recently I fainted in my dream and when I woke up I had all the symptoms of having fainted—your head is buzzy,

266

your body is like after an anaesthetic. You start hearing sounds, little spots coming into your mind, like lights and things . . . It is the state of mind I'm in, it is because of all the pressures on me.''

This woman's dreams, like several others in this book, highlight the very physical quality of some experiences in the sleeping body. While her daytime body soldiers on, one has the impression of another body which is reeling under the strain. Metaphors of fainting and drunkenness convey the sensation. Spinning, falling, flying, having a headache, shouting, taking initiatives—there is often a clear sense of things happening in a body, although it is not the body lying asleep in bed. We have met the term ''energy body'' which is used by many different disciplines to describe an energy field in and around the visible body. Whether or not you accept the concept of such an invisible energy, it can provide a useful model—metaphorical if not literal—for exploring dreams. It provides a tool for investigating what might be happening in the body during certain dream states. Thinking in terms of body ''energy'' can be combined with an understanding of emotional and other factors to contribute to a process of self-healing through dreams. The topics of these final chapters—astral travel, lucid dreaming, soul, reincarnation—can seem airy-fairy, but they do feature in women's dreams and should not be ignored. They can become more grounded and down-to-earth by being linked to processes happening in the body. This chapter will draw these threads together with the others we have explored and see how they can all be woven firmly into the physical fabric of life.

ENERGY AND DREAMS

In many teaching disciplines the ''energy body'' is not presented as anything mystical, but rather as an aspect of—or

extension of—the visible body, composed of energy movements in and around it. For example, in the teaching of the
healer Bob Moore, who works in Denmark, the energy body
or field is seen as part of our anatomy. Like the visible body
it is involved in various processes such as circulation and
elimination, and operates according to certain principles and
laws. Many understand the "weird" experiences of dreams
to be the result of activity in our energy field.

Using terms quite compatible with the Kahunas' teachings
about the "shadowy bodies" and Castaneda's "luminous cocoon" around the physical body (mentioned in Chapter 10),
many teachers of esoteric anatomy describe the energy field
as consisting of several different layers or "bodies." Clairvoyants report seeing these around every person. The
"etheric" body is close to the skin and stores energy for the
visible body to use. Then the "astral" body extends up to
three feet around the visible body; this is the layer where
emotional conflicts and blockages are held. The "astral"
layer is also the one involved in "out-of-body" experiences
or "astral travel" as described in Chapter 10, and it is this
faculty in us which is believed to pick up visions of angels,
devils and so on. Such visions can be understood as reflecting
a genuine event or incursion in the "energy field," one
which is however mediated and shaped by the cultural conditioning and emotional blockages which are held in the astral layer. As a result an individual's vision—whether of the
Virgin Mary or of a "spirit guide"—is not taken as gospel
or understood as an accurate perception of entities "out
there."

The "mental" aura is described as forming a sphere, with
fluctuating boundaries, around the head and shoulders; this
is the area which is understood as holding our beliefs and
decision-making activities. The outermost or "soul" level is
seen as encircling the physical body three feet or more away
from it; this layer is believed to carry our "qualities" which
seek to express themselves in our lives in as much as our

problems, resistance and blockages allow them to be channelled into our daily physicality.

Clairvoyants describe seeing these layers, as well as various scars, colours, movements and blockages within them. Details vary, but their accounts broadly agree that within each of these "bodies," and throughout the visible body itself, there are a large number of special points and energy streams and circulations—as in acupuncture. They also describe seven energy centres in the etheric layer, which are often called "chakras": the "root" chakra at the base of the spine; the "hara" centre on the belly; the "solar plexus" chakra; the "heart" chakra; the "throat" chakra; the "pineal" chakra on the brow; and the "crown" chakra on the top of the head. These are seen by clairvoyants as translucent cone- or trumpet-shaped protuberances with the tip of the cone towards the physical body (like a bell with its top attached to the body and its wide end sticking out at right angles); each one is like a vortex within which the energy rotates in a circular fashion, spiralling into and out of the body. They are believed to draw needed energy into the visible body, linking with endocrine glands, and to discharge unwanted energy out of it. Blockages in a chakra are seen as opaque spots; they impair its energy circulation and may impair the person's functioning in the areas of living which the chakra serves.

Different vibrations of colour are thought to correspond to different vibrations of energy, and each chakra is associated with a colour of the rainbow spectrum (from red at the root chakra to yellow at the solar plexus, blue at the throat and violet on the crown). As I described more fully in *Moving Heaven and Earth*, each chakra is also involved with processing a particular quality of energy relating to one aspect of our functioning. Thus the root energy relates to our ability to "take root" in the physical world, in such areas as housing, sex "drive," work, or eating the food we need; the "hara" is the centre of vitality, sexual pleasure, aggression and calm; the "solar plexus" chakra relates to processing and transmuting raw emotions like fear, anger and jealousy, rather as the stomach digests food; the heart relates to compassion, sorrow and joy; the "throat" chakra energy is linked with discrimination and expressing yourself; the "pineal" chakra on the brow is to do with the "mind's eye" or "third eye," intuition and intellect; and the crown with the development of the whole.

Some dreams seem to be concerned with what is happening in this "energy body," with the colour and flow of energy, or with the chakras:

"I dream I look in through a door and there standing in the kitchen in a red plastic bowl on the floor (like people might use if they haven't got a bath) is a person, grown-up but boy-like—a teenage young man/urchin who is born of the same father as me but has a different mother."

The woman who had this dream commented: "This felt to me like a kind of rebirth (admittedly from a kitchen washing-up bowl rather than, like Aphrodite, from the ocean). I felt that it was to do with centring and a source, especially in my life's work. The boy/child figure felt young and strong and intact. One of my dream group commented that this seemed to represent a strong part of myself that has been there all along, unrecognised. This felt right. Another of the group commented on the roundness and the redness of the bowl and wondered whether it was associated with the root chakra. This felt appropriate too. It was like a starting again, washed new, from the ground up. It felt significant that the figure had a different mother from me, as if I were envisaging a less damaged inheritance."

For those who subscribe to this view of the energy body, dreams without a storyline, where colour is emphasised, where geography or anatomy are important, or where there are geometric symbols or rotating elements, may be viewed as reflecting developments, circulations and conflicts in a person's energy field. This kind of interpretation does not clash with understanding dreams as reflecting emotional developments and conflicts, in fact they are quite consistent. If you cut your finger, the pain you feel and the blood that flows are both different aspects of the same experience. Similarly, feeling sadness or any other emotion can be linked to a corresponding movement in your energy field which is a different aspect of the same experience. Emotional events or blockages are seen by clairvoyants in the energy field, and expressing an emotion can release or clear these blockages. A dream may approach the experience from either angle— unleashing the sadness itself ("a sad dream") or showing a symbol for the movement or blockage of that sadness in the energy field. In this way a black dog peeing in a dream might reflect a release of energy from the lower half of your body (the dog peeing suggesting a natural process of release or relief in the "animal" part of the body, the colour black indicating—as it often does—a healthy protection through this change or transition). The release might be of anger, and at another time the anger itself might be expressed in the dream more obviously; these might be two alternative ways of showing the same experience. A dream of a blocked toilet may reflect problems of clearing energy from your root chakra; it might also reflect constipation and/or an emotional blockage, resistance or fear about throwing away household junk, and again all of these might be different aspects of the same problem, a difficulty with elimination and letting go, which may be manifesting both emotionally and physically.

The problem which the dream presents can be tackled on any of those levels: in practical life; in exploring emotions; or in working on "body energy." For example, practically it is possible to experiment with different patterns of eating, sleeping or housecleaning, changing a job or looking at a relationship. Equally it can be helpful to express some of the emotions carried in the dream, such as fear or sadness, as in

many examples in this book. Or one can work on the energy
field directly through massage, healing or meditation. *In Our
Own Hands* gives some simple meditations, and there are
exercises to help the functioning of the chakras in *Moving
Heaven and Earth* and in Diane Mariechild's *Mother Wit*.
There are also simple experiments, like seeing how it feels
to wear clothes of a colour which featured in your dream.
Working on the chakras and body energy can have an effect
on everyday behaviour; equally, changing patterns in daily
life through talking, emotional clearance or new habits, may
help clear the circulation of the chakras. Like all theories and
models of the human make-up, this model of our energy
structure is debated, and taught in slightly varying versions
by different disciplines. Like all dream interpretations, these
too have to be considered tentatively and checked against
what feels right to the dreamer.

Here is an example of a series of dreams which might be
reflecting some inner knowledge in the dreamer about what
is happening in her chakras. Kim had been coming to me for
massage therapy and had quite often described dreams which
seemed interesting and important but which did not lend
themselves to being understood in any of the usual ways.
Then in April 1993 she recounted the following dream:

*"I am in a six- or eight-sided greenhouse. It is gloomy inside
but early summer outside with lush vegetation and a river
nearby. I am with another woman. She leaves and a man
who seems quite wide and solid comes in. I realise I am
wearing a dress which has short sleeves made from a kind
of net or gauzy material with dark spots on it. I know that
the man has malevolent intent and that he is going to rape
me. I keep moving around, talking at him all the time to keep
him at bay. He doesn't speak. Another man who is tall and
pale comes in, and starts talking to him. I slip out the door
and wake up."*

The previous week, as on several earlier occasions, I had done massage work on Kim's chakras. Struck by the lack of strong personal associations or emotions in the dream, by the shape of the greenhouse, and the emphasis on the characters "moving around" it, I suddenly wondered whether it was reflecting the circulation of a chakra. Each chakra rotates at a different rate, and it is the "hara" chakra on the belly which is thought of as having a six-fold circulation. The "wide, solid" man might be thought of as representing a blockage in the chakra which is experienced as problematic, but which is dealt with by fresh input (the other man entering). The spots in the gauze of the dress sleeves might also represent blockages in the chakra funnel, which are seen by clairvoyants as solid, opaque "spots." Interesting too is the dream's emphasis on talking as a protection, since at the time Kim was ill with a disease affecting her thyroid at her throat as well as her eyes. She comments: "In my journal I have written that I remember other dreams of male violence that began when I was first ill with my thyroid." Expression, and especially the expression of anger that had been suppressed and silenced, was an important theme for her during this period.

This possible interpretation recalled a number of other dreams, involving circles, hollows, and circulation, several of which were explicitly linked to her illness. In September 1992 she had had a dream where:

she was walking along a clifftop with another woman when a man appeared and offered for a small fee to show them the "deepest hole in the world." This looked like a large shallow hollow in the ground covered with long grasses rippling in the wind. The dreamer sat and then realised that she was slipping slowly into the hole.

She commented that afterwards, "I laugh about sitting on the deepest hole in the world without knowing it. When asked where it is in my body, I find it seems to be in my belly. During massage I experience there a spiral of shimmering and changing colours, although it is incomplete and comes and goes. At my heart I get an image of a very deep gunshot wound.''

Kim later found on a piece of paper notes about another dream from earlier that year, in which:

she stands between two pools in the grounds of a country mansion talking to a friend who has lost her appetite. One of the pools has poisonous snakes in it, and the dreamer feels bad because she is not helping another friend who is moving in/out of the mansion.

The link to her illness comes at the end of the dream when:

''Someone is going to give me healing but there is a message for me to ring the consultant at St. Bart's hospital. I know he wants to lecture me about my thyroid.''

This reminded me of an earlier dream Kim had told me, in which she had borrowed a grey open-framed tandem bicycle.

Soon after the greenhouse dream, came a dream involving a friend's contact lens case:

''After a massage session I dreamt that I was in the field where the women's camp had been. In the dream there was a big shallow hollow covered with long grasses . . . swirling round. There were women in the dream but the only one I recognised was a woman I had been very attracted to. She gave me her contact lens case which is more complicated than mine (by turning part of the round lid, the lenses which are held in little round cases revolve, thus cleaning the lenses). It was blue.''

Two pools, two wheels on a bicycle, two lens cases, revolving; grasses swirling round: the theme of circulation recurs. The throat or thyroid chakra is associated with light blue, the brow chakra with purplish-blue or indigo, suggesting—in energy terms—a concern with discrimination, expression, or vision. Kim confirmed this and made links to her illness and healing:

"Looking at the dream . . . I located the swirling grasses in my solar plexus and the lens case in my third eye. It seemed to be about vision—cleaning up what I see or how I see. Which led me back to my belief that I could heal myself and maybe don't want to take on that responsibility.

"The image of the still centre (the inside of the lens case lid) with movement on the outside (the outer bit that rotates the lenses) that causes them to be cleaned, reminded me of the friend I am attracted to. How I see her as very centred and clear whilst I rush around being reactive with unrequited love.

"I felt that this centredness of hers is useful for me in reality—it gives me some safety. Also that it is something I want to cultivate in myself and would help to give me a clearer view of life."

In this series, what suggests that the dreams might be at least partly about movements and changes in the energy body is the lack of clearly dramatised character, action and emotion; the prominence of colour; and the recurrent theme of circulation linked to parts of the body. As we have seen, such an interpretation can co-exist with others: in the contact lens dream, for example, it seemed important—following the Gestalt principle—that Kim should acknowledge as her own potential the quality of "centredness" ascribed in the dream to her friend. Just as the emotional dimension of the dream could be taken further—using some of the techniques described in this book—so the information about body energy could be explored by meditating on the symbols and making contact with the chakras.

London psychotherapist Ann de Boursac developed a simple method to start finding out whether a dream can usefully be looked at in terms of body energy. First, select from a dream three or four elements which seem important. Then, with each symbol in turn, imagine the dream symbol in your body—perhaps shutting your eyes to focus on feeling the quality of it. Then draw it, not in a literal way but by expressing its mood or feeling graphically in shapes and colour. Then write by each picture—all on the same page—some words expressing the qualities of each, and jot down times in your life when you embody those qualities. So, the red washing-up bowl from our example might be drawn as a red circle with the words "calm, fluid, containing" and the dreamer might be aware of times in her life when she is like that. A blocked toilet might be drawn as a huge tangled mass, with the words "stuck, squashed, too much," and so on. Now take a few minutes for some relaxing breathing and to become aware of your body; a good exercise is to start at the bottom of your spine and slowly move your awareness up the back of your body and then down the front again, noticing any sensations. Then ask yourself where in your body you would place each drawing: pelvis, chest, the whole spine, throat, shoulders, legs, or where? You may find that there is an interesting correlation with the site of one of the chakras, or that the symbol feels like a movement through the body, or something surrounding it or radiating from it. At the end, write on the same sheet of paper a sentence starting, "I need . . . ," based on what you have learnt from the drawings. (It might involve house clearance, improving your self-esteem, expressing yourself differently, having more time alone, getting support, making a separation or resolving a conflict.) Afterwards, take time to talk or write about what came up.

Again this exercise might lead into thinking about practical life changes; into bodywork (such as movement, massage or healing); meditation, role-playing, or any of the other techniques described in this book. Sometimes, however, dreams about body energy may be simply confirming a process that is going on below the surface, offering a progress report on changes happening in our underlying energy structure, which needs little interference. As Ann de Boursac put it: "Instead of seeing the watch-face, sometimes you see the cogs underneath. They may be hard to read, and may make sense only when you see the results on the face." In these cases all we need to do may be to trust the self-healing that is happening in the body, and wait until the results of the changes filter through into daily life.

It is different again when the cogs we see turning do not seem to be showing processes to do with this life, but unresolved conflicts from previous lives.

REINCARNATION

Jenny Cockell in her book *Yesterday's Children* gave an account of the chain of events that followed her recurrent dreams of being a woman called Mary in Ireland in the 1930s. This "Mary" was about to die and was very worried about who would care for the children she would leave behind. I saw Jenny Cockell, interviewed on a television documentary, explain that "the memories were a little bit like pieces of a jigsaw." She had images of a cottage in a village, of which she was able to draw a map. Hypnosis "sharpened up a great deal of the detail" and once the village was identified—Malahyde, north of Dublin—the hypnotist Jim Alexander was able to walk round it following her descriptions. They identified the cottage she described; one occupant in the 1930s was indeed called Mary and had died young. They located her death certificate, and traced the children's separate placement in orphanages. Starting with an appeal in an Irish newspaper, they eventually tracked down all the children, many of them now pensioners. They were all re-united for the television programme.

A strange story, but the issue of reincarnation is taken very seriously in some healing circles. The purpose of Jenny Cockell's dreams was apparently to complete a practical task and resolve unfinished business from a previous life by bringing back together a family of orphans scattered more than fifty years earlier. However, in other cases the need is seen as more to do with resolving inner conflicts. Roger Woolger, author of *Other Lives, Other Selves*, runs workshops internationally using a psychotherapeutic approach to past lives. The theory is that painful experiences in past lives may have left us with problems in this life; recalling the past-life memory, and re-living the pain, may help to heal the experience. A woman interviewed in the *Guardian* newspaper described how this approach had cured a chronic back pain which she had previously blamed on a childhood fall. In Roger Woolger's workshop she found a memory of a witch hunt in America: "I was in the middle of a circle of people chanting 'Kill the witch'. I was so desperate I ran off: I ran and ran to a ravine and fell. My back broke in the middle." Since doing the reincarnation work she had had no more back pain.

Like many "spiritual" issues and phenomena, an interest in reincarnation can become a glamorous hobby and a way of evading current problems. But there is a different way of approaching reincarnation, which links it to the body and to practical issues in the present. I will give the examples of two women whose dreams put them in touch with experiences suggesting past lives, experiences which were useful physically and practically for resolving issues in this life.

The first woman had read the Castaneda books (described in Chapter 10), and her unusual dreaming experiences began with her looking at her hands in a dream, as Castaneda is instructed to do by his teacher Don Juan. Two other aspects of her life situation are relevant. One is that during the time she had these experiences she was involved in moving house, and eventually bought a holiday chalet by the sea. The other is that during this time she was having difficulties at work in saying "no" to pressures from colleagues about projects she did not want to be involved with. She was afraid of losing her job, and at one point, when running through the debate in fantasy, she imagined one of the people at work condemning her to death in French. At another time, during meditation, she had a vivid image of a French Revolution Tribunal.

In one experience she found herself in a room with a bed in it. She looked at a photograph on the mantelpiece "and as I look at the figures in it, they keep changing and I realise I'm seeing all these people's past lives, back and back and back. Then I go up to the ceiling and then out of the house. I think, 'I'll fly to Paris. I'll look for the person I was during the French Revolution.' " She landed in a big hall where there was a long queue of people. In the queue was a poet. His name was Henri something. Arriving next to him she introduced herself: "I'm you in a much later life." He responded warmly; they went outside to a summerhouse-type building and made love.

Afterwards she asked a psychic about this experience and was told that she had lived during the French Revolution and had been brought to a tribunal where people were trying to manipulate her. She had refused, and had died as a result. This past situation provided a parallel to her current situation at work, where she felt people were trying to manipulate her and she was again saying "no." The "past life" experience helped her understand why it might be that saying "no" in her work context was so frightening and felt like a life or death issue. This encouraged her to stand her ground. She

was able to recognise that in her current work environment
she was actually surrounded by people who wished her well;
that she could say "no" and still be accepted by her colleagues. Making that past connection had cleared a fear
which was blocking her from standing up for herself in the
present. She was also prompted to re-connect with a long-
standing interest in reading French poetry, and in writing
herself—as if meeting the figure in the dream had enabled
her to reclaim a neglected part of herself.

Some months later, while she was in the middle of house-
hunting,

*she looked at her hands in a dream and decided to fly. She
flew out of London over the rooftops looking for somewhere
to live. She settled on a hill with a big tree on it, which she
could recall clearly on waking.*

*Some time later, in a dream, she found herself in a holiday
chalet and looked at her hands. She thought to herself: "I
can go anywhere. I'll go to the sea." She was paddling.
There were oak trees by the sea. She walked further and saw
a big building.*

This woman later bought a holiday chalet. What she found
striking was that when driving to the holiday chalet she noticed a hill which seemed identical to the one in her dream.
She thought no more about it until one day when she was
walking by the sea near her chalet and found herself on exactly the same piece of beach, with the oak trees, that she
had seen during her flying experience. She saw the same
building that she had seen in the dream, and found out that
it was a priory. She subsequently had more "memories"
about having lived in that area a few hundred years before.
Her images suggested that it had been a painful time which
had left her with unresolved issues about close relationships
now. Being in the holiday chalet at that place gave her an
opportunity to face, and work through, some of those issues.

In these examples, the gift of the dreams is to bring forward scenes which will help the dreamer to do what she needs to do in this life. It is not a question of flying away, but of living better, here, now.

The next example also shows "reincarnation" dreams being brought into the physical life of the present. Marie Perret had the following dream:

"I'm painting the head of a woman. It seems to be superimposed on top of another head. All around the head is dark red and I feel a lot of sadness and am crying as I paint. This is also a deep relief. The woman I paint seems to have mediterranean olive skin and dark hair . . . Then there are other people there . . . I say that all of this is to do with past lives."

Marie Perret linked this dream to the way that in waking life she was finding herself painting "one spontaneous portrait after another, over and over again." She felt that, in this painting process, she was:

"often releasing memories from past lives centuries ago. At the time of painting and in the weeks before I often went through very strong emotions, partly my own resistance, but also sorrow/anger/fear/revenge/self-dislike—all related to past lives—and related often to moments when there had been a crucial event. A moment when a belief was created. E.g. being the last one in a family of pioneers burying her last son, thinking 'There's really no God. Life is just suffering and pain. How could God do this to me?' And such memory structures would surface as part of an opening up and freeing."

Marie Perret identified a precise process whereby before and after the painting she would experience the gradual emergence of a memory from a previous life, associated with a particular emotion. At times, she felt that she could relate the memories and emotions to certain parts of her body. The

physical act of painting helped to bring out the memories
more clearly and vividly; and the colours and feeling of the
picture would help her link the past life to an area of the
body, a chakra, or a part of the energy field where a memory
was held. Reich suggested that childhood memories from this
life can leave a mark in the body, as a tension or block stored
in the muscle structure; and that linking in to that part of the
body can lead to recalling and releasing the memory and the
tension, together with any associated emotions (as described
in Chapter 6). Marie Perret describes a similar process with
past life memories. She found that by attuning to a past life
memory held in her energy structure, and unlocking her feelings about it, she was then able to shift a pattern or blockage
which she had been carrying with her as a burden. While
contacting and painting a memory she often had very intense
physical sensations:

"The last time it was as if my awareness became focused
on a point, and connected to this was a high-pitched sound.
Then I seemed to have a very heightened sensitivity, being
able to smell, see and just know a lot of details. This has
happened a few times with past lives, I think that it is like
going into the mental space where the memory is held . . . I
often feel very relieved to see and to get these pictures out.
The actual paintings are not really works of art!"

Such experiences would lead Marie Perret to a strong sense
of release. By locating and feeling a memory she would gain
a sense of letting go of the past experience, and would find
behind it "a deeper space . . . connected to a lot of freedom
and joy."

In the gradual process of a past-life memory building up,
dreams played an important part:

*"I'm in front of a circular hole in the ground that is con-
creted over. Then suddenly as we watch the ground gives
way and we fall to another level. Inside is a large white room*

with a tiled earthern floor—it is clean, well-preserved and cool. As if it had been preserved like a museum, at a special temperature, etc. There has been a herd of dogs and sheep living there—we let them out, they are young and in good health and run in the sunshine.

"Then I seem to be undoing a mummy that is lying on a table, and yet as I unwrap the cloth I find a kind of flat statue in the shape of a woman—full of engravings. It seems to be cracked at different places, and there are earrings, and flat pieces of wood with symbols painted on.

"A male friend is next to me, with his arm round me supporting me as I do this.

"Then I seem to be outside and talking to someone about this area of the earth that had always been boarded off."

Marie Perret describes her reactions on waking: "This dream was so intense that when I woke up I felt I had to make the statue in clay, which I did—and what turned out was very surprising. It was a woman who was connected to moon worship, and who came from a very ancient civilization in the Middle East . . . A woman who was in some way a priestess. The dream was linked to the hara chakra as the statue held a moon over this part of her body. It felt so incredible to make the statue because it felt like manifesting and bringing forward to the light of day what had seemed like a fragment of a very delicate parchment. Some hidden memory that surfaced from the dream world. What is important in artwork that is linked to the unconscious is that it gives one the chance to bring into form, to make tangible what has been formless and intangible. In doing this one slowly develops a trust in one's inner world until one day you realise 'Well, I have so many hundreds of paintings, so many statues—and yes, perhaps the reality that I have contacted for myself can have some meaning, can be of some help to others.'

"For some reason I think of Mary Daly here and her writings . . . it links to her thoughts about 'women who are mad enough to "step outside" but who do not wish to be cruci-fied for doing so'—the idea of women, human beings, being able to find from within themselves a meaning, a sense, a his/her story that allows them to evolve and grow freely in the present. This is the opposite of belief systems that have tried to clamp man-made ideas and ideals on society."

The process Marie Perret describes is a very physical one. Rather than looking to external belief systems, she seeks a meaning, a "her story," from within, which involves finding knowledge stored in the body. She links the memories in this particular dream to the energy centres at the root chakra (linked with grounding/the earth) and the hara chakra at the belly, the seat of vitality:

"the animals being freed is a feeling of my own instinct/vital energy which had been held back; I come into an area which had been boarded off . . . this space—this preserved place—had been kept safe, a dimension of my own con-sciousness that had been blocked off but was now re-accessible."

While the hara is the centre of vitality, the pineal chakra at the brow is the seat of intuition and intellect; Marie Perret finds that it is through blending her vitality and thought pro-cesses in doing her practical art work that she achieves un-derstanding: "I . . . feel that coming into contact with wisdom is linked to a balance in the hara chakra—and a balancing between the hara and the pineal . . . Wisdom and understanding about one's reality often comes in *doing*." She also feels that the body is an important factor: "This process that . . . I would call a search for my own individuality, my own wisdom and power beyond conditioning, has also been about reowning my body. All of these past life memories are somehow held as blockages in the mental aura which affect the physical body. And as I have gone deeper and deeper and have changed my attitudes, so I have got a better and better contact with my body.''

She clearly feels that carrying unresolved painful memories from past lives creates a blockage in the bodymind which cuts us off from our physicality and from a fuller awareness of ourselves; the process of clearance she describes gives the chance for a better sense of self and body.

And so we begin and end with the body. It seems that even apparently esoteric experiences—like visions, astral travel and reincarnation—belong in the context of the body and the practice of living. While many dream theories seem to compete with each other, as if it were a question of either/or, they are perhaps simply addressing different and partial aspects of our whole experience. The sexual, the intellectual, the emotional, even the ''spiritual,'' can be brought into the total physical framework of our bodymind. Do we have to search for one approach, or can we go beyond the limitations of received theories and beliefs to see dreams as being as varied as the experiences of waking life, as diverse as all our sensations and thoughts, a house with many doors, a forest with many paths? From regression to reincarnation, from politics to toothache, women have found that different dreams call for different approaches; and sometimes several different paths can be used to find a way to the heart of the same dream, as the next example shows.

THE ANSWER LIES NOT IN ONE BUT IN MANY: INTEGRATION

"I am with my lover, and his ex-girlfriend is sitting in the sink, blocking it. Instead of getting angry I simply turn the

tap on so that she has to move or will get wet. She sits herself behind the sink and starts sorting some long stalks of greenery with little pink flowers at the top.

"Then I am standing in the back garden of a little house with daffodils everywhere—all over the garden and bursting from every window of the house. I hold a daffodil in my hand and gesticulate: 'Oh, to be in England now that April's here!' "

This woman worked on her dream on five different occasions. What is striking is that each time she used a different approach, and each time she gained in understanding. Apparently contradictory approaches did not in fact conflict, but complemented each other to reveal a rich web of memories, emotions, inspiration, thoughts and "energy movements," all of which seemed to be contributing to the shaping of this simple dream. The first person who helped her with the dream was a therapist whose background was broadly psychoanalytic. The woman reports:

"I told him the dream. He was interested in some of the symbols, for example the flowers by the sink. Mostly I talked about my hatred and anger towards 'H,' the ex-girlfriend, and the damage she has done to my relationship over the years. My anger at my lover for being a soft touch—falling for her 'poor me' number again and again. 'I hate her! I hate her!' Then I explain to him that this is in the past: 'H' is a spent force now and my relationship is more secure; my feelings are at base about my mother's preference for my younger sister ('Poor little thing') and how wretched and unloved that made me feel."

Here the therapist emphasised acknowledging difficult feelings like anger, jealousy and hatred, and recognising the significance of childhood history. Later that week, however, this woman found that an entirely different face of the dream presented itself to her, when a friend came round in a temper:

"She flounced in the door, plonked herself in the armchair and made some comment about my place being a mess. I was tempted to make some cutting comment back, but I said to myself, 'Wait a minute, her anger is nothing to do with me.' I thought of the tap in the dream, and imagined clear water flowing over me, washing off her anger. Then I was able to make a joke of it, she relaxed, and things were okay between us. Later I meditated on the symbol of the water, and found it useful in a number of situations."

This kind of approach to a dream—finding a symbol which gives hope and then using it in a meditative way—is part of the legacy of Jung's work. Whereas her first dreamwork looked at the "negative" feelings, here a positive aspect of the dream came forward, offering her a new model of behaviour. Already in the dream the use of the tap is suggesting that she is capable of breaking the cycle of jealousy and reaction, transcending her anger to respond in a calm and impartial way. This is the other side of the coin, almost an opposite message, and yet equally clear within the dream itself. There were further revelations to come, this time when she told the dream to another friend:

"She reminded me that everything in the dream is me. I realised that one of the reasons I hate H so much is because she reminds me of a part of myself: manipulative, greedy, needy, seductive. 'I hate that. What can I do about it?' She replied: 'Put your arm round that part of you.' I started to notice the times I was behaving like H, sucking emotional responses out of other people. I had never really been able to admit it before, probably because before this I had not seen a possibility of forgiving it or changing. Perhaps I was outgrowing that part of me."

Here we see the understandings of Gestalt in use, when the dreamer—with some discomfort—recognised H as a part of herself. In another context she might have literally role-played or "spoken as" that part of herself, but in this case she simply lived with the dream's insight and applied it to her life.

So far the dream had been linked to her past (her jealousy of her sister), to an external drama in her relationship (H), and to an internal drama (about her own manipulative side). All those "interpretations" could co-exist. But there were still further layers of the dream to unpeel. At a workshop with Ann de Boursac she was led through the "dream energy" exercise described on page 277, which involved drawing dream symbols and finding where in the body they seemed to belong. She drew H in the sink; the water; and the daffodils at the end:

"H was a tangled mass of yellow and black lines, and the words to describe the symbol's qualities were 'tight, knitted, grabby.' I wrote that I am like that 'when I feel empty.' The daffodil was a springy 'V' shape in yellow with a black border; it looked ready to get up and fly away. Its qualities were 'expansive, open,' and I realised I am like that 'when I feel safe/loved.' When asked where in my body I would place the drawings, I felt immediately that the tangle was in my solar plexus, a blockage there. The water (long wavy lines in blue and white) seemed like the possibility of flow down my spine which could unblock that. The daffodil scene seemed like the possibility of a different way of expressing from the front of my body—less blocked, more generous. The expansive 'V' shape was like the shape of my out-stretched arms at the end of the dream."

Here this woman's intuitive feelings about her dream—expressed in free drawing—fit in with theories about the "energy body." According to these, the colour associated with the energy of the solar plexus chakra is yellow, so it is the place where one might expect to find a "tangled mess of yellow and black." It is also the chakra associated with raw feelings like anger and jealousy (present in the dream) which need to be dealt with before they can be transformed; black is a powerful, absorbent colour which could help this process of transformation. The solar plexus can then become the place from which love starts to express (the more generous mood of the daffodil scene, also in yellow and black?). It might also be thought relevant that a daffodil, like a chakra, is trumpet-shaped, so that the clear yellow trumpet of the daffodil perhaps presents the possibility of an unblocked solar plexus chakra.

With this locating of the dream's themes in the underlying "energy" structure of the body, one might think that its message had been exhausted. However, some days later the dreamer learnt more from a visit to a healer who worked directly on her energy field:

"I explained to him that I had been so exhausted for months that I was worried about my health. He said he could see the problem right away: my defence system was not working and I was leaking energy from my solar plexus. (I had not mentioned the dream or anything.) He placed his hand on my solar plexus at the back and held it for ages. He said that he sensed I was struggling hard to prove myself all the time, pouring out energy indiscriminately. His words and the feeling of the hand on my back sent a wave of relief over me and I cried deeply. I had sensations in my solar plexus, and then in my heart area. Eventually he said he felt a movement of energy down from the top of my head, starting the process of healing the leaks. Afterwards I felt wonderful, though physically shattered, and had to lie down when I got home.

That was two weeks ago. Since then my back has felt like a waterfall (the dream tap?). I have also started to become aware of ways I pour energy out pointlessly, trying too hard, getting panicked, trying to please people. By pouring it out, I guess I also need to suck loads back all the time to replenish; that is when I get like H, needing to charm and impress people. It feels sloppy and abusive of myself and others, like a desperate child trying to get love by tantrums or wheedling. It isn't appropriate any more. Next time H came up in the conversation, instead of getting emotional or manipulative, I just looked my lover in the eye and said, 'I would like to be the only woman in your life.' After some deliberation he said, 'You are.' He might have said no, but at least it felt good to ask a direct question and get a direct answer.''

The last time this woman worked on the dream was in her dream group:

''I asked for help with the last part, the daffodil scene. They were surprised about the line from the poem—very English—something I usually turn my back on. They were struck by the sense of plenty with all the daffodils brimming. I remembered then that my younger sister had a teenage crush on that poet, so the dream is taking me back to then. I was always afraid that if I stretched myself/got attention I would be taking something away from her and would get 'slapped down' . . . The group pointed out that in the dream I was reclaiming that teenage time, taking the stage myself and having fun with my sister's favourite poet. I talked about ways of being expansive without dominating others: a more free, generous way to be rather than all the tugging and struggling. I felt the group support me in that. One of them said it reminded her of the water flowing from the dream tap. It was perhaps most of all their presence as caring friends—letting me be—letting me have attention in the group—no axes to grind—being a bit like the water themselves—it made me feel that change is possible and that the expansive teenager yearning to spread her wings is okay after all. They

made a place for her in the group and that made me feel she
can have a foothold in the world.''

Here, the role of the group was important in giving a social
reality to the changes this woman was going through, which
seemed to be affecting her simultaneously on many different
levels involving physical and energetic factors; internal and
external conflicts; past memories and present relationships;
and her sense of social identity. For this reason it is perhaps
not necessary to ask whether the woman in the sink represents ''H'' *or* the dreamer's sister *or* part of the dreamer's
own personality *or* a blockage in her solar plexus. All these
interpretations can co-exist. Can this woman's solar plexus
turn from a knot of tangled energy to something as clear as
a daffodil? Can she resolve her jealousy, past and present,
and start to give and receive love? Can she stop trying so
hard and start behaving more directly and expressively?
These are not incompatible ways of looking at the dream,
but like different sides of a diamond which she is holding in
her hand. This book has described a series of different ways
of understanding dreams, and each has added a new perspective to the other.

GODS, SYMBOLS AND ENERGY

The possibility that some dreams may be reflecting movements in the dreamer's energy field adds a fresh viewpoint
on religious and mythological interpretations. It suggests that
sometimes a numinous element in a dream—translated on
waking as Virgin Mary, Goddess, Devil, hero, Shadow, Wise
Man, Cosmic Egg, child-saviour archetype or Jesus Christ—
might actually represent a particularly powerful energy con-
figuration or resource around or in the dreamer's body, which
is becoming available for her to access. Christians dream of

Christian deities, Moslems dream with Islamic symbols, suggesting that profound night experiences are mediated through the symbolic clothing available in the dreamer's culture—even before the waking process of interpreting and assigning meaning to the dream. How often is the language of personification, religion and myth used to clothe what are in essence physical processes?

We have seen several examples of spinning dreams, and falling dreams. According to Kilton Stewart in the journal *Fire*, a Senoi child with such a dream would be told

> "Falling is the quickest way to get in contact with the powers of the spirit world, the powers laid open to you through your dreams ... The falling spirits love you. They are attracting you to their land, and you have but to relax and remain asleep ... you may be frightened of their terrific power, but ... you are only receiving the powers of the other world, your own spiritual power which has been turned against you, and which now wishes to become one with you if you will accept it."

Using the term "falling spirits" personalises the forces at work in the dream, as if they reflect the activities of denizens of "another world" who can behave in friendly or unfriendly, helpful or unhelpful, ways—rather like the citizens of this world. This makes the dream experiences seem more manageable, more known. What if we let that language of personification fall away? Then we are left with forces or energies at work. For "the falling spirits love you" one could read: "this is a benign and necessary energy processing experience which needs your cooperation—go with it!" Like the physical body, the energy body is continually involved in processes of circulation, digestion, assimilation, self-healing and elimination, and these may impinge on our dreams just as digesting cheese on toast may. And just as the physical body is kept going by external resources of food, light, heat, and human contact, so the energy body is fed by external sources of energy in sun, earth, atmosphere, other people and the natural world generally. So, a magical dream helper may represent an emerging strength in your personality and a powerful external resource which you are accessing in your energy field; and these may again be different ways of saying the same thing.

As Jane Roberts put it in her Seth book *The Nature of Personal Reality*, "Images as you *think* of them are based upon your own neurological structure, and your interpretation of these." She points out that perception without images seems impossible to us, and yet: "in some dream situations you enter a state of awareness quite divorced from . . . sense data. Images as such are not involved, though later they may be manufactured unconsciously for the sake of translation." Perceiving our experiences more directly, and gaining new understandings, becomes harder if we get attached to a fixed system of dream symbol interpretation—whether psychological, religious, or mythological. The question for me is always how we can use dreams to free and empower ourselves rather than to get trapped in new systems and beliefs.

Reading and Notes

Cockell, Jenny, *Yesterday's Children*, Piatkus, London, 1993.

Ernst, Sheila, and Lucy Goodison, *In Our Own Hands: A Book of Self-Help Therapy*, The Women's Press, London, 1993, pp. 180–85 (first published 1981).

Goodison, Lucy, *Moving Heaven and Earth: Sexuality, Spirituality and Social Change*, Thorsons SF, San Francisco, 1992.

Mariechild, Diane, *Mother Wit: A Feminist Guide to Psychic Development*, Crossing Press, Trumansburg, New York, 1981.

Roberts, Jane, *The Nature of Personal Reality*, a Seth Book, Prentice-Hall, New Jersey, 1974, p. 455.

Stewart, Kilton, "Dream Theory in Malaya," *Fire*, 1, July 1967, published by Fire, 4 St. George's Terrace, London NW1, p. 5.

Woolger, Roger J., *Other Lives, Other Selves*, Bantam, New York, 1988. Also interviewed in the *Guardian* by David Rowan, 16 December 1991.

13
Bridging Night and Day

The patriarchal approach to dreams has been to set them in a world apart and suggest that world can be grasped only through a series of mystical systems or therapeutic theories. In this way we have become estranged from half of our experience. Can we reach across the divide between conscious and unconscious, night and day, to own our dreams as a part of life no more and no less mysterious than the rest?

This chapter explores ways of bringing the creations of night and day together. This involves recognising that our dreams are not a strange land but our own home ground of which we have been disposessed. The colonisers have often been professionals—or peers—armed with the tools of "interpretation."

THE TOOLS OF INTERPRETATION: WHOSE DREAM IS IT ANYWAY?

The fascination with dream dictionaries reflects a need to have someone tell us what our dream means. Does it have a hidden, unpalatable, shameful or sexual message? Is it a sign of archetypes at work and something wonderful about to happen? In this book I have questioned whether a dream has any one fixed meaning, and whether, even if it has, another person can tell us about it. Having your dream interpreted by another can in some cases be a way of being robbed of it.

A classic example of this is in the traditional relationship between psychoanalyst and patient. Freud's writings reveal several examples where he presses a dream interpretation on to an unwilling patient. In *A Case of Hysteria* he describes the treatment of a young woman named Dora whose dreams reflect her feelings about receiving sexual approaches from a friend of her family, a married man Herr K. Freud's interpretation of these dreams shows much skilful detective work. However, his account makes painful reading because some of his remarks seem coercive, for example, his insistence that Dora is actually in love with Herr K. She is in a no-win situation as the more she denies this, the more he is convinced it is true:

"My expectations were by no means disappointed when this explanation of mine was met by Dora with a most emphatic negative. The 'No' uttered by a patient after a repressed thought has been presented to his conscious perception for the first time does no more than register the existence of a repression and its severity; it acts, as it were, as a gauge of a repression's strength."

We seem here perilously close to the old chestnut that sometimes when a woman says "no" she means "yes." One wonders how often patients yielded through attrition, in an unequal contest which a woman patient of a male professional could not hope to win. Even if the unacceptable interpretations were correct in Dora's case, she is evidently not ready to use them. The process of having them forced on her is unlikely to help her recover from real-life experiences of having her wishes over-ridden and her world view dismissed.

Good practitioners working in the Freudian tradition nowadays are adamant that such imposing of interpretations is bad practice and is simply no longer done. But Rosemary Dinnage's *One to One: Experiences of Psychotherapy* gives differing accounts of women's experience. One describes how in analysis she felt pressure to assent to interpretations and remembers "the feeling of being a sort of prisoner in interrogation—you know, whether he's guilty or not he eventually shouts, 'I did it! I did it!' " Another woman describes asking herself why she was getting up at six in the morning to go to her session "and what for? For another person to tell me I'm lying! But at the same time . . . you know that you're avoiding something and you know that today something will be found out . . ." The important thing, especially for women, seems to be finding out appropriate things, without feeling invalidated in the process. As another of the women quoted in the book puts it: "You do have a capacity to see yourself, and they override it, they undermine it. My sense of myself is tremendously important to me, and if I'm enclosed somewhere with someone and no verification, then I'm at this person's mercy."

The dilemma of weighing up the pros and cons of seeking professional help was expressed dramatically in one dream which was sent in. This woman had started making a special effort to record and think about her dreams, as she was seeing a famous and expensive therapist for short-term help with them.

She dreamt she was late cooking supper for her family and, rushing up to the kitchen, was grateful to find that an older woman—resembling the therapist—had already prepared supper. Then she saw what the meal was—peanut butter sandwiches—and thought that this had not after all been much help: "Peanut butter sandwiches! I can do that myself!"

The next day in her session she realised that the therapist
was again telling her little that she did not already know
about herself, and as she left it came to her: " 'Peanut butter
sandwiches! I can do this myself! I don't need to pay great
amounts of money to tell me what I already know about
myself!' . . . I had learned that week that any time I wanted
to remember and understand a dream I could, by putting out
the effort."

Many dreamers writing in this book have been helped by
professionals, but this woman's dream makes an important
point: we can also do it ourselves.

There is an imbalance of power between therapist and client, and any professional practitioner however good—
whether Freudian or humanistic, Gestalt or Jungian—can
make a misjudgement about a dream. The result may be that
the dreamer feels misunderstood or even pressurised. She
may feel that by turning to a self-help dream partnership or
group, she is escaping such experiences. But sadly the same
thing can happen with peer dreamwork, however experienced
or well-intentioned your friend or group may be. Like any
therapist, a peer helper may be influenced by sore points the
dream touches in her own life, or by her feelings about the
dreamer, or by information or assumptions she holds about
the dreamer's life which suggest connections to the dream.
("This reminds me of when you were rude to me on the
phone last week . . ." "You were talking about difficulties
with your boyfriend, does the broken-down car represent
your relationship?") Group members may misunderstand or
misjudge things, or unconsciously gang up to assert their
consensus about a dream's meaning, so that a dreamer again
feels that an interpretation is being imposed on her. To guard
against this, it is important for group members to listen to
each dream afresh without value judgements or preconceptions, and allow time to absorb and respond to it before
thinking about connections to the dreamer's life. As Robin
Shohet pointed out in *Self and Society*, it is important:

that the dreamer feels in charge of what she/he wants to share and of the whole process and should say if something does not feel right. One way of working is for the dream sharer to pick out someone whom they would like to facilitate their work. (It is important that the chosen person feels able to say no.) This has some advantages in pursuing one approach but should not rule out other members being able to follow a strong hunch. After a group has been together a while the group tends to tune in together to the dreamer.

As this sense of resonance develops, people become versed in each other's dream symbols, like being familiar with a painter's or a musician's work. Rather than interfering or imposing, they learn how to listen, can begin to pick out themes and ask relevant questions. Beth Shaw comments:

"I really like the continuity of the dream group . . . that this small group of people knows that dream side of me, and yet there's still more to say, more to hear, more to unravel . . . Each of us seems to have our own unique dream vocabulary, dream landscape and 'blind spots.' The dream group is very useful at gently pointing out those blind spots: 'Hang on, you said you passed a skeleton in the cupboard . . . that happened in that other dream, does that mean anything to you in your life at the moment?' "

The quality of work in a dream group depends on the quality of the relationships. We are vulnerable even in a peer group to believe someone else knows best. Our culture encourages competitive rather than group-sharing skills; it requires good will and hard work to allow the mini-society of the dream group to develop a sense of community where each person is accorded respect and autonomy. *In Our Own Hands* explored ways of dealing with difficult issues which may come up in a self-help group: one person may dominate by talking too much or by withholding; the group or individuals in it may be very resistant to working deeply; unexpressed feelings between group members may get in the way; there may be fears or taboos; group members may lack confidence in their skill and ability to help each other, and so on. Such problems can be tackled within the group, and there is also the possibility of calling in skilled help for a session or two to sort them out.

There are very many different ways of working with dreams, which suit different people. For some people guided visualisation, group drawing and story-telling, for example, may be easier than acting a monster or experiencing childhood emotions. The important thing is for each person to have the space to find their own way of working and their own pace to open up—as in the following example:

"I was in the dream group a long time before I could ask for help with my dreams . . . I'd choose a dream, work out beforehand what I wanted to say about it and then sort of 'sew it all up.' Though I felt desperate for help, I couldn't allow myself to receive it. Came the day when I finally said, Here's a dream and I don't know what to make of it one bit. They said 'Thank goodness for that, maybe we can be of some help then', and so I started letting them help me."

When trust develops which allows people to help and be helped, group dream work gives a feeling of deep satisfaction. The basic necessity is for listeners to have their sets adjusted for maximum receptivity. The person who holds the key to the dream is the dreamer herself.

CHILDREN'S DREAMS

Children's dreams are illuminating, because for them the chasm between night and day has not yet yawned open; they can still bridge the two. Young children have not yet been robbed of their dreams. Freud believed they were the only ones to have undistorted dreams—presumably because they had not yet learnt the necessity or the means to disguise their feelings through indirect dream symbolism. I believe that adults can also dream directly without disguise, but there is sometimes a breath-taking candour about children's dreams. Linda Dove records the following two dreams which her children told her:

"Abbie had a pretty straightforward seven-year-old's dream the other day—she dreamt she slept through Christmas and woke up on Boxing Day!

"And Mia had a heart-wrenching one—she dreamt she and Abbie were sitting on the couch opening their Christmas stockings. Abbie had present after present after present and opened them eagerly. Mia had just one and it turned out to be just wrapping paper. Apparently the dream was so real it spoilt the real stocking-opening on the couch later."

It does not occur to children that their dreams are not theirs, or that someone else knows best about them. With encouragement, they engage enthusiastically with their nighttime world. This same Mia evidently took active steps to prevent more nightmares like the one above, because she wrote to me, "I herd you are working on a book about dreams. I am macking a dream-catcher to make bad dream go away and good dream go through." The dream catcher—I was sent one—is made of a piece of twig bent and tied in a circle, with thread stretched in a web across the circle. It is decorated with feathers, beads and shells and you are meant to hang it over your bed, though I have mine at my window as I imagine dreams coming in that way. The idea is based on a Native American tradition, and the materials are marketed as a kit in the USA; but it would be easy to make one from available odds and ends and natural objects.

In traditional Freudian theory, even a nightmare can be construed as wish-fulfilment, because it can be seen as the re-enactment of a feared punishment, to get it out of the way as it were. More recently ideas about nightmares have been influenced both by Jung's positive emphasis and by the alleged practices of the Senoi people, who are said to discuss their dreams every morning and encourage their children to confront dream enemies and to cultivate "dream friends" to help them do this. An example of how these ideas can be used creatively with children is given in the following account by Anne Wade of helping her son Felix with his dreams:

"I talked to Felix about dreams from an early age. I shared my feeling of going to sleep with pleasurable anticipation.

"He generally enjoyed his dreams, but he had two series of nightmares when he was about three. One was of a witch, and one of a lion. I reminded him that they were his figures, and he had the power to deal with them as he chose, that it's better not to turn one's back or run away but to try and remember, while you're asleep, that you can make them do as you want. Sometimes you may want to make friends with them. Sometimes it's enough to tell them what they must do.

"He was sleeping on a sunbed alongside our bed, and was free to come in with us when he wanted. I got him a little torch with a wristband, so he could wear it and find it if he woke, and which only stayed on as long as the switch was being pressed. He had various other torches, including a light-sword which was very helpful in combatting dream enemies, but they were expensive to use as they tended to get left switched on.

"He dealt with the witch by taking a selection of weapons to bed one night; he woke with great disappointment because she hadn't appeared, and he didn't feel she would do so again. I pointed out that he had won: she had run away, because he was stronger than she was, and if he decided he wanted to talk to her, no doubt she would come back and do so.

"He may have been affected by my awareness that it's useful to hang on to negative figures and transform them rather than lose them into the unconscious. But I think that may be less important for children, whose fantasies are so active and mobile, and who have many avenues for this inner growth through play and imagination. Anyway, I felt it was vital that I affirmed his ways of handling them without intruding except when he asked for help.

"He dealt with the lion partly by taking weapons to bed, but also a selection of torches, and by making friends with him. He went on to develop a large contingent of dream friends, spiced with the odd dream enemy who was a nuisance rather than a problem . . . I have a note he wrote some time later: 'Dream friends are animals who used to live under the bed.' "

Anne Wade regretted that her son's dream figures became more rigid and elaborated during an inhibiting and pressurised year at school. However, there are also teachers imaginative enough to use dreams in the classroom. In *Fantasy and Feeling in Education* Richard Jones regrets that our educational practices in the West have "developed intrinsic postures of dourness with respect to what really matters to children—what excites, bemuses, and impassions them," and suggests that this is what makes school so typically boring. In contrast, he cites the example of an elementary school teacher working in the USA in the first grade, Elena Werlin, who instituted a "dream-time" in her classroom. The children accepted the idea calmly, and she insisted on quiet, reminding them that silence would help them recall their dreams.

It is clear from Elena Werlin's own article describing this work that her intention was not to analyse the children's dreams, but rather to make a space where their imaginative and emotional faculties were allowed, and could be included in classroom activities. She also made a habit of asking the children at least four times a week to "close their eyes and get pictures to a story, a piece of music, or just in silence." She shared with them some of her own dreams, and told them about the pictures she saw when listening to music or sitting in silence. She expresses her hope that:

". . . over the year I will be able to help the children use their preconscious thoughts for enriching the way they listen to the music, draw, work with clay, make up stories, dramatize them, or just in classroom conversations."

For example, one girl had a short dream about a witch chasing her while she was "trick-or-treating"; this was used as the basis of a story to which the whole class contributed. Sometimes Elena Werlin would ask for certain types of dreams, for example about animals, or their parents, or about her: this seemed to help the children to bring forward dreams which might otherwise have seemed too threatening.

Through her work she developed with her class a common culture of words, images and characters which could be used creatively whether to learn spelling or to deal with classroom tensions. She gives the example of a boy named David, who in the first month of school often had tantrums. On one occasion when he was angry with her—and she admits the feeling was mutual—she said to him: " 'I wish I could send you to that giant you dreamed about. He'd make you behave!' David countered: 'If you did, I would kill the giant.' Then we threw a few joking barbs at each other and the sun could shine again. I think this helps David to express his annoyance verbally instead of physically." This exchange is also "held" by the rest of the children hearing it and being able to place it in a shared vocabulary of symbols and characters: "They know David's dream and can participate vicariously. David and I have shown that we're both bigger than his giant and it makes a nice demonstration to all concerned how anger can be used in a safe way . . ."

As Richard Jones points out, this approach encourages children to believe that their feelings and images have a central place in school and in the learning process. Such pioneering work shows that night imagination can come out of the shadows and interact creatively with daytime collective life.

DREAMS INTO ACTION

Having a bridge to your night awareness means the possibility of being guided into action by your whole self and not just by your waking consciousness. Being able to use dreams to make decisions and fresh starts or use a dream to gain insights into current relationships, means allowing dreams to interact with life—a process which is not common in our society. In our culture, letting your unconscious mind guide you can be seen as "superstitious," while following your conscious mind is seen as "rational"—despite the evidence that its choices often take us in a wrong direction. Dreams, psychotherapy and the emotional life are usually seen as an internal and private matter.

In contrast, feminist therapy has suggested that social oppression causes most of the conflicts, low self-esteem and powerlessness which bring women into psychotherapy, and that as a response therapy alone is not enough: action is needed. Recognising the isolation of many women, this approach also stresses the importance of women getting together to develop solidarity which can empower their actions. Running groups for activists in California, Jeanne Adelman-Mahoney told me that she worked on two assumptions: first, that distress and many of the events of the inner life have a social cause; and secondly, that all else being equal, we feel better when we're doing something about it. Despite some advances and changes in social attitudes, the fundamental social inequalities between men and women remain: in reality things have not improved that much for women since the rebirth of feminism in the 1960s. Women's position at work, at home and in the street is still often under-paid, under-valued and under threat of violence, and this reality is reflected in women's dreams.

Although they have been challenged as valid field research, accounts of the alleged Senoi practices offer a useful model or metaphor for bridge-building between dream world and social world. In their lively interplay between the two, the Senoi are claimed to have recognised dreaming as the deepest type of thought which provides solutions to the problems of the day. Kilton Stewart, in the journal *Fire*, was prompted to wonder whether "modern civilisation may be sick because people have sloughed off, or failed to develop, half their power to think. Perhaps the most important half." He also points out that through daily communal dream-sharing and discussion, the individual's deeper self can be acknowledged and validated by a sympathetic social authority; in this way the maximum energy is freed from conflict and anxiety, and made available to engage in socially constructive action. What happens in a women's dream group is perhaps something similar on a smaller scale: by establishing a mini-social authority which validates our innermost experiences, we become less internally divided and more empowered in the outer world.

Here is an example from contemporary London showing this process at work, as dreams bring forward issues which call for action in the daytime world of the present, and help to empower that action. A women's group of young women with learning difficulties, meeting regularly at the Elfrida Rathbone Centre in London at sessions facilitated by Jane Gilmore, devoted several afternoons to looking at their dreams. Some of these reflected feelings of vulnerability, fear and concern for physical safety:

"This man try to force me to do sex while I am sleep in bed and dreaming. I wake up from my dream and saw him there on top of me and I try to scream but I could not because I was scared stiff."

"I was in the train at Holborn Station. The train went fast into the tunnel and it was wobbling from side to side and it wasn't very nice at all. The train nearly crashed in the tunnel. I couldn't see but the front of the train fell off the track. My legs and arms and face got squashed and my glasses and watch got broke."

Many of the group's dreams, however, spoke about things they wished for, in particular sexual relationships:

"Last week I met George Michael down the road and went over to him, asked for his autograph ... He was wearing a suit, nice colour. He looked handsome, gorgeous. I felt great I gave him a kiss gave him a red rose. Then he had a nice car took me in his car drinking champagne, feeling wonderful. Then he took me to meet his family."

"Jane was in my dream in Spain. She was in the hurry because this Man stop her and Kiss her. She feel in love him and she met me at the Beach and told me I said Wow about time what you did today Well I Met My Boyfriend called Pete was kiss me in the water I was Naked he was Naked too So we had a good time doing Sex. I was touching him on his back he put his finger through my hair ..."

"I dream to get married in Trinidad and have a big house and sit in the sun with husband and three children and made West Indian food. The house is near the beach ... and there

are lots of people running about. I have three children, three girls—one is six and seven and three. They look a bit like their Dad and me. My favourite food is ackee and salt fish, rice and peas and chicken.''

In sharing their dreams, the young women were able to identify an issue which concerned them. The dreams about sex and about Trinidad, which had never been realised in real life, enabled them to interpret their dreams as reflecting some things they want to do in waking life. However, as Jane Gilmore pointed out, ''it became apparent that they don't feel as empowered in 'real' life as they do in their dreams. Carers (parents, teachers, and institutions) somehow protect them so much that they feel stifled or denied rights to have sexual feelings or indeed have sex.'' In the past there has been a tendency to regard people with learning difficulties as ''child-like'' and they have been denied the rights due to them as adults with sexual needs like everyone else. Attitudes change slowly. In this case the group decided they wanted to have a further session to discuss parents and carers of people with learning difficulties in relation to sex and sexual relationships. The dreams brought them directly into action in the world to try to change something they were not happy about.

MAKING DREAMS COME TRUE

At the end of his *The Instant Dream Book*, Tony Crisp gives an eight-step summary of ways to approach your dreams. Answering questions like ''Am I Active or Passive in My Dream?,'' ''How Can I Alter the Dream to Find Greater Satisfaction?,'' and ''Am I Limiting Myself?'' will, it is suggested, lead to greater success and satisfaction in sexual relationships and life in general. His is a useful and well-written book, but it reflects the tendency to reduce dreamwork to a formula. The positive life changes which can emerge from dreams happen organically, in their own way and their own time; they cannot be predicted, preconceived, or goal-oriented. While Freud and Freudians, Jung and Jungians have their own agendas about dreams, the newer humanistic psychotherapies—ostensibly more open and flexible—have tended to see dreams as fodder for what Robin Shohet calls "the Change/Self Improvement ethic." This sometimes presents itself as a kind of psychological "rags-to-riches" ideology, suggesting that by superhuman effort we can somehow crawl up a slippery ladder at the top of which spiritual and emotional satisfaction (and of course material success) beckon.

What is missing in all these approaches is doubt. The scramble to change and improve oneself though dreamwork may not be that different from the scramble to change and improve oneself through courses in successful marketing, management skills, self-presentation, assertiveness and "positive thinking." Do we want to get on that train? Is this how people really change? I myself like the quote I found on a leaflet produced by the Situationist movement: "People do not change: they only stand more revealed." This suggests a different process from scrambling up a ladder. What is interesting to me is how little we really know or understand about dreams; or indeed about how individuals or societies change. All existing dream theories are partial: all useful at times, as I hope I have shown in this book, but also provisional. Can we live experimentally with the not-knowing? Good practitioners, in dreams as in other fields, are rarely dogmatic. Can we accept that there may be many other levels operating than those we are aware of? What we see and understand about dreamwork—as about other aspects of human activity, imagination, relationships and interaction—is perhaps only the tip of an iceberg. The best we can do is to work at staying in a state of openness and readiness in order to pay attention, to be surprised and to learn.

This means clearing some obstructions. We need to clear the dead weight of authorities who have defined our experience and left us with a clutter of terminologies all claiming to be absolute. Our dreams and symbols are alive, and we can respond accordingly, rather than fitting them into the cupboards and drawers inherited from our own history, habit, and the received knowledge of others.

Another powerful and—I have suggested—damaging legacy lies in Western culture's splits between "conscious" and "unconscious," day and night, "rational" and "irrational," sun and moon, life and death, "man" and nature, spiritual and mundane, "divine" and "mortal." These divisions in themselves imply value judgements and have set a mould into which our experience is inevitably cast, unless we challenge them. Some women's experiences hint at a shift from this eternal polarised twosome to a worldview based on inclusion and circulation. In the dream notes she sent, Marie Perret suggests that "life is a circulation between heaven and earth"; to allow the unknown to become known, we need to stay open:

"...we need this constant renewal. We cannot live with static religions, with man-made ideas which attempt to impose the known on the unknown ... And the unknown is always evolving. There's a constant movement and interplay ... the physical being transformed by the non-physical and the non-physical being enriched by the physical."

If we did not rigidly hive off spirituality into churches, and dream-thinking into a separate nighttime world, our day-thinking might be rather different. As Paricia Monaghan wrote in a letter, "The resourcefulness of the mind in the dreamlife, the wonderful fluidity of the stories it presents, represents the greatest reserve of metaphor available to us."

It is not only a question of being conversant with our dreams, but of having access to that imaginative resource, that dimension of ourselves, to deal creatively with life as a whole. Reconciling the imaginative with the practical, the divine with the physical, transforms our sense of connection with our own bodies, other people, and the world around us.

One of the joys of writing this book has been my appreciation of the many honest, surprising, perceptive and courageous accounts that women have given me of their dreams, which are the backbone and the soul of the book. So I will end with a dream from Marie Perret about this process of questioning received structures and finding our own creativity. She writes:

"Being creative means to let go of the security of the known, to follow our intuition, and then to act on what we believe to be true. It is not easy to do this, because if we challenge existing structures, outside or within ourselves, we are confronted by our own fears, our own conditioning . . . Around the time I started to paint I had a vivid dream:

"I was sitting on top of a mine shaft that went deep into the earth. I was told that I was going on a journey. I replied that I was afraid of what was between the black and the white."

"The black" here, as so often, seems to stand for the unconscious. In this book I have suggested that our culture's rigid divisions between conscious and unconscious, waking and sleeping, light and dark, are not absolute but a reflection of social divisions between male and female, white and black. Instilled by conditioning, sustained by existing social structures, those symbolisms in turn reinforce the social attitudes which set women and black people on the other side of a divide. This dream questions this divisive worldview and speaks of the dreamer's intention to challenge the separation of conscious from unconscious, looking (with some fear) for what lies "between." She is looking beyond the stereotypes towards a different truth. Her journeys, which she describes as "learning to see in the darkness" were concerned with finding ways to work on her paintings, but what she says holds equally true for all our journeys of exploration into the dream world:

"Now, with hindsight, I see the purpose of these journeys. To recover our own power, to be able to trust ourselves and link to our own wisdom (not simply rely on outside authorities), we need to find a way to free ourselves from the conditioning we have received that has robbed us of these things. If we can do this . . . this is the journey to open the heart."

Reading and Notes

Crisp, Tony, *The Instant Dream Book*, Neville Spearman, Suffolk, 1984, pp. 210–13.

Dinnage, Rosemary, *One to One: Experiences of Psychotherapy*, Penguin, London, 1992, pp. 16, 45, 63 (first published Viking, 1988).

Ernst, Sheila, and Lucy Goodison, *In Our Own Hands: A Book of Self-Help Therapy*, The Women's Press, London, 1993, pp. 240–75 (first published 1981).

Freud, Sigmund, *A Case of Hysteria: Three Essays on Sexuality: And Other Works*, translator and editor James Strachey, The Hogarth Press and the Institute of Psycho-Analysis, London, 1953, pp. 3–122 [Vol VII of *The Complete Psychological Works of Sigmund Freud*].

Jones, Richard M., *Fantasy and Feeling in Education*, Harper Colophon Books, Harper and Row, New York, Evanston and London, 1970, p. 245.

Shohet, Robin, *Dream Sharing: How to Enhance Your Understanding of Dreams by Group Sharing and Discussion*, Turnstone Press, Wellingborough, 1985, p. 74.

Shohet, Robin, "The Peer Dream Group," *Self and Society*, Vol IX, 3, May/June 1981, ("Dreams" issue) published by Self and Society, 39 Blenkarne Road, London SW11 6HZ, p. 119.

Stewart, Kilton, "Dream Theory in Malaya," *Fire*, 1, July 1967, published by Fire, 4 St. George's Terrace, London NW1, p. 7.

Werlin, Elena G., "An Experiment in Elementary Education," R. M. Jones (ed.), *Contemporary Educational Psychology: Selected Essays*, Harper and Row, New York, 1967.

INDEX

Lucy Goodison started work at the BBC and left to become active in community-based politics. She trained in massage, and for fifteen years ran workshops in bodywork, dance and dreams at the Women's Therapy Centre in London. She co-authored (with Sheila Ernst) the bestselling *In Our Own Hands: A Book of Self-Help Therapy* (The Women's Press, 1981). She gained her doctorate for research into female religious symbolism in ancient Crete, as described in her major work *Moving Heaven and Earth: Sexuality, Spirituality and Social Change* (The Women's Press, 1992; abridged, Pandora, 1991). As a freelance journalist she specialises in issues of mental health and learning difficulties.